D1282818

The Plays of T. S. Eliot

The Plays

of

T. S. Eliot

DAVID E. JONES

University of Toronto Press

Toronto

The Plays
of
T. S. Eliot

DAVID E. JONES

Edward

University of Toronto Press
Toronto

First published 1960
Reprinted 1962
First published as a paperback 1965
by University of Toronto Press

© *David E. Jones* 1960

Printed in Great Britain

FOR
OXFORD HOUSE PLAYERS

with whom
I explored several
of the plays
in production

Contents

Foreword

I T is just ten years since I first read *Murder in the Cathedral* and
so received my introduction to Eliot's plays. In that time I
have acted in it, directed it, 'taught' it in grammar school,
university, and adult classes, and gone on to a similar, though
not so extensive, exploration of the other plays in the theatre and
the study. I use the word 'exploration' deliberately. Work of this
stature goes on yielding new insights year after year so that one
is engaged in a continual exploration of it.

This book is an attempt to set down some of the results of my
exploration of the plays so far. Although it has, I hope, something
to offer people already familiar with Eliot's work, it is intended
primarily for those who are just beginning their own exploration
of the plays, whether in the theatre or the study—for those who
have seen or read one of the plays and sensed a richness which will
repay closer consideration. It tries to present the chief facts
relevant to such a study and to point the way down various
avenues.

The study of Eliot does not end with his work. Just as each of
his plays can be fully understood only in relation to the others
and to his poetry and prose, so his work as a whole has its full
meaning only in the larger context of the cultural tradition of
Western Europe. To understand Eliot, is, in fact, to understand
not only the core of Western culture, but also an important part
of Eastern culture. In following up the allusions and references in,
or the implications of, his work, one is liable to find oneself
reading anybody from Heraclitus to F. H. Bradley in the realm
of philosophy or from Aeschylus to Anouilh in the realm of

drama. One will almost inevitably go to the *Divina Commedia*, the *Bhagavad-Gita* and the writings of St. John of the Cross. Eliot is a pathway into each, in that not only does he provide the occasion for going to them but also an insight which makes them more meaningful to the present-day reader. He forms a link between our world and theirs. If the ramifications of this study seem a deterrent to the beginner, they need not be. They can serve rather as an incitement, since there is a satisfaction to be gained at each stage of the exploration as well as the prospect of a lifetime's enrichment.

One of the aids to further study I have provided is an extensive bibliography of writings about the plays. My own debt to this body of criticism, I have indicated so far as possible, but no critic can be sure just how much he owes to his reading of other critics. One of my debts is so great that the whole book is a testimony to it. I mean, of course, my debt to Mr. Eliot's own critical writings. He is his own most perceptive—and most severe— critic. Setting out with a very keen sense of the gulf between my own critical perception and his, I was at first inclined almost to let him write the book for me, so to speak. It was in danger of becoming a mere conglomeration of passages from his works. I, therefore, decided to limit myself, for the most part, to quotations from those of his works which are not readily accessible, and to do little more than refer to the two collections of his critical writings, *Selected Essays* and *On Poetry and Poets*, which every student of the plays will want to have constantly to hand.

No other English dramatist except Dryden has written at such length or with such good sense about the problems of his craft. And, in our time, no one else has given such careful thought to the problem of reviving poetic drama. Much of the value of Mr. Eliot's criticism springs from the fact that he is speaking about problems that he is engaged in solving in hard fact, and, obviously, no one can speak of a problem with deeper understanding than the man who is struggling with it.[1] But the fact that gives such criticism its peculiar value is also the fact that imposes limitations upon it. Such a critic speaks out of his own predicament; what he says will be conditioned by his needs of the moment.[2] It will not

---

[1] Cf. *On Poetry and Poets* (Faber and Faber, London, 1957), p. 106.
[2] *Ibid.*, p. 26.

be surprising, therefore, if we find ourselves disagreeing with Mr. Eliot's later estimates of his plays. *He* sees them in the light of what he is trying to do at the moment. *We* may value them for themselves and not merely as steps in the development of a new form of poetic drama. For this and kindred reasons, I have occasionally ventured to disagree with Mr. Eliot's own pronouncements.[1]

I hope that whenever I have done so, or whenever I have pointed out what seem to me flaws in his work, I have preserved a tone of humility. It is not easy to avoid a tone of superiority when finding fault, but to do so seems to me an important aspect of the discipline of criticism. And I should be particularly sorry if such a tone crept into anything I have to say about Mr. Eliot's work, for I have learnt far too much from it to feel anything but humility and gratitude.

D. E. J.

University of Minnesota
   April, 1959

[1] He himself has given ample warrant for such disagreements. Cf. *The Use of Poetry and the Use of Criticism* (Faber and Faber, London, 1933), p. 130; *On Poetry and Poets*, pp. 30–1 and 122; *World Review*, November, 1949, pp. 9 and 22; *Adam*, No. 200 (November, 1949), p. 16.

Acknowledgments

To name all the people who have helped me with the preparation of this book would take more space than my publishers, co-operative as they are, could allow me. As it happens, most of them—the many assistants of the British Museum Reading Room, the New York Public Library, and the University of Minnesota Library, to specify merely the libraries I have used most—are to me anonymous, and their best reward, in any case, is the sense, which I hope they all have, of doing their jobs well. But a few people I can and must name: they are my good friends Marjorie Benham, Edith Williams, and Howell Roberts, for whose help and encouragement I am glad to have this chance of saying 'Thank you' in print; my sister Aylwen, whose patience in typing and retyping has been little short of heroic; and my colleague Sumner J. Ferris, whose generous assistance in the checking of references and in proofreading saved me from many errors.

Like every student of Eliot, I am indebted to Mr. Leonard Unger for his very useful compilation *T. S. Eliot: a selected critique* (Rinehart and Co., Inc., New York, 1948) and for his essays on Eliot conveniently gathered together in *The Man in the Name* (University of Minnesota Press, Minneapolis, 1956). My debt would go deeper were it not that my personal acquaintance with him began only when my book was nearly complete. As it is, the chapter on *The Elder Statesman* owes a good deal to his lectures on Eliot's poetry.

I am deeply indebted to Mr. Eliot and Messrs. Faber and Faber, Ltd., his English publishers, for permission to quote profusely

Acknowledgments

from his works. (For the same courtesy, I am obliged to Harcourt, Brace and Company, Inc., as the American publishers of all his major works before *On Poetry and Poets* and *The Elder Statesman*, and to Farrar, Straus and Cudahy, Inc., as American publishers of these latest works.)

Acknowledgments are also due to Mr. Christopher Fry for quotations from his plays, *A Phoenix Too Frequent* (copyright 1946, 1953 by Christopher Fry; reproduced by permission of Oxford University Press) and *Thor, With Angels* (copyright 1952, 1953 by Christopher Fry); to Mr. E. Martin Browne for the passages from his article on 'The Dramatic Verse of T. S. Eliot' published in *T. S. Eliot: A Symposium*, ed. Richard March and Tambimuttu (Editions Poetry London, 1948); to Chatto and Windus, Ltd., for the passages from *Drama from Ibsen to Eliot* by Raymond Williams; to William Collins Sons and Co., Ltd., for the quotations from the text of Shakespeare edited by Peter Alexander; to the Cresset Press for the passages from *The Art of T. S. Eliot* by Helen Gardner; to the publishers of *The New Statesman* for the passages from Miss Gardner's review of *The Confidential Clerk*; to the Oxford University Press for the quotations from *The Achievement of T. S. Eliot* by F. O. Matthiessen; to the editor of *The Sewanee Review* for the passages from Louis L. Martz' article, 'The Wheel and the Point'; and to Mr. Grover Smith, Jr., for the passages from his *T. S. Eliot's Poetry and Plays* (University of Chicago Press). I am glad to have this opportunity of expressing my admiration for, and acknowledging my debt to, Mr. Ronald Peacock's *The Art of Drama* (Routledge and Kegan Paul).

D. E. J.

Chapter One

Poetry in the Theatre

'The tendency . . . of prose drama is to emphasize the ephemeral and superficial; if we want to get at the permanent and universal we tend to express ourselves in verse.' [1]

As a form of literature, drama has limitations which at first seem excessively restrictive, though in the end they reveal themselves as a source of strength. The author can say nothing in his own person except through appendages like the prologue, the epilogue, or the choric commentary. Within the play itself, the characters can, for the most part, say only what is characteristic of them. How then is the author to convey the quality of insight, the moral or philosophical vision, which makes for art?

Of course, the portrayal of human action can in itself induce keener emotions than any other form of art, emotions not as powerful perhaps as those induced by music but keener because focused upon the predicament of people like ourselves. However, the kind of significance which gives drama universal and permanent validity cannot be defined, or even suggested, by

[1] Part of the argument of one of the interlocutors in Eliot's 'Dialogue on Dramatic Poetry' of 1928 (*Selected Essays*, Faber and Faber, third enlarged edition, 1951, p. 46). For statements by Eliot in his own person on the advantages of the use of verse in drama, see 'The Need for Poetic Drama', *The Listener*, 25 November, 1936, p. 994; *Poetry and Drama*, p. 34 (*On Poetry and Poets*, pp. 86-7); and the earlier version of the same passage in 'The Aims of Poetic Drama', *Adam*, No. 200 (November, 1949), pp. 15-16, which makes several points omitted in the later version.

action alone. A mimed wedding, for instance, may arouse strong feelings in the onlookers, but the feelings will be different in each onlooker because they will be merely the outcome of association, and the associations will be different for each. The control of the audience's reaction which allows the creation of a significant, aesthetic pattern must come from additional factors. In mime. these may reside in the quality of the performance, but this cannot easily be communicated to other performers. In ballet, they may reside in the choreography, the décor, and the music as well, and these are more permanent elements, assisting the perpetuation of the performance. In drama, the corresponding elements are the direction, the setting, and the text. Of these, the text is the only element which is likely to be preserved intact, though it will be differently interpreted from production to production, especially in different regions and different ages. The setting may be re-produced, of course, but there is no assurance that it will be permanently associated with the text, and the total reproduction of a performance on film involves translation into what is essentially a different art-form.

Thus, the only element in drama over which the author has anything like permanent control is the text. And here he is faced with the problem of conveying his sense of the significance of the action through the mouths of characters who, by the rules of the game, must, for the most part, be unaware of that significance, During the greater part of the history of drama, dramatists have found a solution in the use of dramatic conventions. The chorus is the most obvious conventional mouthpiece for the author, but there are subtle means of commentary within the action itself. A character may be depersonalized temporarily to convey a piece of information or suggest a point of view which will orientate the reactions of the audience. In a theatre governed by conventions, the audience will make the necessary adjustment to the movement out of character quite unconsciously. Conventions are thus seen to be liberating agencies, allowing the author to supplement the action by information and insights which will illuminate it. They are basically tacit agreements between author and audience that characters shall behave or speak in a way which is not true to life but which will broaden the scope of the drama. We do not normally voice our inmost thoughts when alone ('O, that way mad-

2

ness lies'), but we give a franchise to Hamlet since that is the only way in which we can be admitted to his heart-searching. 'I am invisible', says Oberon, and we take him at his word, or rather Shakespeare's. Why strain at a gnat when the very basis of theatre is make-believe? The sole proviso is that the outcome shall be worth while, that either entertainment or enlightenment will follow. And, in fact, the more active one's participation in the make-believe, the more enjoyable it is.[1]

Of the conventions of language, far and away the most important is poetry. This is the subtlest means of transcending the limitations of drama, and the one which leads to the greatest enrichment. As Ronald Peacock points out:

'It extends the range of expression over that available to prose, for a subtle instrument follows the subtleties of nature, revealing more of persons, their motives, thoughts and situations than blunter tools could achieve. But everything in art being a matter of mutual assimilation, the extension of meanings through increased poetic power reacts on the dramatic quality; if verse, or poetry, makes the expression of the drama more complete it makes it more dramatic. For all these reasons we find confirmation in the fact, always assumed but rarely stated, that although verse is not indispensable to fine dramatic art the greatest plays have nevertheless all been in verse.'[2]

Not the least of the achievements of the Elizabethans was their forging of a mode of drama which could range from something like complete verisimilitude to the farthest reaches of fancy and move smoothly from the one extreme to the other in the same play, from the earthiness of the 'rude mechanicals' to the ethereality of the fairies, from Caliban to Ariel. Elizabethan drama was, of course, a happy accident rather than a deliberate creation, a hybrid form, mixing convention and naturalism, prose and verse, making the best of both worlds. But it was the dominance of poetry which opened the way to the exploration of areas of

---

[1] In his essay on Marie Lloyd (1923), Eliot refers to 'that collaboration of the audience with the artist which is necessary in all art and most obviously in dramatic art' (*Selected Essays*, ed. cit., p. 458).

[2] Ronald Peacock, *The Art of Drama* (Routledge and Kegan Paul, London, 1957), p. 225. Cf. Eliot, *Selected Essays*, p. 52.

thought and feeling never before charted. Great poetic drama is an extension of sensibility.

By approaching from the quasi-philosophical angle, I may have seemed to imply that dramatists ultimately arrived at conventionalized verse drama as the solution to the problems of dramatic form. The historical facts, so far as we know them, point to a very different development. Most early forms of drama were in verse and made full use of conventions, being more like narrative supplemented by action than action supplemented by words. Prose gradually encroached and conventions were shorn away over the centuries. Just as language began as a highly synthetic form and evolved by a process of analysis, so drama, as a manifestation of language, began as a very complex form and developed by simplification. In the arts, however, development does not necessarily mean improvement.

As the form of language most suited to the more serious dramatic genres, verse went unchallenged until the eighteenth century. Only when naturalism became the dominant mode was poetry ousted from its rightful place in the theatre. Naturalism implied the reproduction of the surfaces of life; in its extreme form, it aimed at scientific impartiality, something which is alien to art because it excludes the author's vision, his attitude to, and interpretation of, the events portrayed. Poetry, the means by which this vision can best be expressed, was excluded as a too obvious organization of language.

Most of the great dramatists of the last hundred years have sought to evade the limitations of naturalism without resorting to poetry. Ibsen, Strindberg, and Chekhov, had recourse to symbolism; Pirandello explored the nature of theatrical reality, using shock-tactics to pierce the barrier between actors and audience postulated by naturalism; Giraudoux and Anouilh followed Cocteau in seeking to achieve a more universal and permanent significance by building upon ancient myth or by creating their own quasi-mythical worlds; Synge distilled the power and glory of uncontaminated peasant speech; Shaw devised his own kind of discussion-play in which he could develop his manifold sociological interests; and O'Neill experimented laboriously with almost every kind of theatrical convention. Others, under the influence of the theories of Adolphe Appia and Gordon Craig,

4

have tried to achieve heightened significance by the use of the devices of modern staging and the techniques of modern production, by relying on décor, lighting, rhythmic movement, and other adventitious aids. The German Expressionists went some way towards fulfilling Craig's desire to see the actor replaced by the marionette; they reduced him to the level of a component more or less on a par with the décor, and in this way portrayed the dehumanization of man in mechanized society.

Cocteau has been the most eloquent spokesman for the conception of poetry as a synthesis of all the elements of theatre, the poetry *of* theatre ('poésie de théâtre') as opposed to poetry *in* the theatre ('poésie au théâtre'). This is an attractive theory, but its results in practice are tenuous and transient. As developed by Ronald Peacock, however, it takes into account a permanent and peculiar characteristic of drama; 'the poetic quality in a play', he writes,

'is not just a matter of the linguistic text. The pictorial and expressive sensuousness of drama is exceedingly vivid. Present images, not the vaguely shifting ones of memory, strike us, and the voices and language affect our feelings with a continuously pursued purpose. The drama, and the poetry, reside not in one or the other of these phenomena but in all of them. And the paradox of all art holds here, too; the meaning—the aesthetic situation in which the play and ourselves are established together—is beyond the sensuous imagery, but the only way into it is through the imagery. We repeat, what moves us in a play is not the words, or any other particular, but the whole situation. We are moved by Lear deserted, of which his ragings, however sublime their language, are but the symptom. We are moved by Macbeth and his wife haunted by remorse and fear; moved by Hamlet desperately trying to see his mother through a murk of sin and disloyalty. The symptoms—the images and the language—have to be vivid, but their vividness, of whatever intensity, still serves the total image and the sense of distilled human reality we see captured in it. By means of its simultaneous creation of picture and language drama reflects a feature of life itself, which is both pre- and post-linguistic. It is lived partly *outside* words but also partly *as* words. The two layers interpenetrate, but they do not

5

necessarily coalesce, though the degree of coalescence might be held as an index of culture. These conditions of separation, interpenetration, and coalescence are all felt strongly in the form of drama, contributing depth to its sensuous complexity. It is elemental first, then spiritual, then linguistic. It repeats thus the hierarchy of culture, projecting always the world and existence that are before language, and carrying their power into the world-after-language.' [1]

This deep-searching analysis provides a kind of overall qualification of what I have to say. But it leaves certain distinctions to be made. Mr. Peacock is talking about the drama as the word made flesh—the actor supporting the words by the emotion and bodily action they imply—rather than the mechanical parts of theatrical performance. The heart of drama is this intimate co-operation between dramatist and actor. By the very nature of his medium, the dramatist depends upon it. Unless the actor's imagination warms to the author's, there can be no theatrical experience, for there is nothing to *share* with an audience. Actors have been known to claim that they needed only 'two planks and a passion', but for a sustained, articulate performance they need also a text about which the passion may take shape. Drama as we generally think of it starts with the text and ends with the actor finding the passion that underlies that text. I suggest that it is no accident that the plays Mr. Peacock cites are verse plays. Towering passions can be realized best in the medium of poetry.

We shall return to Mr. Peacock's penetrating analysis of poetic drama. For the moment, having glanced at his work as an important extension of Cocteau's view of drama, we turn again to Cocteau, and suggest that permanent significance cannot inhere in methods of staging and production which change as the architecture and mechanics of the theatre change. As Mr. Peacock admits, Cocteau found the fulfilment of his ideal of 'poésie de théâtre' in film, where setting and direction are integral parts of the actual creation and not merely means of interpretation, adjuncts of performance.[2] The permanent part of a play is the words,

---

[1] Ronald Peacock, *The Art of Drama* (Routledge and Kegan Paul, London, 1957), pp. 244-5.
[2] *Ibid.*, p. 239.

6

and words raised to their highest power are poetry. Perhaps the axiom of one of the interlocutors in Eliot's 'Dialogue on Dramatic Poetry'—'All poetry tends towards drama, and all drama towards poetry' [1]—is, as one of his antagonists says, 'a neat and dangerous generalization', but it contains an element of truth. For one thing, it militates against the all-too-frequent assumption that poetry is merely something added to a play—a decoration. Poetic drama is not prose drama with a top-dressing of poetry. It is not the passages of beautiful description or profound meditation which make Shakespeare's plays poetic, but the whole conception. As Eliot puts it:

'The writer of poetic drama is not merely a man skilled in two arts and skilful to weave them together; he is not a writer who can decorate a play with poetic language and metre. His task is different from that of the "dramatist" or that of the "poet", for his pattern is more complex and dimensional . . . . The genuine poetic drama must, at its best, observe all the regulations of the plain drama, but will weave them *organically* (to mix a metaphor and to borrow for the occasion a modern word) into a much richer design.' [2]

If the pleasure we feel in watching a poetic play is no different from that felt at a poetry recital, the poetry is superfluous. In the theatre, poetry 'must justify itself dramatically'. [3] In genuine poetic drama, the poetry and the drama are fused; the language *is* the essential action: first, in the sense that it often does what it says, and, secondly, in the sense that it is the most important part

---

[1] *Selected Essays*, p. 52.

[2] Introduction to G. Wilson Knight, *The Wheel of Fire*, (Oxford University Press, 1930), p. xix. It follows that a poet coming to the theatre as Eliot did will have to discover the laws of a new kind of poetry. He gives a succinct account of his discovery in his introduction to *Shakespeare and the Popular Dramatic Tradition* by S. L. Bethell (King and Staples, London, 1944), one of his most important statements on the nature of poetic drama. For a shorter account, see 'The Social Function of Poetry', *The Adelphi*, Vol. 21, No. 4 (July–September, 1945), p. 153. This passage differs considerably from the revised version in *On Poetry and Poets*, p. 17. The discovery referred to here of the need to cultivate a third voice, the dramatic voice of poetry, is amplified in the lecture on 'The Three Voices of Poetry' delivered in 1953 and reprinted in *On Poetry and Poets*, pp. 89 ff.

[3] Eliot, *Poetry and Drama*, p. 12 (*On Poetry and Poets*, p. 72).

of the play, making explicit what is really happening. To see how the language can do what it says, let us compare a passage of dramatic prose with a passage of dramatic verse. The prose is Falstaff's justification of his addiction to sherris-sack:

'A good sherris-sack hath a twofold operation in it. It ascends me into the brain; dries me there all the foolish and dull and crudy vapours which environ it; makes it apprehensive, quick, forgetive, full of nimble, fiery, and delectable shapes; which delivered o'er to the voice, the tongue, which is the birth, becomes excellent wit. The second property of your excellent sherris is the warming of the blood; which before, cold and settled, left the liver white and pale, which is the badge of pusillanimity and cowardice; but the sherris warms it, and makes it course from the inwards to the parts extremes. It illumineth the face, which, as a beacon, gives warning to all the rest of this little kingdom, man, to arm; and then the vital commoners and inland petty spirits muster me all to their captain, the heart, who, great and puff'd up with this retinue, doth any deed of courage—and this valour comes of sherris. So that skill in the weapon is nothing without sack, for that sets it a-work; and learning, a mere hoard of gold kept by a devil till sack commences it and sets it in act and use.'[1]

This makes brilliant use of imagery, going about as far in this direction as it is possible to go in prose, and once or twice the words begin rhythmically to do what they say (e.g. 'the sherris warms it, and makes it course . . . doth any deed of courage'). But for the most part Shakespeare is content here to give a physiological account of the 'twofold operation' and describe its effects. The overall movement is the logical movement of prose.

The verse is from Christopher Fry's *A Phoenix Too Frequent* and marks the moment when, having accepted a bowl of wine, Dynamene, the young widow who has sworn to follow her husband into Hades, begins to discover how good life can be:

> A mystery's in the world
> Where a little liquid, with flavour, quality, and fume
> Can be as no other, can hint and flute our senses

[1] *Henry IV*, Part II, IV. iii. 97 ff. All references to Shakespeare are to *The Complete Works* edited by Peter Alexander (Collins, London, 1951).

> As though a music played in harvest hollows
> And a movement was in the swathes of our memory.
> Why should scent, why should flavour come
> With such wings upon us? [1]

This gives us the sensation itself and makes us understand its significance for Dynamene. The movement follows the very effect of the wine as it wakens the dulled senses of the fasting woman to the wonder of the Creation. The comparison with the movement of Shakespeare's prose illustrates in a small way the distinction drawn by Henry Reed in a broadcast talk:

'though valuable functions may be performed by prose, they will always be subsidiary by contrast with those of verse; and only the presence of rhythm will effect that state of communication from writer to spectator where the limited number of words can be disposed into speech that can bring the density and complexity of character and the progress of psychological action bearably and intelligibly before us.' [2]

Rhythm is one of the two most distinctive features of poetry; the other is imagery. 'Images in verse', wrote T. E. Hulme, 'are not mere decoration, but the very essence of an intuitive language'.[3] In other words, they are a mode of apprehending reality. Moreover, they enable the poet to say more than one thing at a time and endow his thought with the sensuousness and concreteness of direct experience. Something of the impact of the other four senses can be added to hearing. In Burns' line 'My luv is like a red, red rose,' the simile conjures up the visual splendour of the rose, its fragrance, and its velvety softness, as means of conveying how his love appears to him. In simile, a comparison is explicitly made and the terms of the comparison remain distinct. Burns' love has certain rose-like qualities, but she is not identified with the flower. In metaphor, a more complex form, the comparison is implicit

---

[1] Christopher Fry, *A Phoenix Too Frequent* (Oxford University Press, 1949), p. 20.
[2] Henry Reed, 'Towards "The Cocktail Party"—II', *The Listener*, 17 May, 1951, p. 804.
[3] T. E. Hulme, *Speculations*, Essays on Humanism and the Philosophy of Art, ed. Herbert Read (Kegan Paul, Trench, Trubner; London, 1924), p. 135.

and the terms are identified. In Cleopatra's greeting of Antony—

> com'st thou smiling from
> The world's great snare uncaught? [1]—

the world is imaged as a snare which Antony has eluded. The poetry expresses the significance of the action, or, as we phrased it earlier, makes explicit what is really happening. In fact, the metaphor sums up the theme of the play, illustrating the truth of Wilson Knight's view of Shakespeare's plays as 'expanded metaphors'.[2]

An extended example of the use of imagery occurs in a passage in Fry's *Thor, With Angels*, where Merlin prophesies the coming of Augustine:

> When, years ago,
> The Romans fell away from our branching roads
> Like brazen leaves, answering
> The hopeless windy trumpets from their home,
> Your tribes waged winter upon us, till our limbs
> Ached with the carving cold. You blackened
> The veins of the valleys with our dried blood. And at last
> Your lives croaked like crows on a dead bough
> And the echoes clanged against you. But I can hear
> Faintly on the twittering sea a sail
> Moving greatly where the waves, like harvest-home,
> Come hugely on our coast: the men of Rome
> Returning, bringing God, winter over, a breath
> Of green exhaled from the hedges, the wall of sky
> Breached by larksong. Primrose and violet

---

[1] *Antony and Cleopatra*, IV. viii. 17–18. The metaphor is Biblical, of course, and carries religious overtones. Cf. Ecclesiastes IX. 12 and Proverbs IV. 2.

[2] G. Wilson Knight, *The Wheel of Fire*, revised edition (Methuen and Co., London, 1949), pp. 14–15. I say that 'the metaphor sums up the theme', but it would be truer to say that it presents the negative aspect. The positive aspect is put by Octavius in another snare image:

> she looks like sleep,
> As she would catch another Antony
> In her strong toil of grace.

> (V. ii. 343–5)

Between them, these images suggest the significance of the whole action of the play.

And all frail privileges of the early ground
Gather like pilgrims in the aisles of the sun.[1]

The action is given an extra dimension by the development, in a kind of verbal counterpoint, of the equivalence between the return of the Romans bringing the message of Easter and spiritual rebirth, on the one hand, and the return of spring with its renewal of Nature, on the other. In such a case we see how poetry can introduce into drama sensory experience which cannot be shown on the stage (that is, can be an extension of purely dramatic experience) and, at the same time, can interpret the action by setting it in the larger context of moral or spiritual vision.

It has been easier to isolate illustrative passages from Fry than from Eliot because, from the first, Eliot tended to eschew the more obvious effects of poetry in the theatre, partly, perhaps, as a result of his innate austerity and his anti-Romanticism, but even more, certainly, as part of his strategy for evading the present-day inhibitions about poetic drama. For whatever reasons, however, he has tended more and more to sacrifice the sensuous richness of poetry in order to demonstrate the deeper, organic unity which poetry can bring to drama. 'If you write a play in verse,' he observed to Ezra Pound, 'then the verse ought to be a medium to look THROUGH and not a pretty decoration to look AT.' [2] In other words, poetry is to be a mode of apprehending the experience embodied in a play, and imagery, the essence of intuitive language, is to be strictly functional. Una Ellis-Fermor notes how in *The Family Reunion* the imagery has

'the function of revealing much of the thought or the spiritual experience which would else prove well-nigh inexpressible within the limits of dramatic form . . . . Here . . . . is a play in which this peculiar function of imagery is exercised so fully that it would be hard to find a parallel outside the narrative or reflective poetry of mystical experience; yet it is an integral part of the action and thus essentially dramatic in function.' [3]

[1] Christopher Fry, *Thor, With Angels*, (Oxford University Press, 1949), pp. 32–3.
[2] 'Five Points on Dramatic Writing' (A Letter to Ezra Pound), *Townsman*, I, 3 (July, 1938), p. 10.
[3] Una Ellis-Fermor, *The Frontiers of Drama* (Methuen and Co., London, 1945), p. 94. I am indebted to this valuable little book for several ideas in this

Metaphoric use of imagery is, however, but a localized and tangible form of a mode of apprehension which goes much deeper. What happens in a single metaphor, happens in the play as a whole in poetic drama, though there is not necessarily such a connection between the metaphor and the whole play as we noted in the 'snare' metaphor from *Antony and Cleopatra*. This is an extension of the view that Eliot puts tentatively when he says:

'It is possible that what distinguishes poetic drama from prosaic drama is a kind of doubleness in the action, as if it took place on two planes at once. In this it is different from allegory, in which the abstraction is something conceived, not something differently felt, and from symbolism (as in the plays of Maeterlinck) in which the tangible world is deliberately diminished—both symbolism and allegory being operations of the conscious planning mind. In poetic drama a certain apparent irrelevance may be the symptom of this doubleness; or the drama has an under-pattern, less manifest than the theatrical one.' [1]

Eliot has in mind something slightly different from the pattern or chains of imagery, which one might call the over-pattern to distinguish it from the under-pattern of which he speaks. This becomes evident later in the same essay, when, speaking of Marston's *Sophonisba*, he develops this view:

'as we familiarize ourselves with the play we perceive a pattern behind the pattern into which the characters deliberately involve themselves; the kind of pattern which we perceive in our own lives only at rare moments of inattention and detachment, drowsing in sunlight'. [2]

This pattern may be related to the pattern of imagery and may become explicit through it, but it may, on the other hand, be quite distinct from the imagery and lie at a much deeper level. It may lie at the root of the action and have the quality of myth, an archetypal pattern of human experience or an ineffable vision

---

first chapter. With this quotation, compare Eliot's remark: 'Hell, though a state, is a state which can only be thought of, and perhaps only experienced, by the projection of sensory images' (*Selected Essays*, p. 250).

[1] *Selected Essays*, p. 229.

[2] *Ibid.*, p. 232. Cf. *Murder in the Cathedral*, p. 13, and *Four Quartets*, p. 13.

of supernatural reality. It may emerge above the surface of lifelike action and reveal itself as symbolism or allegory, or it may remain submerged. In the later plays of Eliot the tendency has been for it to remain submerged.

Whether projecting above the surface or submerged, however, this pattern is the bedrock of the play, the principle of its unification, and all parts of the play are subordinate to it. Character is just such a subordinate part, and therefore, as Mr. Martin Browne points out:

'the poet fails, quite deliberately, to satisfy one of the expectations of the contemporary audience. He does not depict character with psychological realism. For him, experience is universalised, and therefore character is a symbol. However acute his observation of character may be—and no one's could be more so than Eliot's—he will, with deliberate austerity, reduce his depiction of it to those factors which further the development of his pattern. The individual, seen through the poet's eye, is still an individual unique in his personality—a true character: but he is presented not for his individuality but as typifying some aspect of man.' [1]

The poetic dramatist tends, in the economy of his art, to develop only those aspects of his characters which illustrate his theme. This, perhaps, is the aspect of poetic drama which gives most difficulty to audiences conditioned to naturalistic drama.

The basic pattern is an aspect of the organic unity of poetic drama, an organization not just of parts but of the whole in a manner analogous with music. As Eliot has pointed out in a broadcast talk to schools:

'To work out a play in verse is to be working like a musician as well as like a prose dramatist: it is to see the thing as a whole musical pattern .... The verse dramatist must operate on you on two levels at once, dramatically, with the characters and plot. The requirements for a good plot are just as severe as for a prose play .... It is fatal for a poet trying to write a play, to hope to make up for defects in the movement of the play by bursts of poetry which do not help the action. But underneath the action, which should

[1] E. Martin Browne, 'The Poet and the Stage', *The Penguin New Writing*, ed. John Lehmann, No. 31 (Penguin Books, 1947), pp. 83–4.

13

be perfectly intelligible, there should be a musical pattern which intensifies our excitement by reinforcing it with feeling from a deeper and less articulate level. Everybody knows that there are things that can be said in music that cannot be said in speech. And there are things which can be said in poetic drama that cannot be said in either music or ordinary speech.' [1]

Othello is probably the most perfect example of musical organization in poetic drama. In Acts I and II we have the exposition of the two main themes: the noble, expansive music of Othello's love and its sensuous richness are contrasted with the cramped, corrosive music of Iago's hate and its intellectual sterility. The development section, in which this contrast becomes conflict, rises to its climax in the temptation scene, then subsides to a prolonged *agitato* which gives way to an *adagio* in the 'willow scene'. In Act V the feeling mounts swiftly to the height of human agony, and then after a brief recapitulation of the Othello music in a minor key—Othello attempting to see himself in a noble light[2]—the 'sound and fury' fade away like the coda of a great symphony.

This kind of order—an organic order growing from within, not a mechanical order imposed from without—is not possible to prose. Because poetry is an artificial medium not tethered to verisimilitude, it has greater scope and flexibility. It can range from near-naturalism to extreme formalism; it 'may lean towards the lyrical, or the meditative, or the philosophical, or whatever, without cutting loose from its anchor in the dramatic scheme'.[3] On the other hand, as Eliot observes: 'A really dramatic verse can be employed, as Shakespeare employed it, to say the most matter-of-fact things.' [4]

Usually, however, the poet, in the theatre as outside it, speaks above the 'common measure'. Coleridge pointed out that:

'If metre be super-added, all other parts must be made consonant with it. They must be such, as to justify the perpetual and distinct attention to each part, which an exact correspondent recurrence of accent and sound are calculated to excite.' [5]

[1] 'The Need for Poetic Drama', *The Listener*, 25 November, 1936, p. 994.
[2] See Eliot, *Selected Essays*, pp. 130–1. [3] Peacock, *op. cit.*, p. 226.
[4] *Poetry and Drama*, p. 20 (*On Poetry and Poets*, p. 78).
[5] *Biographia Literaria*, Chapter XIV (Everyman's Library edition, p. 150).

14

This heightened awareness is perhaps the essential distinction of poetic drama in performance. The poetry is a kind of extra dimension, and poetic drama aims not only to excite us with the action but also to reveal the significance of the action, using for its purpose the state of keener perception which poetry induces.

This heightened awareness stems partly from the power of poetry to give access to deeper levels of being. Rhythm seems to act as a kind of release, somewhat after the fashion of hypnosis, and the images which rise from the depth of the unconscious yield a kind of sensuous apprehension of experience not available to prose. It seems, for instance, as if only through poetry can the deep reserves of significance in myth be tapped, and this may be because metaphor and myth are cognate modes of apprehending reality, the difference between them being in scale rather than in kind.

Eliot is reported to have said that poetry is 'the mode in which reality is experienced most profoundly'.[1] It alone makes possible the creation of a complex artistic structure which corresponds to the totality of human experience and reproduces the different levels—sensuous, logical, psychological, and spiritual—upon which life is lived. As Eliot says: 'It is in fact the privilege of dramatic poetry to be able to show us several planes of reality at once.'[2]

Different planes of reality may co-exist in prose drama, as in *The Wild Duck*, but in prose they are a more or less deliberate contrivance and constitute a conception developed for the play in hand. It is a conception which is logical, almost mathematical, rather than intuitive and organic, as is the conception of poetic drama. Moreover, the symbolism of prose drama is not readily transferred from one play to another; the symbolism of each play tends to be unique. The poetic dramatist's apprehension of experience, on the other hand, is not an *ad hoc* contrivance; it is something native to him, corresponding to, if not identical with, his permanent conception of life. Thus, whereas the symbolic systems of Ibsen's prose plays are mutually exclusive, the poetic

[1] Alessandro Pellegrini, 'A London Conversation with T. S. Eliot', translated by Joseph Frank and reprinted from *Belfagor* in *The Sewanee Review*, LVII (1949), p. 287.
[2] 'The Aims of Poetic Drama', *Adam*, No. 200 (November, 1949), p. 16.

worlds of Shakespeare's plays, although they have quite different atmospheres, belong to the same planetary system, belong, so to speak, to the universe of a great poetic dramatist. And because that universe is a poet's conception of the universe we all inhabit, we find that it helps us to understand ourselves and our world.[1]

This might seem a great weight to put upon metrical organization, and Mr. Ronald Peacock argues against

'the view that all poetry depends only on one kind of metaphor or "symbol"—the poetic image in a verse text. (This latter is the error of those who decry Eliot's plays as against his earlier poems; they do not see the transference of metaphorical power from words alone to scene and persons) . . . . Certainly imagery is all-important, but what counts for drama is the principle of metaphor and symbol not only in language and verse but in all the varied imagery of which as an art it makes use. A character or characters, the events and actions, the setting, and more frequently still the play as a whole, are all of them in some way symbols radiating their power through all the details of the imagery and creating a unified pattern of metaphor and symbol.'[2]

This is very perceptive, but does not, I suggest, make allowance for the fact that, in practice, this kind of integration is achieved only in verse drama. Verse alone seems to bring into play the mode of apprehension which works in such depth. Mr. Peacock's acute observation about Eliot's plays makes light of the important fact that they are in verse, even if it is a verse which makes increasingly less use of poetic imagery.

Nowadays, discussion of poetic drama is apt to involve certain semantic difficulties, which are neatly summarized by Mr. Peacock:

'One has always to distinguish between at least three major current meanings of "poetic". It indicates a text in verse, which meaning derives ultimately from classical times. It means, secondly, the romantically poetic, and this refers rather to certain themes and attitudes irrespective of verse or prose forms, as we observe in fairy tales and in an author like Maeterlinck, whose plays are

[1] Cf. *Poetry and Drama*, p. 35 (*On Poetry and Poets*, p. 87).
[2] *The Art of Drama*, p. 217.

intensely romantic though in prose. Thirdly, it means lyrical and musical style, primarily in verse, but also in prose. These variants, taken together, show how impossible it is to *restrict* the meanings of "poetic" either to verse compositions, or to romantic ones; the various influences and usages are by now inextricably inter-twined.' [1]

I agree that the present situation is difficult, but I do not agree that 'The alternative is to *broaden again* the notion of the poetic'.[2] If this suggestion were followed, the word 'poetic' would rapidly lose what precision of meaning is left to it. The 'poetic' inheres in poetry; any looser usage is merely by analogy from the mode of apprehension which is peculiar to poetry and does not fully operate in any medium but poetry.

Probably few, if any, plays exhibit all the qualities of poetic drama we have tried to define. But many of these qualities—certainly, the organic unity, the crystallization of meaning in the imagery, the capacity for lifting the action onto the plane of universal significance—may be conveniently illustrated in a passage from *Macbeth*. Macduff and Lennox have just been admitted to Macbeth's castle on the morning after the murder of Duncan, and Macduff has gone to call the king, leaving Lennox and Macbeth to make small talk. After an abortive start—he can get 'no change', as we would say, out of Macbeth, whose mind has followed Macduff to the murder chamber—Lennox launches out, as anybody in his place would, on the weather. Naturalism, however, quickly begins to give way to supernaturalism and tension increases in preparation for the announcement of the murder. After a slight relaxation of tension—as a response to an account of happenings so strange that Lennox is careful to dis-tinguish hearsay from his own experience, Macbeth's brusque ' 'Twas a rough night' is almost comical—after this relaxation designed to sharpen its impact, the announcement peals out with all the power rhetoric can command. I begin to quote at the exit of Macduff:

LENNOX   Goes the King hence today?
MACBETH   He does: he did appoint so.

---

[1] *Ibid.*   [2] *Ibid.*

LENNOX	The night has been unruly. Where we lay,
	Our chimneys were blown down; and, as they say,
	Lamentings heard i' th' air, strange screams of death,
	And prophesying, with accents terrible,
	Of dire combustion and confus'd events
	New hatch'd to th' woeful time; the obscure bird
	Clamour'd the livelong night. Some say the earth
	Was feverous and did shake.
MACBETH	'Twas a rough night.
LENNOX	My young remembrance cannot parallel
	A fellow to it.

Re-enter MACDUFF

MACDUFF	O horror, horror, horror! Tongue nor heart
	Cannot conceive nor name thee.
MACBETH } LENNOX }	What's the matter?
MACDUFF	Confusion now hath made his masterpiece.
	Most sacrilegious murder hath broke ope
	The Lord's anointed temple, and stole thence
	The life o' th' building.
MACBETH	What is't you say—the life?
LENNOX	Mean you his Majesty?
MACDUFF	Approach the chamber, and destroy your sight
	With a new Gorgon. Do not bid me speak;
	See, and then speak yourselves.

(*Exeunt* MACBETH *and* LENNOX)

Awake, awake!
Ring the alarum bell. Murder and treason!
Banquo and Donalbain! Malcolm! awake!
Shake off this downy sleep, death's counterfeit,
And look on death itself. Up, up and see
The great doom's image! Malcolm! Banquo!
As from your graves rise up and walk like sprites
To countenance this horror! Ring the bell.

(*Bell rings*)

Enter LADY MACBETH

LADY M.   What's the business,
            That such a hideous trumpet calls to parley
            The sleepers of the house?

                                        (II. iii. 50–81)

The central action of the play, the murder of Duncan, involves
an assault upon the divinely ordained order of the universe and a
disruption of it. Macbeth's action is like a pebble thrown into a
pool sending out ripples. The repercussions of his evil deed are
felt throughout the universe because of man's central position in
it. Man, made 'a little lower than the angels' and having dominion
over the lesser orders of Creation, straddles the boundary between
nature and supernature, combining in himself the physical existence of the animal creation and something of the spirituality of the
angelic orders. What he does affects everything lower down
on the ladder of Creation, the great Chain of Being. This is what
gives human nature its significance. If the passions 'outrun the
pauser, reason', and the brute part of man gains the upper hand,
the true order is turned topsy-turvy at its key-point, the link
between heaven and earth, and the lower orders of Creation
'fall' in sympathy. This is what happens when Macbeth gives in
to his 'vaulting ambition'. Following the murder, 'the frame of
things' has begun to disjoint, as is clear from Lennox's account of
the unnatural happenings of the night.[1]
The implications of Macbeth's deed begin to emerge even
more clearly in Macduff's manner of announcing the murder.
Disorder ('confusion') has made inroad upon the divinely ordained order ('broke ope/The Lord's anointed temple'). Macbeth
has decided to 'jump the life to come' and the judgment it will
bring.[2] But the imagery, telescoping time, reminds us of the
judgment that he cannot avoid. Standing probably, in the Elizabethan theatre, upon the upper stage, Macduff calls up the 'sleepers
of the house' to witness 'the great doom's image', the Last Judgment. Rising in their night-shirts[3] and flocking on to the stage
by every entrance, perhaps even through the traps, they present a

---

[1] This disorder is only touched upon here, but Shakespeare thinks it of
sufficient importance to devote half the next scene to it (II. iv. 1–20).

[2] I. vii. 1–28.   [3] Cf. lines 125 ff. in this scene.

visual resemblance to the spirits rising from their graves on the Last Day, and the theatrical image complements the verbal image. The climax of this double-action comes when Lady Macbeth enters and asks, with terrible irony,

> What's the business,
> That such a hideous trumpet calls to parley
> The sleepers of the house?[1]

It will indeed be a 'hideous trumpet' which summons her to the Judgment. Thus, the whole tenour of the play—the damnation of Macbeth and his wife—is epitomized in this scene. The poetry makes explicit what is really happening.

Now, while the consummate artistry of this is Shakespeare's, the possibility of it was latent in the Elizabethan conception of the universe. With the loss of this conception under the impact of the scientific revolution of the seventeenth century and the break in the theatrical tradition of poetic drama which resulted from the closing of the theatres in 1642—when they reopened in 1660 the native tradition was overlaid with French classicism—poetic drama was drained of vitality. In keeping with the temper of the age, the theatrical current turned towards prose drama and ultimately towards naturalism. The old system of conventions was scrapped in favour of the single convention—though nobody thought of it as a convention—that what happens on the stage is a 'slice of life'. Divorced from the reality which prose drama now purported to convey, verse drama tended towards sheer bombast; it became the vehicle for the heroic, the grandiose. The Romantic penchant for the flamboyant, *le culte du moi*, did nothing to correct this, and, consequently, verse drama became closet drama, to be played in the theatre of the mind, confined neither by the limitations of the actual theatre nor by the limitations of the human nature which the theatre represents. By this time, the task of restoring human reality to verse drama and reconciling it with the theatre had become formidable.

---

[1] The discrepancy between the sound of the bell and the word 'trumpet' poses a problem. The primary meaning of 'trumpet' here is possibly 'alarm' or 'proclamation', but even if it has this more general meaning, clearly the metaphoric quality is still lively enough to be obtrusive. Perhaps Shakespeare intends to jar us by the discrepancy so that we do not miss the irony.

Most attempts at reviving poetic drama have failed in the very first requirement; the poetic idiom employed has not been sufficiently alive. It has usually been a pale imitation of Elizabethan blank verse, and, consequently, a wholly artificial language without roots in the idiom and rhythms of living speech. As Eliot reminds us,

'No poetry . . . . is ever exactly the same speech that the poet talks and hears: but it has to be in such a relation to the speech of his time that the listener or reader can say "that is how I should talk if I could talk poetry" . . . . The music of poetry . . . . must be a music latent in the common speech of its time.' [1]

If this is true of all poetry, how much more true is it of speech designed to be spoken on the stage as the speech of living men: 'The dependence of verse upon speech is much more direct in dramatic poetry than in any other'.[2] Yet it is in precisely this particular that poetic drama has gone astray since the seventeenth century. The failure of the plays of the great poets of the nineteenth century is usually attributed to their lack of theatrical experience. Eliot, however, suggests that:

'It is not primarily lack of plot, or lack of action and suspense, or imperfect realization of character, or lack of anything of what is called "theatre", that makes these plays so lifeless: it is primarily that their rhythm of speech is something that we cannot associate with any human being except a poetry reciter.' [3]

So Eliot's own work for the theatre and the important phase of modern poetic drama which he initiated started from a revitalizing of the rhythms and idiom of dramatic poetry. He had successfully done this for non-dramatic poetry before coming to the drama, but here his problem was intensified by the modern self-consciousness about dramatic poetry, which is the result of the loss of the tradition of poetry in the theatre. Naturalistic prose being the dominant theatrical medium, much of Eliot's energy has gone into circumventing the prejudice against poetry on the one hand and the conscious enjoyment of it on the other. As Eliot points

[1] 'The Music of Poetry', *On Poetry and Poets*, p. 31.
[2] *Ibid.*, p. 33.　　　　　[3] *Ibid.*, p. 34.

out,[1] the conscious enjoyment of it is liable to be as bad as the dislike, because it induces the wrong state of attention. This is the outcome, then, of the loss of one artistic convention.

Certain other artistic conventions, however, have been more durable, perhaps because they are firmly rooted in the soil of theatrical reality. Unsophisticated audiences, such as were to be found until recently in the English music-hall, have no difficulty in accepting conventions like the soliloquy. They are aware of whether they are being entertained, but hardly at all of the techniques by which they are being entertained. Popular audiences react instinctively to the subtle changes of Shakespearean technique. It seems to be only the dramatic critics and the cultural sophisticates ('A little learning . . .') who have any difficulty in making the necessary adjustments. The galleryite at the Old Vic will probably take Prince Hal's 'I know you all' as Shakespeare meant him to take it; it is only the intellectual with naturalistic preconceptions of character who will let it sour the whole play for him. Thus, Eliot was to have little difficulty in restoring some of the conventions of the older drama in *Murder in the Cathedral*, a play written for an unsophisticated audience.

But, as one of the interlocutors in his 'Dialogue on Dramatic Poetry' observed, 'it is as much the lack of moral and social conventions as the lack of artistic conventions that stands in the way of poetic drama to-day.' [2] We have no common standards by which to measure the significance of man's actions, and this is the very root of poetic drama. Man's actions, I suggest, are not significant in themselves, but only by reference to values outside man. The most complete mode of reference is poetry, and the values inhere in a religious conception of life, in the belief that the goal of existence is God. It would seem that a religious attitude to human life is necessary for the writing of true poetic drama. Apart from the plays of Auden and Isherwood, all the important poetic drama of the last thirty years in England has been religious in basis. And the drama of Auden and Isherwood may in the long run reveal itself as no more than an interesting phenomenon of the thirties because it has no such basis. The really significant phase of modern poetic drama began when the drama went back to its origins

[1] *Poetry and Drama*, p. 13 (*On Poetry and Poets*, p. 73).
[2] *Selected Essays*, p. 54.

inside the church and from there moved into the commercial theatre by way of the smaller specialized theatres, such as the Mercury. In this movement, Eliot has been so much the leader as to seem at times an isolated figure, moving steadily forward on his own.

Chapter Two

Eliot's Approach to Drama

*The Experiments—'Sweeney Agonistes' (1926-7)
and 'The Rock' (1934)*

I N one respect, Shakespeare is the worst thing that has happened to English drama. Milton and Keats, in a different sphere, testified to the overwhelming effect he had upon them; after reading him they felt drained of creative energy.

> Then thou our fancy of itself bereaving,
> Dost make us Marble with too much conceaving,

complained the young Milton ('On Shakespeare' in 1630), though he graciously turned his complaint into a near-Metaphysical compliment. 'On sitting down to read King Lear once again', Keats uttered something like a prayer:

> When I am through the old oak forest gone
> Let me not wander in a barren dream
> But when I am consumed with the fire
> Give me new Phoenix-wings to fly at my desire.[1]

In the sphere of poetic drama, the devastation has not been just momentary. The attempts at drama by the poets of the nineteenth century were largely bedevilled by his magnetic pull. By 1916

---

[1] *The Letters of John Keats*, ed. Maurice Buxton Forman (third edition, Oxford University Press, 1947), p. 89.

Yeats had decided that 'If our modern poetical drama has failed it is mainly because, always dominated by the example of Shakespeare, it would restore an irrevocable past.' [1]

Eliot saw quite early in his career as playwright that the only solution to the problem was to go back beyond Shakespeare to earlier forms of dramatic verse and indeed to the root principle of English prosody—organization by stress rather than numerical division into syllabic units. And already, in his non-dramatic poetry, he had tackled another aspect of the problem. In English, as perhaps in most modern languages, the vital tension of poetic rhythm arises out of the subtle interaction of ordinary speech rhythms with the basic metric pattern. As a poetic innovator, Eliot started from the principle that the language of poetry must be related to everyday speech. When it departs too far from living speech rhythms and current idiom, it loses its vitality. Poetry tends to distil a language of its own out of the language of common speech and this tends to become a fashion and to ossify, so to speak. Thus, although it has initially a living relationship to the spoken language, it may soon become divorced from it, for it tends to stand still, while the living language is constantly changing. Every so often, therefore, a renewal of poetic rhythm and idiom is necessary; and, as Eliot points out:

'the task of the poet will differ, not only according to his personal constitution, but according to the period in which he finds himself. At some periods, the task is to explore the musical possibilities of an established convention of the relation of the idiom of verse to that of speech; at other periods, the task is to catch up with the changes in colloquial speech, which are fundamentally changes in thought and sensibility.' [2]

Donne was such an innovator, Wordsworth another, and in the twentieth century the task fell to Eliot. And if this renewal was necessary in non-dramatic poetry, how much more necessary was it in dramatic poetry, where the accent of speech must be dominant. Almost all dramatic poets since Shakespeare had used

[1] 'A Note on "At the Hawk's Well"' (December, 1916), *The Wild Swans at Coole, Other Verses and a Play in Verse* (The Cuala Press, Churchtown, Dundrum, 1917), p. 47. Cf. Eliot, *On Poetry and Poets*, pp. 150–1.
[2] 'The Music of Poetry', *On Poetry and Poets*, p. 35. Cf. *ibid.*, p. 31.

blank verse. As early as 1928, however, Eliot saw that 'We must find a new form of verse which shall be as satisfactory a vehicle for us as blank verse was for the Elizabethans.'[1] At other times, he has suggested that the Elizabethans exhausted the resources of blank verse as a dramatic medium[2] and that subsequent poets, notably Milton, in exploiting it for non-dramatic purposes have robbed it of the flexibility which it 'must have if it is to give the effect of conversation'.[3] By the twentieth century, blank verse was completely out of touch with current speech rhythms. When he came to work in the theatre, therefore, Eliot felt that one of his prime tasks was the creation of a plausible verse to replace blank verse, the creation of a form moulded to modern sensibility—a new bottle for a new wine.

From the first, Eliot's critical doctrine of the impersonality of poetry[4] inclined him to the use of *personae* and incipiently dramatic situations; if the situations did not become fully dramatic, it was because the characters were evading action instead of taking it. *The Love Song of J. Alfred Prufrock*, for example, is a suppressed drama. We have what Raymond Williams calls 'the dramatisation of consciousness, the dramatic realisation of a mind',[5] but it is a mind which shrinks from the commitment of action. In *Portrait of a Lady*, there is a momentary advance into the world of action; there are scenes and dialogue before the protagonist withdraws completely into himself; there is, in short, a partial objectification of the drama. This technique is elaborated and immensely complicated in *The Waste Land*, which, with its series of scenes dissolving into one another or cutting from one to another in a manner analogous to film, is a dramatization of the consciousness of Europe in a framework of myth:

> And I Tiresias have foresuffered all
>
> .   .   .   .
>
> I who have sat by Thebes below the wall . . .[6]

[1] *Selected Essays* (1951), p. 57.
[2] *On Poetry and Poets*, pp. 34–5. Cf. pp. 159–60.
[3] *Poetry and Drama*, p. 24 (*On Poetry and Poets*, p. 80).
[4] Cf. *Selected Essays*, pp. 17–22.
[5] *Drama from Ibsen to Eliot* (Chatto and Windus, London, 1952), p. 224.
[6] *The Waste Land*, ll. 243–5 (*Collected Poems*, p. 70). Cf. Eliot's note on l. 218 (p. 80): 'What Tiresias *sees*, in fact, is the substance of the poem.'

The logical end of this movement is drama, and it is not alto-
gether surprising that Eliot felt committed to it as early as 1924.
Arnold Bennett recorded in his journal a visit from Eliot on 10
September, 1924, in which he said that

'he had definitely given up that form of writing [poetry, with
particular reference to *Wastelands*, as Bennett called the poem]
and was now centred on dramatic writing. He wanted to write a
drama of modern life (furnished flat sort of people) in a rhythmic
prose "perhaps with certain things in it accentuated by drum-
beats". And he wanted my advice. We arranged that he should do
the scenario and some sample pages of dialogue.'[1]

The collaboration seems not to have developed, but the idea
recorded here may well be the germinal idea for Eliot's first essay
in dramatic form.

Sweeney Agonistes (1926-7) remains incomplete—'Fragments of
an Aristophanic Melodrama'. We are probably not meant to
place a strict interpretation upon the word 'Aristophanic'. Certainly, the resemblance to Greek Old Comedy does not go deep.[2]
The 'Fragment of a Prologue' performs the same general functions
as the Aristophanic prologue; it sets the scene, creates a mood, and
initiates the exposition. The 'Fragment of an Agon', however,
does not follow the carefully articulated form of its prototype.[3]
There is essentially no conflict because there is no mutual understanding, no common ground, so to speak, upon which contend-
ers could meet in debate. Part of Sweeney's 'agony' consists in
his inability to communicate his insight to the others. The play is

[1] *The Journals of Arnold Bennett*, Vol. III, 1921-8, ed. Newman Flower
(Cassell and Company, London, 1933), p. 52.
[2] For this and several other observations on *Sweeney Agonistes* I am indebted
to Mr. Roy Arthur Swanson of the Department of Classics, University of
Minnesota.
[3] A beginning can be made towards finding broad equivalences. The section
up to the song 'Under the bamboo tree' (pp. 126-7) might be considered as
the strophe; the two songs (pp. 127-9) as the epirrheme, with the dimin-
uendo of the second serving as a pnigos; the next page and a half (129-31)
up to 'Cheer him up?' as the antistrophe; but Sweeney's 'story' (129-32) does
not constitute an antepirrheme, for it does not correspond to the epirrheme. If
it did, however, the last lines of the chorus and of the play would serve as an
antipnigos. (All references to *Sweeney Agonistes* are to *Collected Poems 1909-
1935*.)

Aristophanic, however, in the more general sense that it presents a satirical view of contemporary life. It is a melodrama both in the primary sense of a play interspersed with songs and in the secondary sense of a play in which the emotions are inflated and the situations overdramatized. This inflation and this overdramatization comprise another aspect of the satire.

In the development of Eliot's art *Sweeney Agonistes* is perhaps most important as an experiment in the introduction of contemporary rhythms and diction into poetic drama, but it also captures an aspect of the contemporary world. As Dilys Powell says: 'It is the union of the ultimate economy of diction with a conception of the ultimate spiritual destitution.' [1] Eliot parodies the popular song of the jazz era.[2] He reproduces the slightly artificial rhythm of a telephone conversation, which arises from the fact that the speakers cannot see each other, and this is reinforced by that ridiculous modern affectation, the telephone voice, and by the excessive politeness of prevarication:

> Hello Hello are you there?
> Yes this is Miss Dorrance's *flat*—
> Oh Mr. Pereira is that you? how do you do!
> Oh I'm *so* sorry. I *am* so sorry
> But Doris came home with a terrible chill
> No, just a chill
> Oh I *think* it's only a chill.[3]

The characters are lower in the social scale than those in the later comedies, and Eliot has caught the vacuous repetition of limited intelligence very neatly:

DUSTY: It's a funny thing how I draw court cards—
DORIS: There's a lot in the way you pick them up

[1] *Descent from Parnassus* (The Cresset Press, London, 1934), p. 75.

[2] 'Under the bamboo', p. 128. This is 'based on a song by Bob Cole and J. Rosamond Johnson first published in London in 1905; Mr. Eliot's tune is obviously different, but he has borrowed from the original song the title and the last two lines of the chorus' (Sears Jayne, 'Mr. Eliot's Agon', *Philological Quarterly*, XXXIV, 1955, p. 401). In Eliot's hands, however, it becomes a parody, satirizing the facile escapism of popular lyrics. It also makes a sophisticated-revue-like reference to 'culture':

> Where the Gauguin maids. . . .

[3] *Collected Poems*, p. 120.

DUSTY: There's an awful lot in the way you feel
DORIS: Sometimes they'll tell you nothing at all
DUSTY: You've got to know what you want to ask them
DORIS: You've got to know what you want to know.[1]

Mr. Grover Smith points out that the similar repetition in the 'fatuous dialogue between Klipstein and Krumpacker', as he calls it, might owe something to the 'bouncing' of a line from one speaker to another in the comic turn of the music-halls.[2] That Eliot was ready to learn from such a source, we know from an essay in *The Sacred Wood:*

'The Elizabethan drama was aimed at a public which wanted *entertainment* of a crude sort, but would *stand* a good deal of poetry; our problem should be to take a form of entertainment, and subject it to the process which would leave it a form of art. Perhaps the music-hall comedian is the best material.' [3]

And perhaps it was the material he was using here—there is certainly something of the crude vigour of the vaudeville sketch in the fragments—but quick-fire repetition is, of course, a standard theatrical device for achieving the speed necessary to comic effect while ensuring intelligibility. Molière, for example, employs it with a touch of parody at the beginning of *Les Fourberies de Scapin*, and Eliot himself uses it to get the ball of comedy rolling at the beginning of *The Cocktail Party*. But there, as in *Sweeney Agonistes*, he uses it creatively; it emphasizes the emptiness of party chatter and the vacuity of the society he is depicting.

Clearly, one of Eliot's chief concerns in *Sweeney Agonistes* was to come to terms with the speech of the time. Having done this, perhaps his purpose was fulfilled. Possibly, however, he found that the situation he had developed was not yielding promise of a complete play. Even so, it has adumbrations of the plays to come. For instance, he uses a chorus to voice communal feeling, and he approaches what is to be his central theme—that of spiritual

[1] *Ibid.*, p. 122.
[2] Grover Smith, Jr., *T. S. Eliot's Poetry and Plays* (University of Chicago Press, 1956), p. 115. The dialogue referred to is on pp. 123-5 of *Collected Poems.*
[3] *The Sacred Wood* (Faber and Faber, third edition, 1932), p. 70.

conflict and growth in an exceptional person and its relation to, and repercussions in, the lives of more ordinary people.

Like all Eliot's plays, it has a pattern of relationships worked out in terms of spiritual awareness:

'My intention was to have one character whose sensibility and intelligence should be on the plane of the most sensitive and intelligent members of the audience; his speeches should be addressed to them as much as to the other personages in the plays—or rather, should be addressed to the latter, who were to be material, literal-minded and visionless, with the consciousness of being overheard by the former.' [1]

The exceptional character is Sweeney, but Sweeney is to some extent the type of modern sensual man, whose spiritual growth is stunted by the parched soil of the Waste Land. His wrestling is a far cry from that of Milton's Samson.[2]

Attempts to divine the pattern of a total play seem to me pointless speculation. The links between the fragments are few and not particularly significant. The temptation to read significance into them, however, is strengthened by the fact that several of the characters appear, or seem to appear, in Eliot's earlier poetry. In *Sweeney Erect*, when the hero, at his morning ablutions, 'Tests the razor on his leg' and 'The epileptic on the bed' has a fit, a Doris

> towelled from the bath
> Enters padding on broad feet
> Bringing sal volatile
> And a glass of brandy neat.[3]

If it is the same Doris in *Sweeney Agonistes*, she has moved from Mrs. Turner's establishment and set herself up in a flat for which

---

[1] T. S. Eliot, *The Use of Poetry and the Use of Criticism* (Faber and Faber, 1933), p. 153.

[2] The one possible point of contact between them is a figure of speech:
> To live a life half dead, a living death
>
> > (*Samson Agonistes*, l. 100)
>
> Death is life and life is death
>
> > (*Sweeney Agonistes*, p. 131)

Collected Poems, p. 43.

Pereira pays the rent. Mrs. Porter, 'The Queen of Hearts' [1] is linked with Sweeney in *The Waste Land:*

> But at my back from time to time I hear
> The sound of horns and motors, which shall bring
> Sweeney to Mrs. Porter in the spring. [2]

Marvell's 'winged chariot' is modernized and heard only intermittently and appears to give easy access to a not-so-coy mistress. Day's 'noise of horns and hunting' has become a much less romantic sound and it will bring, not 'Actaeon to Diana in the spring', but Sweeney to Mrs. Porter, who no doubt presents something of a contrast to the goddess of chastity and who, instead of being glimpsed in her naked beauty in a forest pool, is to be seen washing her feet in soda water. [3]

Sweeney himself is the hero of two poems and makes a brief appearance in two others. [4] He seems to be representative of modern man, a debased image of humanity. In *Sweeney Erect,*

> Gesture of orang-outang
> Rises from the sheets in steam. [5]

And in *Sweeney Among the Nightingales,*

> Apeneck Sweeney spreads his knees
> Letting his arms hang down to laugh,
> The zebra stripes along his jaw
> Swelling to maculate giraffe. [6]

This seems to be what mankind has come to:

> The lengthened shadow of a man
> Is history, said Emerson
> Who had not seen the silhouette
> Of Sweeney straddled in the sun. [7]

---

[1] *Ibid.*, p. 121.

[2] *The Waste Land*, ll. 196–8 (*Collected Poems*, p. 68).

[3] The lines from Day are quoted by Eliot in his note on l. 197 (*Collected Poems*, p. 80).

[4] *Sweeney Erect, Sweeney among the Nightingales, Mr. Eliot's Sunday Morning Service*, and *The Waste Land* (*Collected Poems*, pp. 42, 57, 56 and 68 respectively).

[5] *Collected Poems*, p. 42.

[6] *Ibid.*, p. 57.   [7] *Ibid.*, p. 43.

While some attend *Mr. Eliot's Sunday Morning Service*,

> Sweeney shifts from ham to ham
> Stirring the water in his bath.[1]

Sweeney is modern, secular man, who employs the Sabbath in physical relaxation.

F. O. Matthiessen thought that 'The hero [of *Sweeney Agonistes*] is so different a character from the "apeneck Sweeney" of the poems that Eliot might better have given him a different name'.[2] But it seems to me that the character seen in the dramatic fragments may be essentially the same as the character implied in the poems. Some of the difference may spring from the fact that he has been developed and given a chance to speak for himself, so that we begin to see inside him. But even more of the difference may be the result of functional necessity. If light is to be thrown upon the shabbiness and monotony of the world of the play, someone in it must be aware of the shabbiness and the monotony, and Sweeney fulfils this function, while retaining the name, perhaps as representative of modern man.

I cannot find so much evidence of pattern in the drunken maunderings of Sweeney as Mr. Sears Jayne does.[3] Sweeney is striving to be articulate and he is more aware than the others of the horror of the boredom, but he has not transcended the condition of life depicted in the play. In emphasizing this, I am a little at variance with the author's statement quoted earlier. Perhaps, however, when Eliot wrote those words some years later he was for the moment ignoring, or had even forgotten, that the pattern is not quite so clear-cut in the play itself. In such an effective representation of a drinking-party as we find here, it is hardly likely to be.

Not yet too drunk to 'make a pass', Sweeney's first words are a muted suggestion of seduction, if not rape:

SWEENEY: I'll carry you off
           To a cannibal isle.
DORIS: You'll be the cannibal!

---

[1] *Collected Poems*, p. 56.

[2] *The Achievement of T. S. Eliot* (third edition, Oxford University Press, 1958), p. 159.

[3] 'Mr. Eliot's Agon', *Philological Quarterly*, XXXIV (1955), pp. 395–414.

SWEENEY: You'll be the missionary!
You'll be my little seven stone missionary!
I'll gobble you up. I'll be the cannibal.
DORIS: You'll carry me off? To a cannibal isle?
SWEENEY: I'll be the cannibal.
DORIS: I'll be the missionary,
I'll convert you!
SWEENEY: I'll convert *you*!
Into a stew.
A nice little, white little, missionary stew
(p. 126).

Although the tone is entirely flippant, this is a curious anticipation of the killing of another 'missionary' by the cannibals, the crucifixion of Celia in *The Cocktail Party*. It starts Sweeney's train of thought towards the escape from civilized life ('There's no telephones . . .') offered by 'a crocodile isle', an aspiration which is echoed by most of the other men in wistful chorus: 'We won't have to catch any trains . . .' (p. 129). Sweeney's egg, which is what suggests 'life on a crocodile isle', also finds its way into the first song, much to Doris's disgust ('I don't like eggs . . .'). This playful throwing about of ideas reinforces the tone of sophisticated flippancy which marks the first part of the scene.

In Sweeney, however, the gaiety soon gives way to an over-emphatic, almost maudlin moralizing, as is very common in drunkenness. On the island there will be

Nothing at all but three things

.   .   .   .

Birth, and copulation, and death.
That's all the facts when you come to brass tacks:
Birth, and copulation, and death.
I've been born, and once is enough.
You don't remember, but I remember,
Once is enough (p. 127).

The purely secular life of modern society is reduced to its bare bones, and the reiteration of 'once is enough' indicates its reluctance to be reborn in the spirit.

Unaware that she is condemning contemporary city life shorn

33

of its 'civilized' trappings and thus revealed as a pagan existence, Doris rebels against 'life on a crocodile isle' as described here and in the songs:

> DORIS: That's not life, that's no life
> Why I'd just as soon be dead.
> SWEENEY: That's what life is. Just is
> DORIS: What is?
> What's that life is?
> SWEENEY: Life is death.
> I knew a man once did a girl in (p.129).

It is this glimpse of an abnormal world which has given him his insight.

On the basis of the intimate knowledge shown in 'This one didn't get pinched in the end' (p.130) detective-story addicts in the audience may begin to construct the theory that Sweeney himself is the murderer, and that his explanation—

> He used to come and see me sometimes
> I'd give him a drink and cheer him up (pp.130-1)

—is a 'cover-up'. Certainly, Sweeney seems to have known the impulse to murder:

> Any man might do a girl in
> Any man has to, needs to, wants to
> Once in a lifetime, do a girl in (p.130),

but this reads satisfactorily as a recognition of the universality of sinful impulse: 'There, but for the grace of God, go I.' If, as seems likely, then, Sweeney's knowledge of the murder is second-hand, he clearly has sufficient sympathetic imagination to understand the murderer's predicament:

> He didn't know if he was alive
>   and the girl was dead
> He didn't know if the girl was alive
>   and he was dead
> He didn't know if they both were alive
>   or both were dead

If he was alive then the milkman wasn't
      and the rent-collector wasn't
And if they were alive then he was dead.

(p. 131)

As Grover Smith points out, in the first instalment of Eliot's 'Eeldrop and Appleplex', a sketch contributed to *The Little Review* in 1917, there occurs 'a curious forecast of this theme':

'In Gopsum Street a man murders his mistress. The important fact is that for the man the act is eternal, and that for the brief space he has to live, he is already dead. He is already in a different world from ours. He has crossed the frontier. The important fact that something is done which can not be undone—a possibility which none of us realize until we face it ourselves.' [1]

There is no evidence that his experience will lead Sweeney across the frontier, as it is to lead Harry in *The Family Reunion*. And, after all, it is an experience gained at a remove. Sweeney seems to lose interest in or give up his attempt to communicate his insight and to subside into morose indifference:

But if you understand or if you don't
That's nothing to me and nothing to you
We all gotta do what we gotta do
We're gona sit here and drink this booze (p.131).

He has, however, moved the other men to link his story with their own experience:

When you're alone in the middle of the night and
      you wake in a sweat and a hell of a fright
When you're alone in the middle of the bed and
      you wake like someone hit you in the head
You've had a cream of a nightmare dream and
      you've got the hoo-ha's coming to you
Hoo hoo hoo
You dreamt you waked up at seven o'clock and its
      foggy and it's damp and it's dawn and it's dark

---

[1] Eliot, 'Eeldrop and Appleplex, I', *The Little Review*, Vol. IV, No. 1 (May 1917), 9, quoted by Grover Smith, pp. 117–18.

> And you wait for a knock and the turning of a lock
> for you know the hangman's waiting for you.
> And perhaps you're alive
> And perhaps you're dead
> Hoo ha ha . . .
> KNOCK KNOCK KNOCK (p.132)

To some extent this is communal expression of terror such as we find in *Murder in the Cathedral* and *The Family Reunion*, but the comic overtones of the idiom employed ('hell of a fright', 'cream of a nightmare dream', 'hoo-ha's'), the overdramatization, and the resemblance to the bad-night patter in *Iolanthe*,[1] prevent one from taking it quite seriously. Are the boys 'laying it on' to scare the girls, and are they perhaps suddenly scared in turn at the abrupt interruption of reality when the knock they say they are waiting for really comes? The capitals might be construed as stage directions.[2] Like the ringing of the telephone (p.120), however, the knocks are used as a contribution to the rhythm of the play and are, therefore, included in the pattern of the verse. There is probably some playful experimentation in the play, though this does not preclude a deeper seriousness.

The fragments present a picture of the boredom and emptiness of modern life with its evasion of fundamental realities—fate knocking at the door (Pereira and the Devil to pay?), the *memento mori* of the 'coffin card'.[3] Terror of the unknown is reduced to the melodramatic 'hoo-ha's' of the chorus. Even Sweeney's intimations of mortality arise from contemplation of a sensational murder of the kind reported in detail in the *News of the World*, the Sunday newspaper which boasts 'the largest circula-

---

[1] Pointed out by Henry W. Wells in *New Poets from Old* (Columbia U.P. New York, 1940), p. 75.

[2] Cf., however, the normal stage directions on pp. 122–3.

[3] The inference that the knocking is symbolic is supported by the fact that the players of the 'game of chess' in *The Waste Land* are also waiting for a knock upon the door (*Collected Poems*, p. 66). The reading of the cards in that poem (pp. 62–3) also satirizes this modern superstition as a survival of ancient religious augury debased to a form of popular escapism. Eliot probably intended the 'coffin card' to have some precise significance in the complete play. For Doris, certainly, it is a cloud in the party atmosphere (see pp. 129–30).

tion in the world'.[1] In his glimpse of the murderer's dilemma, however ('He didn't know if he was alive . . .'), we see the germ of Harry's spiritual awakening in *The Family Reunion*. The epigraphs are, in fact, much more applicable to the later play. And Sweeney's relation to the others—

> I gotta use words when I talk to you
> But if you understand or if you don't
> That's nothing to me and nothing to you

—is a rudimentary form of the impossibility of communication between Harry and his obtuse uncles and aunts.[2] As Miss Helen Gardner observes,

'Sweeney's incapacity to express the horror at the heart of life in any terms he feels to be adequate, or that his hearers are likely to understand, suggests that the subject of the fragments is not even the contrast of inanity and despair, but the gulf fixed between those capable of awareness and those who are not: "You don't see them, you don't—but *I* see them." It is difficult to see how such a subject could be developed at all except by repetition; for it is impossible to imagine any change in the attitudes of Doris and Dusty and their guests. The theme of Mr. Eliot's early verse finds supreme expression in *The Waste Land*, to which *Sweeney Agonistes* appears a rather sterile appendix. Confined within the limits of scenic presentation, with this limited circle of people, the "boredom", which in *The Waste Land* seems universal, is capable of dismissal as an accident of a certain class and period; and the "horror" is either trivial, and rather obviously symbolic, as in the telephone bell and the knocking, or grotesque as in Sweeney's anecdote from the *News of the World*.'[3]

[1] In an essay of 1927 Eliot pointed out the persistence of the popular appeal of the thriller throughout the ages:
'*The Spanish Tragedy*, like the series of Hamlet plays, including Shakespeare's, has an affinity to our contemporary detective drama. . . . It is only surprising that there are not more examples of this type of play, since there is evidence of as lively a public interest in police court horrors as there is to-day' (*Selected Essays*, p. 81).
We shall observe some exploitation of this interest in *The Family Reunion*.
[2] Cf. *The Family Reunion*, pp. 28–30.
   The Art of T. S. Eliot (The Cresset Press, London, 1949), pp. 131–2.

The fragments show, however, that Eliot could adapt his gift
for satiric portraiture through speech to the requirements of
drama, in which over-subtlety is apt to be lost:

DORIS: Here's the two of spades.
DUSTY: The *two* of *spades*!

            THAT'S THE COFFIN! !

DORIS: THAT'S THE COFFIN?
        Oh good heavens what'll I do?
        Just before a party too!
DUSTY: Well it needn't be yours, it may mean a friend.
DORIS: No it's mine. I'm sure it's mine.
        I dreamt of weddings all last night.
        Yes it's mine. I know it's mine.
        Oh good heavens what'll I do.
        Well I'm not going to draw any more,
        You cut for luck. You cut for luck.
        It might break the spell. You cut for luck

                                (pp.121-2).

This illustrates also the comic exaggeration which characterizes much of the play and should underline the danger of taking
too seriously a symbolism which makes fun of itself ('News of an
absent friend?—Pereira'; 'The Queen of Hearts!—Mrs. Porter';
'Of course the Knave of Hearts [who, we recall, "stole some
tarts"] *is* Sam!'). It is perhaps the neatness of much of the characterization within the limited space and the comic poise secured
through the balance of speech rhythm and metre which are the
most significant achievements of the fragments. The raciness is
peculiar to the milieu, but the technical assurance looks forward to
The Cocktail Party.

Eliot's next excursion into drama was *The Rock* (1934), a pageant play written in aid of a church building fund and aptly taking
the building of a church as its framework. Here Eliot was writing
under the direction of Mr. E. Martin Browne, who wrote the
scenario.[1] In his Prefatory Note to the play, Eliot said that of only

[1] Martin Browne was himself working to order. See his comments in *T. S.
Eliot: A Symposium for his Seventieth Birthday*, ed. Neville Braybrooke (Farrar,
Straus and Cudahy, New York, 1958), p. 57.

one scene—presumably, the last scene in Part I, the one scene entirely in verse [1]—was he 'literally the author', and suggested that for only this scene and the choruses was he responsible,[2] And in a letter to *The Spectator* in June, 1934 he tried to correct the impression that might have been created by a review which had appeared in it:

'The "play" makes no pretence of being "a contribution to English dramatic literature" [terms used by Derek Verschoyle in his critique]: it is a *revue*. My only serious dramatic aim was to show that there is a possible *rôle* for the Chorus.' [3]

He has chosen therefore to preserve only the choruses and they are reprinted in the *Collected Poems*, but some knowledge of the pageant is necessary to their full understanding and, since it is no longer in print, an account of the action may be helpful.

The structure, Martin Browne has said, was borrowed from a C. B. Cochran revue,[4] but it is used creatively for much of the pageant's length. The central action, the building of a church in contemporary London, is opened out to emphasize that the building of a church is not a matter of merely piling up stones. It ranges back and forth in time to show the continuity of the ecclesiastical tradition, the persistence of the past into the present, and the way in which the present is built upon the past. This new church is built upon the foundation of *the* Church and *the* Church is built upon the Rock ('tu es Petrus, et super hanc petram . . .', Matthew xvi. 18). The Chorus of seven men and ten women,

[1] *The Rock* (Faber and Faber, 1934), pp. 42-7.
[2] For Eliot's account of the conditions under which he collaborated in the work, see *On Poetry and Poets*, p. 91. Apart from the stimulus which, he says there, it gave to his writing of poetry in general, the peculiar importance of *The Rock* is that it engaged Eliot in theatrical activity for the first time—he had had no part in the production of *Sweeney Agonistes* by Rupert Doone at the Group Theatre—and initiated the long collaboration with Martin Browne from which he was to learn how to solve many of the problems of stagecraft. Possibly, too, it was a pledge of his interest in drama which encouraged the organizers of the Canterbury Festival to commission *Murder in the Cathedral*.
[3] *The Spectator*, 8 June, 1934, p. 887. The review had appeared on June 1st.
[4] In an interview by Burke Wilkinson, *The New York Times*, 7 February, 1954, Section 2, p. 1, col. 6.

wearing half-masks to emphasize their impersonality,[1] 'speak as the voice of the Church' (p. 7), and the 'Rock' himself is one of the *dramatis personae*.

After a chorus in which the spiritual sickness of contemporary society is diagnosed—'Knowledge of words and ignorance of the Word'—the Rock enters, led by a Boy, and exhorts the audience to 'Make perfect your will'. Then he invites us to see 'the work of the humble' and this introduces choruses contrasting the work of the men building churches with the plight of the unemployed. Eventually our attention is focused upon a small group of workmen who are 'discovered' digging and building the foundations of a church. Most of them are indifferent about the building they are working on. To them, it is just another job. But Ethelbert, the foreman, is alive to its significance:

'Us 'ere, I says, Fred, is doin' somethink which is more'n just bricks and mortar . . . . There always 'as been someone buildin' a church. Always someone buildin', buildin', buildin' . . . . You and me, Fred, and you, young Edwin, are doin' somethin' for God and somethin' for 'umanity what always 'as to be done. There's somethin' strong and lastin' about a buildin'. You needn't believe in God but you've got to believe in a buildin'. It goes up and up in the sky, and on and on through the years, and it speaks with its lights and its bells in the night and in the sunshine—and it stands when you and I are dust, what built it for the glory of God —and that church 'as been put up with 'ands, buildin', buildin', buildin',—all through the years—in the ruddy rain and 'eat and 'ail and snow—workin' in bricks and mortar, goin' on forever and ever and ever, buildin' the church of God' (pp. 13–14).

If we refuse to be disconcerted by the stunted idiom, a caricature of working-class speech for which Eliot himself may not be responsible,[2] we glimpse here the great theme which is symbolized by the presence of the Rock as a character appearing at crucial moments throughout the play. This theme begins to issue

---

[1] E. Martin Browne, *T. S. Eliot: a symposium*, ed. March and Tambimuttu, p. 198. Photographs of the production are reproduced in *Theatre Arts Monthly*, Vol. XVIII, No. 12 (December, 1934), pp. 927–8.

[2] The pub scene in *The Waste Land* (*Collected Poems*, pp. 66–7) shows that Eliot is capable of reproducing working-class idiom faithfully.

in dramatic incident a couple of pages later, when Ethelbert helps to effect the necessary transition:

'There's some new notion about time, what says that the past —what's be'ind you—is what's goin' to 'appen in the future, bein' as the future 'as already 'appened. I 'aven't 'ad time to get the 'ang of it yet; but when I read about all those old blokes, they seems much like us . . .' (pp. 15–16).

A group of Saxons enter and the workmen witness the acceptance of Christianity in Britain, the foundation of the English Church:

> Thus your fathers were made
> Fellow citizens of the saints, of the household of GOD,
>   being built upon the foundation
> Of apostles and prophets, Christ Jesus Himself the
>   chief cornerstone.[1]

The building of a single church is not an isolated act; it is part of the larger process of founding and maintaining the Church temporal. The difficulties of building the church in this sense are perennial—'the Church must be forever building, and always decaying, and always being restored' [2]—but the example of earlier men and the difficulties they overcame gives strength. The builders discover, in fact, that they are aided by the vast host of the Church spiritual. Rahere, a builder and monk of the Middle Ages, appears and promises them that

'Those who helped me, both visible and invisible, shall help you. If you will have faith, all the angels and saints of God shall pray for you, and your work shall be blessed' (p. 28).

And Rahere's men enter and work 'above', while 'below, the bricklayers resume their tasks with a will' (*ibid.*).

Similar parallels are illustrated between the difficulties of the modern church-builders and those of the Israelites rebuilding Jerusalem, and between the plan of sabotage proposed by a contemporary political agitator and the Danish Invasion: 'The Church must be forever building, for it is forever decaying within

---

[1] p. 19 (*Collected Poems*, p. 162).   [2] p. 20 (*Collected Poems*, p. 163).

and attacked from without.' [1] Sometimes, the parallelism is telescoped. In a scene reminiscent of German Expressionism and very like the kind of drama the younger poets of the time, notably Auden and Spender, were attempting—it is the only scene entirely in verse—squads of Redshirts and Blackshirts enter 'in military formation' and offer their solutions to the problems of contemporary society:

REDSHIRTS (*in unison, with military gestures*).

> Our verse
> is free
> as the wind on the steppes
> as love in the heart of the factory worker
> thousands and thousands of steppes
> millions and millions of workers
>   all working
>   all loving
> in the cities
>   on the steppes
> production has risen by twenty point six per cent
> we can laugh at God!
> our workers
>   all working
> our turbines
>   all turning
> our sparrows
>   all chirping
> all denounce you, deceivers of the people! (p. 43).

(The parody of free verse and the parody of communist claims—free love increasing 'production', the sparrows backing up the workers in denunciation—go together.)

BLACKSHIRTS (*saluting*). Hail!

> We come as a boon and a blessing to all,
> Though we'd rather appear in the Albert Hall.
> Our methods are new in this land of the free,
> We make the deaf hear and we make the blind see.
> We're law-keeping fellows who make our own laws—
> And we welcome SUBSCRIPTIONS IN AID OF THE CAUSE! (p. 44).

[1] p. 21 (*Collected Poems*, p. 164).

The Chorus are not deceived by these 'new evangels' (p. 44). But if the new creeds of Communism and Fascism can be easily dismissed, the old creed of Capitalism has a stronger hold upon the members of society who now throng the stage. When at the command of the Plutocrat the Golden Calf is brought on, the crowd forgets everything else and falls to struggling over its dismemberment. The difficulty that Moses encountered in establishing God's law is the difficulty of the modern church-builders also. Ethelbert feels that everything is working against them. But in response to his cry 'O Lord help us!', the Rock is revealed 'standing brooding on the pinnacle':

THE ROCK.

> There shall be always the Church and the World
> And the Heart of Man
> Shivering and fluttering between them, choosing and chosen,
> Valiant, ignoble, dark and full of light
> Swinging between Hell Gate
> and Heaven Gate
> And the Gates of Hell shall not prevail.
> Darkness now, then
> Light.
>
> Light (pp. 47–8).

And, as if to point the relevance to the modern, everyday world, the lights go up in the theatre to mark the end of Part I.

Part II neatly takes up the theme by going back to the time before there was light. Presumably, this Part began in darkness and light came up on cue:

In the beginning GOD created the world. Waste and void. Waste and void. And darkness was upon the face of the deep.

And when there were men, in their various ways, they struggled in torment towards GOD.

Blindly and vainly, for man is a vain thing, and man without GOD is a seed upon the wind: driven this way and that, and finding no place of lodgement and germination.

They followed the light and the shadow, and the light led them forward to light and the shadow led them to darkness.[1]

[1] p. 49 (*Collected Poems*, p. 172).

This fine chorus rapidly surveys the history of the world to the time of Christ, the coming of the light of revelation and the foundation of the Church: 'Then it seemed as if men must proceed from light to light, in the light of the Word.' [1] But they did not, although their backslidings were momentary until our own time, when

Men have left GOD not for other gods, they say, but for no god;
   and this has never happened before
That men both deny gods and worship gods, professing first
   Reason,
And then Money, and Power, and what they call Life, or Race,
   or Dialectic.
The Church disowned, the tower overthrown, the bells upturned,
   what have we to do
But stand with empty hands and palms turned upwards
In an age which advances progressively backwards? [2]

But the Church is still there to remind men of the truth. The Rock sends 'one who accomplished much, in a time of drought and desolation:/Blomfield, Bishop of London,/Builder of many churches' (p. 53) and thus the action of Part II is initiated. Bishop Blomfield tells the Chorus that conditions were no more favourable to the building of churches in his own time and suggests they take as example the Crusades, which 'were set in motion' by 'a few men of principle and conviction', such as 'can accomplish what men without principle and conviction deem impossible' (p. 55). The scenes thus introduced serve to bring a touch of chivalric colour and give an opportunity for the introduction of liturgical pomp, but they are very tenuously connected with the central theme and are pedestrian in conception and execution.

After this, the action digresses even further from the central theme. A visit to the site by Mrs. Ethelbert serves as an excuse for a toast to the church and a song by her and Ethelbert. A visit by some members of the 'upper classes' gives rise to a discussion of styles of church architecture and leads to a scene of 'Reformation times' in which Romish decoration is stripped from the churches. This in turn gives rise to a fine chorus, 'Son of Man,

[1] p. 50 (*Collected Poems*, p. 173).
[2] p. 51 (*Collected Poems*, p. 174).

behold with thine eyes.'[1] But the near-integration of Part I has been quite lost from view. The great theme of the abiding, ever-renewed Church has been displaced by peripheral commentary.

With the completion of the church by Ethelbert and his men, we return to this theme. Before the dedication,

> you shall be reminded of other dedications
> Out of the distant past of London, out of times less dim:
> So that you may remember
> That the Temple is forever building, forever to be destroyed,
> forever to be restored ... (p. 78).

There follows a dramatization of the legendary dedication of Westminster Abbey by St. Peter, the rock on which the Church was founded. We have returned splendidly to the theme, but the next moment we are off again, this time into a ballet on the legend of Dick Whittington and his cat, justified flimsily as a transition to the dedication of the rebuilt Church of St. Michael, Paternoster Royal. A conversation piece between Wren, Pepys and Evelyn leads to the dedication of St. Paul's and the final chorus spoken around the altar of the new church, 'now furnished and lighted' (p. 83):

> It is now a visible church, one more light set on a hill
> In a world confused and dark and disturbed by portents of fear.[2]

With this hymn of thanksgiving to the 'Light Invisible', a short speech by the Rock, 'now St. Peter' (p. 86), the benediction and communal singing of the Builders' Song, the pageant ends.

Criticism exceeds its brief in finding fault with a piece for not doing what it does not set out to do, but one cannot help regretting that the promise of some of the earlier parts of the pageant is not fulfilled. There are hints of a conception of the Church's struggle for survival through the ages, which, if it had been fully realized in dramatic representation, might have formed a worthy prologue to the series of plays proper:

> And if blood of Martyrs is to flow on the steps
> We must first build the steps. . . .[3]

[1] pp. 74 ff. (*Collected Poems*, pp. 177 ff.).
[2] p. 84 (*Collected Poems*, p. 179).   [3] p. 42 (*Collected Poems*, p. 171).

As it is, much of the latter part is just scene-spinning. One can almost hear the authors asking themselves, What can we do next to give variety? The pageant becomes a sort of extravaganza on the building of churches instead of the dramatic meditation on the building of the Church adumbrated in the opening scenes.

The choruses, unfortunately, suffer from this lack of unification. Some of them, notably VII, IX and X, stand on their own; they have a pattern which makes them sufficient to themselves, and are on a par with Eliot's finer, though not his finest, non-dramatic poetry. But others tend to be just a series of reflections on the spiritual deterioration of modern society:

You, have you built well, have you forgotten the cornerstone?
Talking of right relations of men, but not of relations of men
  to GOD.
'Our citizenship is in Heaven'; yes, but that is the model and
  type for your citizenship upon earth.[1]

What life have you if you have not life together,
There is no life that is not in community,
And no community not lived in praise of GOD.
Even the anchorite who meditates alone,
For whom the days and nights repeat the praise of GOD
Prays for the Church, the Body of Christ incarnate.
And now you live dispersed on ribbon roads,
And no man knows or cares who is his neighbour
Unless his neighbour makes too much disturbance,
But all dash to and fro in motor cars,
Familiar with the roads and settled nowhere. . . .[2]

These extracts illustrate the stiffness of much of the choral writing. It operates upon a wavelength too short for choral

[1] p. 20 (*Collected Poems*, pp. 162-3).

[2] p. 41 (*Collected Poems*, p. 164). Cf. Eliot's observation in a broadcast talk:
'When I see the tendency for the village to be replaced, not by the suburb, for which there is much to be said, but by an endless line of houses along a ribbon road over which passes a ceaseless stream of cars, I wonder what sort of organic unity can be left, what sort of local patriotism and activity can be fostered.'
—'The Modern Dilemma (3): The Search for Moral Sanction', *The Listener*, Vol. VII, No. 168, 30 March, 1932, p. 480.

speech; it is too near ordinary speech, not near enough to chant. The voice is Eliot's public voice, precise, measured, meticulous, and this will not serve for group utterance, where the smaller rhythmic variations of individual speech are ironed out, leaving monotony. From time to time, however, we see this personal rhythm expanding:

Out of the sea of sound the life of music,
Out of the slimy mud of words, out of the sleet and hail of verbal imprecisions,
Approximate thoughts and feelings, words that have taken the place of thoughts and feelings,
There spring the perfect order of speech, and the beauty of incantation.[1]

In such passages we see Eliot reaching towards, if not attaining, the suppleness of the choral writing in *Murder in the Cathedral*. A measure of the distance between the general level of style in *The Rock* and that in the later play can be gathered from a comparison of the last choruses in both.[2] In the earlier play, the style merely flutters; in the later, it soars.

Eliot's description, in 'The Three Voices of Poetry', of the conditions of composition of *The Rock* not only accounts for most of one's discontent with it, but also suggests how it was that, just a year after its production, he was able to achieve the greatest choral poetry yet written in English. Working to a scenario, he was mainly concerned, in writing the choruses, to provide links between the scenes. In this task there was nothing to stimulate a truly dramatic conception, to call forth what he calls the third, or dramatic, voice. Consequently, it was the second voice, that of himself 'addressing—indeed haranguing—an audience', as he puts it, 'that was most distinctly audible'. The members of the chorus were not individuated; they had no character of their own. They merely served as a voice-piece for the author's views. In *Murder in the Cathedral*, on the other hand, the chorus as a whole had

[1] p. 75 (*Collected Poems*, p. 178).
[2] *Collected Poems*, pp. 179–81; *Murder in the Cathedral*, pp. 85–8. Just as the final chorus of the later play has as ground-bass the *Te Deum*, so the final chorus of *The Rock* uses the *Gloria* (see E. Martin Browne, March's *Symposium*, p. 200).

definite character and required Eliot to make an imaginative identification.[1]

However, it is not merely that Eliot was compelled to write in character. The choruses of *Murder in the Cathedral* are integrated with a total dramatic conception. *The Rock* does not realize the unifying conception latent in it. There is no dramatic emotion in the choruses to fuse the parts, only a number of different poetic moods: occasionally a devotional mood, but more often an elegiac mood of mourning for the wholeness of vision now lost to society, or a satiric mood in which the superficiality of modern life is castigated. Each chorus of *Murder in the Cathedral* has an emotional shape determined by its place in the dramatic development, whereas even the best choruses of *The Rock* have no more than an intellectual, self-determined shape.

The choruses are chiefly significant, therefore, as a stage in the creation of a new verse-form. Mr. Martin Browne explains this accomplishment very neatly:

'characterization is not called for. But a contemporary speech-rhythm is essential, and two developments follow. First, the iambic foot of Shakespearean tradition is given up: the stress shifts to the beginning of the foot, in accordance with the change that has come over English speech. This trochaic-cum-dactylic foot is of course no more rigidly adhered to than was the iambic in Shakespeare's later plays. The verse is infinitely varied, with many inverted feet; but the rhythm is strongly maintained.

'The other change is a final freeing of the verse from the counting of syllables. The ten-syllable line of "blank verse," which was almost uniform in Shakespeare's early plays, came to vary from eight to fourteen syllables in his later ones: but still the ten-syllable basis was at the back of the mind of both writer and hearers. Eliot has broken this "blank verse" tradition of syllables by going at once back and forward. He has gone back to the basis established by the mediaeval poets, of a fixed number of *stresses* in the line without any fixed number of syllables. He has gone forward to meet the development of prose-rhythms by the inclusion of a very long, sweepingly rhythmic line having six or eight stresses, but still a part of the verse-structure. Thus a form

[1] *On Poetry and Poets*, p. 91.

of verse much more varied than any before is placed at the service of the theatre.' [1]

But in *The Rock* itself Eliot's demonstration of the new form is not very persuasive. The explanation of the fluency that comes suddenly with *Murder in the Cathedral* is chiefly, I have suggested, the liberating effect of a unifying dramatic conception. In so far, however, as an explanation is necessary in terms of technique, we can most of us supply it from our own experience. After a determined but unsuccessful attempt to achieve mastery of a new technique, we may relax our efforts for a moment, perhaps even desist altogether for a time. When we next apply ourselves, we find that it comes easily; the hard-earned lessons have been absorbed and we make the right approach almost without thinking about it. [2] It is in this way that the choruses of *The Rock* seem to have prepared Eliot for the writing of *Murder in the Cathedral*.

Sweeney Agonistes and the choruses of *The Rock* were, then, only fragmentary essays in verse drama and hardly went beyond the problem of a suitable dramatic speech. Eliot's next work was a full-scale play, and it brought him face to face with the problem of dramatic form.

[1] March's *Symposium*, pp. 197–8.
[2] Eliot himself notes as the lesson he learnt the need for simplification of vocabulary, syntax, and content, in direct proportion to the number of voices written for (*On Poetry and Poets*, p. 91).

Chapter Three

'Murder in the Cathedral'
(1935)

THE choruses of *The Rock* return frequently to the
analysis of the spiritual condition of contemporary
society:

> Waste and void. Waste and void. And darkness on
> the face of the deep.
> Has the Church failed mankind, or has mankind
> failed the Church?[1]

To those who think of the Church primarily as a social organization, it may appear to have failed. But, under its spiritual aspect,
as the body of Christ and 'the noble army of martyrs', it offers
perpetual refreshment for the parched soil of the Waste Land.
In his first play Eliot turned immediately to what was to be the
central theme of almost all his plays—the role of the spiritually
elect in society, the fructification of communal life by the example
of the saint and the saintly. And he began with a full-scale study
of martyrdom.

The problem of creating a dramatic form capable of embodying
the kind of design Eliot had in mind was paramount. One thing
was clear; the example of Shakespeare must be eschewed. Even
if he had provided a suitable example—though probably the

---

[1] *Collected Poems*, p. 174.

sensuous richness of his drama was alien to the theme, in any case—it would have been a dangerous one to follow. Eliot perceived that

'a form which has been perfected by one age cannot be copied exactly by writers of another age. It belongs to its own period. If we wrote in the dramatic form and in the versification of Shakespeare we should only succeed in making rather poor imitations of Shakespeare: we should not be contributing anything to the life of our own time. . . . Hence we have to make use of suggestions from more remote drama, too remote for there to be any danger of imitation, such as "Everyman" and the late mediaeval morality and mystery plays, and the great Greek dramatists.' [1]

Apart from the use of allegorical figures in the temptations scene, Eliot's indebtedness to the *form* of medieval English drama is not great, though he models much of the *versification* upon *Everyman*. For the form he is mainly indebted to Greek tragedy. His play is essentially a series of episodes linked by stasima or choral odes.[2]

It seems likely that Greek tragedy evolved from the chorus, to be precise from the choric dithyrambs, by the gradual isolation of the leaders of the semi-choruses. In Aeschylus, the chorus remains central to the action, not in the sense that it takes part in the physical action, though it does from time to time, but in the sense that it opens up the spiritual dimension of the action. The chorus of *Agamemnon* is completely ineffectual in its attempts to influence the course of the action. Yet the essential action of the play, the operation of deity in human life, is revealed chiefly through the choral odes; it would be only slight exaggeration to say that the episodes are merely illustrations in action of the pattern of divine purpose thus revealed. Certainly, there is no lessening

---

[1] 'The Need for Poetic Drama', *The Listener*, 25 November, 1936, pp. 994-5.

[2] Less important resemblances to Greek tragedy are

(*a*) the use of the Messenger to announce the approach of the chief character (pp. 14-16) as in *The Persians* and *Agamemnon* (in Greek tragedy the Herald performs this function, the Messenger being used, when necessary, to narrate the off-stage action at the climax) and

(*b*) the confining of the action to the period immediately before and after the climactic deed.

of the sense of drama when episode gives way to stasimon; it is merely that the drama opens out to include a survey of the enveloping action, the working out of the curse on the House of Atreus and the evolution of the gods which, for Aeschylus, is focused in this phase of legendary history. The chorus is for him the principal means of transcending the limitations of drama. Sophocles transfers attention to the individual actor and makes the chorus subordinate to him. Although used with extraordinary skill to enhance effect—one of his characteristic uses being to relax tension as a prelude to increasing it yet further—the choral odes in Sophocles suspend the action; they are supplementary to it rather than complementary, as in Aeschylus. And although Euripides occasionally brings the chorus back towards the centre of the physical action, notably in the *Bacchae*, he does nothing to restore its centrality of function; indeed, the choral odes tend more and more in his drama to become lyric interludes, with less dramatic justification than in Sophoclean drama. Thus Aeschylean drama was quickly outmoded and it was the Sophoclean-Euripidean form of tragedy which shaped the European tradition through the mediation of Seneca. The chorus dwindled to a single actor commenting on the action or narrating intervening action, as in *Henry V*.

In a talk broadcast in the year after the first production of *Murder in the Cathedral*, Eliot remarked that:

'in making use of [the chorus] we do not aim to *copy* Greek drama. There is a good deal about the Greek theatre that we do not know, and never shall know. But we know that some of its conventions cannot be ours. The characters frequently talk too long; the chorus has too much to say and holds up the action; usually not enough happens; and the Greek notion of climax is not ours. But the chorus has always fundamentally the same uses. It mediates between the action and the audience; it intensifies the action by projecting its emotional consequences, so that we as the audience see it doubly, by seeing its effect on other people.' [1]

To this end, Eliot restored the full-throated chorus of Greek tragedy after centuries in which it was reduced to a single expositor of the action. (The dramatic poems, like those of Milton and

[1] 'The Need for Poetic Drama', *The Listener*, 25 November, 1936, p. 995.

Swinburne, in which the full chorus was used were plays for reading rather than performance.) He has, in fact, gone back to the fountainhead of European drama and restored the Aeschylean form.[1] He has used the chorus to open out the action into its full significance, as nobody else has done since Aeschylus.

But Eliot has not just copied Aeschylus; he has given the chorus a new significance in the light of the Christian dispensation. In Aeschylus the chorus has a character of its own—it consists of elders of Argos, or libation bearers, or some such personages—but for the most part it is just the author's mouthpiece, his principal means of conveying his vision of the significance of the action. In *Murder in the Cathedral* the chorus is much farther individualized. This is due less perhaps to the influence of naturalism and the modern emphasis on individuality than to the implications of Christianity, with its simultaneous emphasis on the precious uniqueness of the individual and the importance of spiritual community. The chorus represents, in effect, the great mass of individuals which Christ came to save: 'we acknowledge ourselves as type of the common man ...' (p. 87). The martyrdom of Becket is likewise on their behalf. The choruses embody their experience, rather than the author's view of the action. Of course, they speak with his fullness of utterance, not with the limited idiom of real 'scrubbers and sweepers'. But this 'discrepancy' is not far removed from the normal convention of dramatic poetry; what difference there is, can be largely accounted for in terms of the convention of communal speech. They are giving expression to communal feeling, which usually runs deeper than individual feeling, though it is not usually as articulate. The articulateness is poetic illumination, differing from the normal convention of dramatic poetry only in degree.

A theory of the origin of tragedy which was much discussed in the earlier part of the century was that of the Cambridge anthropologists, who thought they had discovered it in the rites of mystery religions representing the passion of a god, his death and rebirth, by which the yearly cycle of the disappearance of the seed into the ground and its re-emergence as new life in the spring was assured. Eliot had already used a seasonal myth as the basis

[1] In his essay 'Four Elizabethan Dramatists' Eliot defines his admiration of Aeschylus—and, incidentally, of *Everyman* (*Selected Essays*, p. 111).

of *The Waste Land* and shown his awareness of the parallel with the Christian story of Easter. It may, however, have been the work of the Cambridge anthropologists which suggested to him the possibility of reinforcing the theological pattern by the pattern of myth in *Murder in the Cathedral*.[1]

The fusion of these elements of Christian drama of the Middle Ages with the pre-Christian drama of the Greeks yielded a highly original form. Although nearer to Aeschylean tragedy than to any intervening form, it has been perfectly adapted to Christian theology and is very much of its time. Milton's adaptation of the Greek form to a Biblical theme is a less radical transformation, for all its touches of the baroque. Eliot's work is nearer the stylization of the Byzantine. Yet it has also a functional simplicity which is peculiarly twentieth-century. It resembles certain of the vocal works of Stravinsky more than anything in English dramatic art.

The form arose out of Eliot's conception of this particular subject and could not be adapted for general use. As we shall see, it allowed more obvious poetic effects than Eliot has since permitted himself in drama. At this time, in fact, Eliot had a different view of the tactics necessary for the reintroduction of poetry into the theatre from the one he has since evolved. In his talk on 'The Need for Poetic Drama' broadcast in 1936, he spoke of

'the necessity for poetic drama at the present time to emphasise, not to minimise, the fact that it is written in verse.'

'Furthermore, in the desire to emphasise those essentials of drama which have tended to be forgotten—the permanent struggles and conflicts of human beings—we wish to remind the audience that what they are seeing is a play, and not a photograph. The theatre, in the effort to get greater and greater realism—that is, greater illusion—and thereby attempting to do what the cinema can do better, has tended to depart so far from poetry as to depart from prose too; and to give us people on the stage who are so extremely lifelike that they do not even talk prose, but merely make human noises. So we want to take the opposite direction, and not let the audience forget that what they

[1] That Eliot was acquainted with the work of Harrison and Cornford, we know from *Selected Essays*, pp. 44 and 62.

are hearing is verse. Blank verse can too easily be made to sound as if it were bad prose, and the more regular the verse the more easily it can be maltreated in this way. So we introduce rhyme, even doggerel, as a constant reminder that it *is* verse and not a compromise with prose.'[1]

This position is very far removed from his recent pronouncements. The success of *Murder in the Cathedral* encouraged Eliot to devote his artistic energies to the problem of reviving poetic drama,[2] and prolonged consideration has led him to change his strategy; he now believes that the poet should do everything he can to prevent the audience from being aware that it is listening to poetry.

In the light of his later development, therefore, *Murder in the Cathedral* seems to be a digression. The creation of a plausible dramatic verse for general use was deferred. There was a tradition of treating historical subjects in verse, and, in any case, characters in a historical piece were expected to speak in a manner somewhat different from that of contemporary speech. Moreover, the play was to be produced for a festival audience prepared 'to put up with poetry'.[3] Under these conditions, Eliot felt free to use rhetorical devices such as balance, antithesis, cumulative effects, and even, from time to time, an elaborate alliteration reminiscent of Old English verse:

> shall I, who keep the keys
> Of heaven and hell, supreme alone in England,
> Who bind and loose, with power from the Pope,
> Descend to desire a punier power?
> Delegate to deal the doom of damnation,
> To condemn kings, not serve among their servants,
> Is my open office.[4]

This massive, almost ponderous, effect is particularly suited to the acoustic peculiarities of churches, where speech must be slowed

---

[1] *The Listener*, 25 November, 1936, p. 995.
[2] The later three of the *Four Quartets* (*East Coker*, 1940; *The Dry Salvages*, 1941; and *Little Gidding*, 1942) constitute all the important non-dramatic poetry Eliot has published since 1936.
[3] *Poetry and Drama*, p. 23 (*On Poetry and Poets*, p. 79).
[4] *Murder in the Cathedral* (fourth edition, 1938), p. 30.

down and enunciated clearly in separate phrases if it is not to be scrambled in transmission. In such a setting the heavy thud of the alliteration in 'Delegate to deal the doom of damnation' is particularly effective as an evocation of the awful solemnity of excommunication.

Being at no pains to hide the fact that he was writing in verse— indeed, being inclined, as we have seen, to obtrude the verse-form upon the audience—Eliot employed a considerable variety of metres as well as two stretches of prose. As Martin Browne points out, he developed the style suitable to each kind of scene:

'The most superficial level, that of the quarrels between Becket and the Knights, is rhymed doggerel. . . . More subtle, and some-times rather crabbed, is a four-stress rhyming verse for the Temp-ters who dramatise the tortuous progress of Becket's inner struggle. . . . There is an easy, near-blank-verse for dialogue with the Priests and Women. . . . And for the Chorus, a very varied series of forms, from the three-stress lines of the women's domestic talk . . . to the long complexes of pleading or of praise. . . . In addition, Eliot has followed the precedent he established with his final Chorus in *The Rock* which is based on the *Gloria* of the Mass and used the rhythms of two more Christian hymns as ground-bass of choral odes.' [1]

And if this experimentation did not lead towards Eliot's ultimate objective, the creation of 'a verse-form capable of enclosing within itself all the moods and characters of the play',[2] nevertheless it yielded magnificent results for this one play. The choruses were the fruit of the previous experimentation in *The Rock*. They are perhaps the greatest thing in a great play. There is nothing else like them in English, to my knowledge. In fact, it seems to me that we have to go back to Greek tragedy to find choral writing with which to compare the best of them.

[1] E. Martin Browne, 'The Dramatic Verse of T. S. Eliot', *T. S. Eliot: a symposium*, compiled by Richard March and Tambimuttu (Editions Poetry London, 1948), pp. 199–200. The Christian hymns referred to are *Dies Irae* (pp. 70–2) and *Te Deum* (pp. 85–8). Eliot's own account of the versification of the play in *Poetry and Drama* (p. 24; *On Poetry and Poets*, p. 80)—he says that he modelled it chiefly on that of *Everyman*—is simplified to suit a lecture audience.
[2] *Ibid.*, p. 201.

The departures from ordinary speech rhythms and idioms were made possible not only by the historical subject, but also by the ritualistic overtones. In *Murder in the Cathedral*, as Peacock points out:

'ritual belongs both to the inner structure of the play and to its performance. Through creating direct links at various points with his audience the poet has made his work into a continuous invitation to celebrate in religious fellowship the spiritual triumph of a saint. . . . The drama becomes again an instrument of community.' [1]

These links are made possible by the re-introduction of some of the conventions of earlier drama. Thomas addresses the audience directly in the sermon and elsewhere, at times informing it of the course the play is to take; for instance, just before the temptations begin, he says:

> Meanwhile the substance of our first act
> Will be shadows, and the strife with shadows.[2]

and after summing up the action of the First Part:

> I know
> What yet remains to show you of my history
> Will seem to most of you at best futility,
> Senseless self-slaughter of a lunatic,
> Arrogant passion of a fanatic.
> I know that history at all times draws
> The strangest consequence from remotest cause.
> But for every evil, every sacrilege,
> Crime, wrong, oppression and the axe's edge,
> Indifference, exploitation, you, and you,
> And you, must all be punished. So must you (p. 45).

Here the audience is unequivocally implicated in the consequences of the action. Similarly, after the murder, the Knights step clean out of the twelfth-century setting to justify their action to the

---

[1] Ronald Peacock, *The Poet in the Theatre* (Routledge and Kegan Paul, London, 1946), p. 4. There is a discussion of the relation of drama to religious liturgy in 'A Dialogue on Dramatic Poetry' (1928) (*Selected Essays*, pp. 47-9).

[2] p. 23. This is ostensibly spoken in answer to a question by the First Priest, but it is of greater importance as a guide to the audience.

twentieth-century audience, and ram home the relevance of the action to the modern situation:

'if you have now arrived at a just subordination of the pretensions of the Church to the welfare of the State, remember that it is we who took the first step. We have been instrumental in bringing about the state of affairs that you approve. We have served your interests; we merit your applause; and if there is any guilt whatever in the matter, you must share it with us' (pp. 81–2).

There is never, in fact, any diffidence about reminding the audience of its physical presence; this is recognized as a basic factor in the play's performance.

An even more important convention is the Chorus. Not only is the full-throated chorus of Greek tragedy restored, as we have seen, but its original function is enlarged in the light of the Christian liturgy. It represents the common people and mediates between them and the action as in Greek drama, but also 'chorus is choir', as Raymond Williams notes, 'the articulate voice of the body of worshippers':[1]

Forgive us, O Lord, we acknowledge ourselves as type of the common man. . . .
Lord, have mercy upon us.
Christ, have mercy upon us (pp. 87–8).

The play constitutes a return to the origin of English drama within the Church as an extension of the liturgy (*Quem quaeritis?*) and a means of religious instruction, and fulfils both these pristine functions of the drama; it instructs us in the meaning of martyrdom and is an extension of the liturgy in that it invites us to celebrate the act of martyrdom as a sign of God's Grace relevant to all sorts and conditions of men.

Throughout most of his career as dramatist, Eliot has been preoccupied with the theme of spiritual election, though it is only in this play that sainthood is in the foreground. In his later plays, the theme has been pushed farther and farther into the background

---

[1] *Drama from Ibsen to Eliot*, p. 228. In *Poetry and Drama* (p. 25: *On Poetry and Poets*, p. 81) Eliot has explained why he felt justified in making so much use of the chorus. Cf. his remark on Milton's use of the chorus in *Samson Agonistes* (*On Poetry and Poets*, p. 176).

as he has sought to portray the contemporary world and show the relationship of sainthood and martyrdom to the lives of the ordinary men and women of today. But from the first, to show this relationship was one of his chief aims in drama.

Murder in the Cathedral is not just a dramatization of the death of Thomas Becket; it is a deep-searching study of the significance of martyrdom. There is no attempt at naturalism or the creation of illusion. Historical detail is severely subordinated to the pattern or design of martyrdom which gives the play its shape as well as its meaning.[1] Part I portrays the temptations the martyr must undergo, first the temptations to compromise and avoid martyrdom, then the temptation to accept it in the wrong spirit, 'to do the right deed for the wrong reason'. After the episode of Becket's return, which is treated in a semi-naturalistic manner, the action moves smoothly onto the plane of a medieval Morality, the plane of abstractions, 'the strife with shadows' (p. 23). The rest of Part I is constructed upon a strict, almost geometric, pattern, reaching its climax in a counterpointing of the temptations from within (the Tempters) and the claims of humanity from without (the Priests and the Chorus).[2] Here the elements of spiritual conflict in Thomas are objectified in a massive antiphony of three choral groups.

---

[1] Eliot may have learned from Tennyson's *Becket* the danger of diffusing interest by a full treatment of Thomas's career. He incorporates only what is germane to his theme, and that retrospectively through the first three temptations. What historical detail there is—and a little reading in the biographies of Becket soon reveals that there is more than leaps to the eye—is skilfully used to point the main theme and relate it to the historical facts (e.g. the Second Tempter's speech on p. 26). For Eliot in the last resort 'history is a pattern Of timeless moments' (*Four Quartets*, p. 43). In an article on 'The Use of Original Sources for the Development of a Theme', *English*, Vol. XI, No. 61 (Spring, 1956), pp. 2–8, J. T. Boulton demonstrates how 'once Eliot decided on the limits of the dramatic action—"I wanted to concentrate on death and martyrdom"—he adhered faithfully to the outline, and often to the detail, of the events described by contemporary witnesses' (p. 3).

[2] pp. 41–4. The suppression of names and the substitution of numbers for the Priests reinforces the geometric pattern. They also gain a kind of impersonality and stand for the body of priests. At the same time, they are sufficiently distinguished to give the actor scope for some characterization. See E. Martin Browne in *T. S. Eliot: a symposium*, ed. R. March and Tambimuttu (1948), pp. 201–2.

The sermon follows as an Interlude between the two parts, giving expression to the self-knowledge that Becket has gained in Part I and showing him beginning to 'make perfect [his] will' in readiness for the action of Part II. Louis L. Martz observes that it 'forms a nodus of theme, symbol, and tradition, of past and present, binding the play's two parts, and binding Becket's search for Peace with our own.' [1] As we shall see, it defines the pattern of martyrdom, 'the eternal design', in theological and emotional terms, in terms of the fulfilment of God's will and the testimony of mankind.

In the original form of the play, Part II begins with a striking device based on the liturgy as a means of rapidly and smoothly covering the passage of time from Christmas Day, on which the sermon is preached, to December 29, the day of the martyrdom.[2] The three Priests enter in procession and announce, each in his turn, the passing of the days. The banners of the appropriate saints are carried in and the Introits of St. Stephen and St. John are heard. In this device, much more than the mere passage of time is suggested. The idea of martyrdom and sainthood is kept before us and we are led from the anniversary of the martyrdom of St. Stephen, 'first martyr', to the day on which, we are given to expect, Thomas will be 'conjoined with all the saints and martyrs gone before'. Moreover, the liturgical form and the last words of the First Priest ('He lays down his life for the sheep') prepare us for celebration of martyrdom. A bridge-passage rounds off this introduction with a brilliant touch of irony. The formalism relaxes; we are being prepared for a style nearer naturalism:

FIRST PRIEST

To-day?

SECOND PRIEST

To-day, what is to-day? For the day is half gone.

[1] Louis L. Martz, 'The Wheel and the Point: Aspects of Imagery and Theme in Eliot's Later Poetry', *The Sewanee Review*, LV (1947), reprinted in *T. S. Eliot: a selected critique*, ed. Leonard Unger (Rinehart and Co., New York, 1948), p. 461.

[2] In the second edition a chorus was substituted as being more generally playable. In the fourth edition the device was restored, but the new chorus was retained.

FIRST PRIEST

To-day, what is to-day, but another day, the dusk of the year.

SECOND PRIEST

To-day, what is to-day? Another night, and another dawn.

THIRD PRIEST

What day is the day that we know that we hope for or fear for?
Every day is the day we should fear from or hope from. One
    moment
Weighs like another. Only in retrospection, selection,
We say, that was the day. The critical moment
That is always now, and here. Even now, in sordid particulars
The eternal design may appear (pp. 56–7).

And at this moment, the Knights, the 'sordid' instruments of
'the eternal design', their significance thus pointed for us, burst
into the scene. The murder is to be presented as part of that design
and not just as an historical event.

Apart, however, from the occasions when the Knights speak
in unison, the action from here up to the murder follows a
comparatively naturalistic line. Then, as soon as they have completed the murder, the Knights step forward, drop into naturalistic
prose and complete informality of manner. Coming hard upon
the agony of the martyr and the tremendous outburst of the
Chorus in which tears 'drown the wind', this abrupt transition
to something midway between a political meeting and a music-
hall act is meant to shock the spectators, to jerk them out of
sanctimonious complacency into a fiercely uncomfortable realization that this man died for them.[1]

The Knights' apologia for their action is far from being an
excrescence, as some critics have suggested. It is an integral part
of the play. It is, in effect, the temptation of the audience, corresponding to the temptation of Thomas in Part I, as is subtly

---

[1] Eliot himself tells us this was meant to shock (*Poetry and Drama*, p. 26).
In the film edition (Faber and Faber, 1952, pp. 13–14), George Hoellering
notes that 'in stage production these speeches amused the audience instead of
shocking them, and thereby made them miss the point'. I'm not so sure that
the audience does miss the point entirely because it is amused—theatrical
reactions are often very complex—and I am sure that the touches of humour
confirm the shock when the play is performed in church, as was originally
intended.

indicated by the doubling of the Tempters and the Knights. As we shall see, the second half of the play is concerned largely with the second half of the pattern of martyrdom, the creation of the attitude of acceptance in the great mass of believers. With and through the Chorus, we of the audience are invited to participate in the celebration of the act of martyrdom and to accept the sacrifice of Thomas as made in our behalf. Before we can do this, however, we, like Thomas, must undergo temptation, in our case the temptation to deny the efficacy of his sacrifice and its relevance to us. Stepping out of their twelfth-century setting, the Knights seek by every means from blandishment to exhortation, cunningly using the techniques of modern political oratory, to make us admit the reasonableness of their action and to acknowledge that we are involved in it, since we have benefited from it.

For the Knights the play is over, and the First Knight suggests 'that you now disperse quietly to your homes' (p. 83). But for most of us in the audience the arguments will have had the opposite effect to that intended by the Knights. We admit that we are implicated in the death of Thomas, but we do not concede the justification of the killing on the grounds argued by the Knights. The benefit we acknowledge is spiritual rather than political and it comes from Thomas's suffering rather than their action. For us, therefore, the play is not over; the effect of Thomas's sacrifice continues. The Priests enter and help us to recover the mood of the martyrdom in a chastened form. From a threnody for the archbishop in the minor key, the recovered verse-form modulates to the major and the great hymn of praise and thanksgiving for the new saint in glory with which the play ends. The pattern of mourning and rejoicing which Thomas distinguished in the death of martyrs, as in the Birth and Passion of Christ, is here fulfilled.[1] By cutting down the historical action to its bare essentials, Eliot has brought 'the eternal design' into stark relief.[2]

The true martyrdom requires the fulfilment of two halves of a pattern. The first half must be fulfilled by the martyr himself; he must learn to accept his martyrdom in the right spirit. For a

---

[1] Cf. the sermon (p. 49).

[2] The sensuous detail excluded from the action of the play returns, however, with the full impact of poetry, in the choruses.

man of many parts, like Becket, this is far from easy; the temptations to ignore the Divine Election are strong. In the days following his return, while he is waiting for the attack which he knows must come, temptations throng his mind. Temptations of the past revive: the appeal to the senses which he partly indulged in his days of wordly prosperity, the lure of temporal power such as he has wielded during his Chancellorship, the prospect of beating Henry at his political game by accepting the proffered alliance with the discontented barons—these are temptations which he has known before and can the more easily master again.[1] But the fourth temptation is of the present and unexpected—the temptation 'to do the right deed for the wrong reason', to become a martyr for the glory of being one. In his agony, Thomas acknowledges the spiritual Pride within him and humbles his will, emerging with the hard-won knowledge that, as he says in the sermon, 'the true martyr is he who has become the instrument of God, who has lost his will in the will of God, and who no longer desires anything for himself, not even the glory of being a martyr' (p. 49).

Although the recognition of the extent of his Pride comes as such a shock to Thomas, Eliot has given the audience a number of pointers. The First Priest portrays him unequivocally as a man of Pride (pp. 16–17) and this emerges in his rejection of temporal power (p. 30). Being a setting up of the self against the will of God, Pride is the deadliest of sins as well as the most insidious. It naturally forms the last obstacle to true martyrdom, but one that Thomas, because of his blindness to this weakness in himself, could not foresee. The Fourth Tempter makes Thomas realize that he has been thinking of martyrdom as a glory which will exalt him above all earthly potentates and, among other things, give him the final victory in the struggle with Henry. The shock of the recognition of the impurity of his motives leads to a nightmarish dilemma:

> Is there no way, in my soul's sickness,
> Does not lead to damnation in pride?
> ... Can I neither act nor suffer
> Without perdition? (p. 40).

[1] This review of the past in the face of death is not unlike what is commonly supposed to happen to a drowning man. Cf. 'Dans le Restaurant' (*Collected Poems*, p. 52) and *The Waste Land*, ll. 315–18 (*Collected Poems*, p. 73).

He has now to recognize that he did not properly understand the words he spoke to comfort the women on his return. As a final turn of the screw, the Fourth Tempter flings them back at him:

You know and do not know, what it is to act or suffer.
You know and do not know, that action is suffering,
And suffering action. Neither does the agent suffer
Nor the patient act. But both are fixed
In an eternal action, an eternal patience
To which all must consent that it may be willed
And which all must suffer that they may will it,
That the pattern may subsist, that the wheel may turn and still
Be forever still.[1]

Thomas has now to make this perception a reality in his life, not just a proposition to which he gives intellectual assent. In losing his will in the will of God, he achieves the reconciliation of all irreconcilables. On the circumference of the wheel, in the realm of phenomena, of physical appearances, action and suffering are distinct, but at the heart of reality, at 'the still point of the turning world', they coincide.[2] For the fulfilment of the 'eternal design', however, for the realization of the pattern, it is necessary for those on the circumference of the wheel to turn towards the centre, to 'consent that it may be willed' and 'suffer that they may will it'. The pattern becomes valid only in so far as men answer with love God's gesture of love in Christ.

[1] p. 40. Cf. p. 21. The Fourth Tempter's speech omits 'for the pattern is the action / And the suffering', presumably as less relevant to this situation.

[2] In Eliot's own mystical experience, as embodied in *Burnt Norton*, from which this phrase is taken (first published a year after the performance of the play and reprinted in *Four Quartets*, 1944), he found

> The inner freedom from the practical desire,
> The release from action and suffering, release
>   from the inner
> And the outer compulsion (*Four Quartets*, p. 9).

Cf. also *Ash Wednesday*, V (*Collected Poems*, p. 100) and *Coriolan*, I (*Collected Poems*, p. 136). See also Appendix II and Harold E. McCarthy's illuminating article on 'T. S. Eliot and Buddhism' in *Philosophy East and West*, Vol. II, No. 1 (April, 1952), pp. 47–53.

Thomas now discovers the reality of the Divine love so completely that he could say with Dante

> ma già volgeva il mio disio e'l velle
> sì come rota ch' igualmente è mossa,
> l'amor che move il sole e l'altre stelle.[1]

He discovers the force of the ultimate law of the spirit:

> E'n la sua voluntade è nostra pace.[2]

It is this peace which he talks about in the first part of his sermon and which gives the whole sermon an almost perfect serenity. In

---

[1] *But now my desire and will, like a wheel that spins with even motion, were revolved by the Love that moves the sun and the other stars* (*The Divine Comedy*, with translation and comment by John D. Sinclair, The Bodley Head Press, revised edition, 1948, Vol. III, *Paradiso*, XXXIII, 143–5). Behind this is the Aristotelian concept neatly explained by Grover Smith:

'Aristotle, in speaking of the nature of movement (analogous to action), compares the good, towards which desire moves, and by which it is moved, to the unmoved center which in a wheel imparts motion to the rim: "For everything is moved by pushing and pulling. Hence just as in the case of a wheel, so here there must be a point which remains at rest, and from that point the movement must originate" [*De Anima*, iii. 10]' (*T. S. Eliot's Poetry and Plays*, p. 188).

This seems to have supplied the image of 'the still point of the turning world', which is obviously related to the image of the wheel. This symbol of the wheel is 'often used in Hindu and Buddhist scriptures to denote the hopeless round of unredeemed life and death' (Kristian Smidt, *Poetry and Belief in the Work of T. S. Eliot*, Oslo, 1949, p. 116). For instance, the *Bhagavad-Gita*, which Eliot calls 'the next greatest philosophical poem to the *Divine Comedy* within my experience' (*Selected Essays*, p. 258) refers to 'the terrible wheel of rebirth and death'. (Cf. *Bhagavad-Gita* ii, 40; ix, 10; xviii, 61. In the translation by Swami Prabhavananda and Christopher Isherwood, Phoenix House, London, 1947, pp. 44, 102, and 172). The image is used at one or two other key-points in the play (p. 18 by Third Priest; pp. 24–5 by Thomas), and recurs in *The Family Reunion*, pp. 30, 101 and 108. In the first of these later appearances it becomes 'the burning wheel', perhaps under the influence of Shakespeare's 'wheel of fire', (*King Lear*, IV. vii. 47), which is a symbol of hell. For further comment on this image, see articles by Louis L. Martz and Leo Shapiro listed in the Bibliography for this play.

[2] *And in His will is our peace.* (*The Divine Comedy*, trans. John D. Sinclair, Vol. III, *Paradiso*, III. 85). Cf. Wordsworth's
> central peace subsisting at the heart
> Of endless agitation (*The Excursion*, IV. 1146–7).

so far as he has identified himself with Christ by submitting his will to the will of God as Christ did ('Thy will be done'), he has found the peace 'which passeth all understanding'. This is the inner logic which binds the two parts of the sermon together.

Thomas has said at the end of Part I: 'I shall no longer act or suffer, to the sword's end' (p. 45), and it is in this spirit of acceptance—he will not seek out, nor will he avoid, martyrdom—that he awaits the Knights:

> Death will come only when I am worthy,
> And if I am worthy, there is no danger.
> I have therefore only to make perfect my will (p. 69).

The act of obedience to the will of God is not made once and for always, though the discovery of what it means to submit wholly and without reserve is a decisive step. It must be renewed from moment to moment.

To lose one's will in the will of God is, as we have seen, to realize the eternal pattern in the flux of time:

> Men's curiosity searches past and future
> And clings to that dimension. But to apprehend
> The point of intersection of the timeless
> With time, is an occupation for the saint—
> No occupation either, but something given
> And taken, in a lifetime's death in love,
> Ardour and selflessness and self-surrender.[1]

It is in such a spirit that Thomas gives his life, accepts his death:

> It is not in time that my death shall be known;
> It is out of time that my decision is taken
> If you call that decision
> To which my whole being gives entire consent.
> I give my life
> To the Law of God above the Law of Man (p. 73).

[1] *Four Quartets*, p. 32. The great moment of 'the intersection of the timeless / With time' is, of course, the Incarnation, as Eliot goes on to make clear (p. 33. Cf. *The Rock*, Chorus VII, *Collected Poems*, p. 173). In seeking to live in Christ, the saint is seeking a repetition of this fertilization of time by eternity. The apprehension of 'the point of intersection . . .' is also the apprehension of 'the still point of the turning world'.

His share in the pattern of action and suffering is here nearing completion:

> We have fought the beast
> And have conquered. We have only to conquer
> Now, by suffering. This is the easier victory.
> Now is the triumph of the Cross (p. 74).

Every martyr is a witness, as the word itself signifies, to the efficacy of Christ's sacrifice, a gesture of love in response to the Divine Love revealed in Christ:

> His blood given to buy my life,
> My blood given to pay for His death,
> My death for His death (p. 75).

Thus, Thomas fulfils his part in 'the eternal design'.[1]

But as martyrdom requires the right attitude to God on the part of the martyr, so also it requires the right attitude on the part of the great mass of men. A martyrdom is not efficacious unless it is accepted by them as 'the design of God, for His love of men, to warn them and to lead them back to His ways' (p. 49). So prone is Man to turn his back upon the love of God revealed in Christ—for the demands it makes are not light—that he must from time to time be shocked into recognizing it afresh by a violence comparable to the Crucifixion:

> the Son of Man was not crucified once for all,
> The blood of the martyrs not shed once for all,
> The lives of the Saints not given once for all:
> But the Son of Man is crucified always
> And there shall be Martyrs and Saints.[2]

None of this violence and bloodshed fulfils its purpose unless it reminds ordinary men and women of God's love. The witness must extend to them. Theirs is a passive witness as opposed to the active witness of the martyr, but they also must suffer the action, if only in the sense of permitting it or consenting to it. 'This is your share of the eternal burden', as Thomas tells the Chorus; this is their part in the pattern of action and suffering.

[1] For an answer to some criticisms of the portrayal of Thomas, see Appendix I.
[2] *The Rock*, p. 42 (*Collected Poems*, p. 171).

In accepting Thomas's witness, they—and we of the audience also if we allow that they represent us—accept anew Christ's sacrifice, and the pattern of Atonement is re-emphasized.

Even the First Priest fails to see the significance of Thomas's death:

> The Church lies bereft,
> Alone, desecrated, desolated, and the heathen shall
> build on the ruins
> Their world without God (p. 84).

The Third Priest has to point out to him—and through him to the audience—that

> the Church is stronger for this action,
> Triumphant in adversity. It is fortified
> By persecution: supreme, so long as men will die for it (p. 84).

It remains for the Chorus, representing the layman,[1] to give their paean of praise and thanksgiving for the sacrifice made in their behalf.

Before they do this, however, they have passed through all the phases of revulsion and fear that attend the Christian witness. Eliot's original title, *Fear in the Way*, was a neat index of this important aspect of the play.[2] When we first see them, they have

---

[1] They introduce themselves as 'the poor, the poor women of Canterbury' (p. 11), refer to themselves at their daily task as 'the scrubbers and sweepers of Canterbury' (p. 86, 'one might almost say, charwomen of Canterbury', *On Poetry and Poets*, p. 91) and finally 'acknowledge [themselves] as type of the common man . . .' (p. 87). They are 'the small folk drawn into the pattern of fate, the small folk who live among small things' (p. 20).

[2] This title would seem to derive from Ecclesiastes xii, which is quoted by the Third Priest (p. 18). The sardonic title *Murder in the Cathedral* was suggested by Henzie Raeburn (Mrs. E. Martin Browne). (See Ashley Dukes, March's *Symposium*, p. 113.) Eliot doubtless foresaw that it would lead some members of the public to expect a thriller. The great popularity of Mrs. Agatha Christie's plays, among them a *Murder in the Vicarage* (1950), would have aggravated the situation if Eliot's play had not meanwhile become one of the best-known plays of our time. There is testimony to Eliot's own acquaintance with thrillers in the echo of a Sherlock Holmes story in the colloquy between Becket and the Second Tempter (see Grover Smith, 'T. S. Eliot and Sherlock Holmes', and Constance Nicholas, in the bibliography for this play), and in the apologia of the Fourth Knight with its prosecution-like analysis of the mystery of 'Who killed the Archbishop?'. We shall see a more developed use of thriller-like interest in *The Family Reunion*.

a premonition of what is to come and of their part in it:

> Some presage of an act
> Which our eyes are compelled to witness, has forced our feet
> Towards the cathedral. We are forced to bear witness (p. 11).

They fear that, like Peter, they will not prove equal to the test:

> who shall
> Stretch out his hand to the fire, and deny his master? who shall
> be warm
> By the fire, and deny his master? (p. 12).

They fear even more the impending 'disturbance of the quiet seasons', the irruption of the unknown, the uncontrollable, into the familiar round of their lives, which they have carefully ordered to create a feeling of security, conveniently forgetting what should make them question this false sense of safety and permanence. They would prefer 'to pass unobserved'. So, even though they recognize that what is about to happen is the design of God, they think of it as a malady, something they would rather do without:

> Some malady is coming upon us. We wait, we wait,
> And the saints and martyrs wait, for those who shall be martyrs
> and saints.
> Destiny waits in the hand of God, shaping the still unshapen:
> I have seen these things in a shaft of sunlight.
>
> .   .   .   .
>
> For us, the poor, there is no action,
> But only to wait and to witness.[1]

To witness, in the Christian sense, means, however, not just to

---

[1] p. 13. With the line 'I have seen these things in a shaft of sunlight' cf. *Four Quartets*, pp. 13 and 33, and *Selected Essays*, p. 232. These references make clear that the intuition of the Chorus is the intuition of the ordinary man, his fleeting glimpse of 'the eternal design'. This passage of the play illustrates the curious alternation of first person plural and first person singular in the choruses. Sometimes the use of the singular invites assignment of the line to a single voice, but at other times it seems to indicate the coalescence of the voices in the expression of communal feeling at the deepest level (e.g. p. 72).

see but to be involved, and in their fear they appeal rhetorically to Thomas:

Archbishop, secure and assured of your fate, unaffrayed among the shades, do you realize what you ask, do you realize what it means

To the small folk drawn into the pattern of fate, the small folk who live among small things,

The strain on the brain of the small folk who stand to the doom of the house, the doom of their lord, the doom of the world? (p.20).

They implore him to return—to France. But he returns to them, and gently rebukes the Second Priest for his chiding of them:

Peace. And let them be, in their exaltation.
They speak better than they know, and beyond your understanding . . . (p. 21).

In their fear, the women apprehend more than the Second Priest in his false security. Indeed, the fear itself is testimony to their understanding that to witness is to be involved, that because of the fellowship in Christ we are all 'members one of another' and in that fellowship action and suffering are but obverse and reverse of the same coin.

As the Tempters gather their forces for a united attack on Thomas—now that he has recognized the vanity of his own aspirations, he is assailed momentarily by an unqualified scepticism about the value of all earthly endeavour—the Chorus's fear mounts, through an oppressive sense of the evil at war with the good in him ('The earth is heaving to parturition of issue of hell', p. 41), to a sudden panic at the possibility that the 'Lords of Hell' will triumph:

God gave us always some reason, some hope; but now a new terror has soiled us, which none can avert, none can avoid, flowing under our feet and over the sky;

Under doors and down chimneys, flowing in at the ear and the mouth and the eye.

God is leaving us, God is leaving us, more pang, more pain than
   birth or death.

.   .   .   .   .   .

O Thomas Archbishop, save us, save us, save yourself that we
   may be saved;
Destroy yourself and we are destroyed (pp. 43–4).

They thus acknowledge that their spiritual welfare depends upon
Thomas. And in the chorus which opens Part II in the later editions
of the play, they admit the need for his sacrifice:

The peace of this world is always uncertain, unless men keep the
   peace of God.
And war among men defiles this world, but death in the Lord
   renews it,
And the world must be cleaned in the winter, or we shall have
   only
A sour spring, a parched summer, an empty harvest.[1]

   But of their own part in the design, the consent implicit in
standing by and doing nothing to prevent the murder, they are
keenly ashamed:

I have smelt them, the death-bringers; now is too late
For action, too soon for contrition.
Nothing is possible but the shamed swoon
Of those consenting to the last humiliation.
I have consented, Lord Archbishop, have consented.

.   .   .   .   .   .

O Lord Archbishop, O Thomas Archbishop, forgive us, forgive us,
   pray for us that we may pray for you, out of our shame (p. 68).

They have now consented to the 'eternal patience' and acknowledged their responsibility for the imminent death of Thomas.
They recognize that they will be involved in the sin of the
murderers, and, as Eliot observed in his essay on Baudelaire,
'the recognition of the reality of Sin is a New Life'.[2]

---

[1] pp. 53–4. The link between 'the peace of God' and martyrdom is also, as
we have seen, present in the sermon, the first half of which deals with the
Christmas message of peace and the latter half with the meaning of martyrdom.
[2] *Selected Essays*, p. 427.

Thomas comforts them with the assurance that

These things had to come to you and you to accept them.
This is your share of the eternal burden,
The perpetual glory. This is one moment,
But know that another
Shall pierce you with a sudden painful joy
When the figure of God's purpose is made complete (pp. 68-9).

Even the evil of their timid inaction will be turned into a good for themselves and all men through the martyrdom which God has ordained. The design takes into account their human weakness; in fact it is through the very weakness which makes martyrdom necessary—man's fallible will, turning him from God—that God brings man back to Himself.[1] The knowledge of the weakness to which he succumbs in the crucial moment springs out of the remorse that comes when he sees its consequences, and this knowledge is the beginning of wisdom and grateful recognition of the love of God. All this is behind the action of the play, but the poetry speaks in the concrete terms of human experience.

As the moment of martyrdom approaches, the Chorus has a vision of a horror beyond all horrors that life can bring, the ultimate horror of the separation from God at the Day of Judgment, the horror of the Void,

Where those who were men can no longer turn the mind
To distraction, delusion, escape into dream, pretence,
Where the soul is no longer deceived, for there are no objects, no tones,
No colours, no forms to distract, to divert the soul
From seeing itself, foully united forever, nothing with nothing
(p. 71).

---

[1] This is the paradox of the fortunate fall, the *felix culpa* or happy fault of traditional theology, in which the sin of Adam is regarded as a necessary preliminary to the sacrifice of Christ and thus indirectly as the source of salvation for all believers. Similarly, the betrayal by Judas and the renunciation by the Jews were necessary parts of the design of Atonement. Christopher Fry puts this succinctly in *Thor, With Angels*:

> The sacrifice of God was brought about
> By the blind anger of men, and yet God made
> Their blindness their own saving (p. 53).

This is the picture of the fate they can expect unless atonement is made. From it the women turn to the comfort of the Saviour's sacrifice about to be renewed in the martyrdom of Thomas.

At the moment of the murder the unknown irrupts into the known, separating them by a vast gulf from the petty safety of the everyday round:

A rain of blood has blinded my eyes. Where is England? where
    is Kent? where is Canterbury?
O far far far far in the past; and I wander in a land of barren
    boughs: if I break them, they bleed; I wander in a land of
    dry stones: if I touch them they bleed.
How how can I ever return, to the soft quiet seasons? (p. 76).

In the rare perception of this moment, they recognize that they share the sin of the whole world which necessitates Thomas's sacrifice:

It is not we alone, it is not the house, it is not the city that is
    defiled,
But the world that is wholly foul.[1]

As yet they do not clearly perceive that the blood will refresh the Waste Land of 'barren boughs' and 'dry stones' and cleanse the world, but with a sure instinct they cry:

Clear the air! clean the sky! wash the wind! take the stone from
    the stone, take the skin from the arm, take the muscle from
    the bone, and wash them. Wash the stone, wash the bone,
    wash the brain, wash the soul, wash them wash them!
    (p. 77).

Fuller understanding of the significance of Thomas's death has come by the end of the play:

We thank Thee for Thy mercies of blood, for Thy redemption
    by blood. For the blood of Thy martyrs and saints
Shall enrich the earth, shall create the holy places (pp. 86–7).

They experience the moment of 'painful joy' prophesied by

[1] p. 77. In the preceding lines, they also recognize the truth of Thomas's claim: 'It is out of time that my decision is taken' (p. 73).

Thomas (pp. 68–9) and acknowledge that Thomas's sacrifice was made on their behalf:

We acknowledge our trespass, our weakness, our fault; we acknowledge
That the sin of the world is upon our heads; that the blood of the martyrs and the agony of the saints
Is upon our heads (p. 88).

Thus, under the impact of the martyrdom, they have moved from apathy and evasion to a lively faith and humble acceptance. As this analysis of the choruses has indicated, the pattern of spiritual development is given wider implications by the overtones of seasonal renewal. From its initial position in the Waste Land of spiritual torpor—'the land became brown sharp points of death in a waste of water and mud' (p. 11), where the death of the year corresponds to the death of the martyr which will come in the winter (December 29) and the 'sharp points' correspond to the 'swords' points' (p. 45) that will kill him—the Chorus fears 'disturbance of the quiet seasons' as something destructive and sterile:

Winter shall come bringing death from the sea,
Ruinous spring shall beat at our doors,
Root and shoot shall eat our eyes and our ears,
Disastrous summer burn up the beds of our streams
And the poor shall wait for another decaying October (p. 12).

As D. E. S. Maxwell notes, 'Their rejection of the return of life with the spring is linked with their repugnance to spiritual rebirth, and to the return of the Archbishop.' [1] The chorus written as an alternative opening to Part II takes up this theme and develops it in the light of the sacrifice to come, so that a positive note emerges in:

And the world must be cleaned in the winter, or we shall have only
A sour spring, a parched summer, an empty harvest (p. 54).

[1] *The Poetry of T. S. Eliot* (Routledge and Kegan Paul, London, 1952), p. 188. In Eliot the pain of spiritual rebirth—the death by water of *The Waste Land*—is often imaged as natural growth. Cf. *The Waste Land*, ll. 1–9 (*Collected Poems*, p. 61), *Gerontion*, ll. 1–2, and 'In the juvescence of the year/Came Christ the tiger' (*Collected Poems*, p. 37), and *The Family Reunion*, pp. 59–60.

But it is not merely a matter of the ensuring of fertility. It is also a matter of securing the divinely ordained order of Nature. In the Chorus's account of its 'subtile forebodings' (pp. 66-8)—the spelling 'subtile', being archaic in England, is apt to remind the English reader of the serpent who was 'more subtil than any beast of the field' [1]—the encroachment of evil is envisaged as a pervasive disorder in the natural world, a Fall in Nature consonant with the Fall of Man wrought by the lures of the Devil impersonating the 'subtil' serpent. This tremendous picture stems from the same conception of divinely ordained order that we saw reflected in *Macbeth*.[2] Based on the Thomistic view of the universe as involved in a teleological movement from potentiality to actuality, this scheme is commonly envisaged as what Pope called 'the vast chain of being', namely, the continuum of created being from the meanest particle of created matter up to the highest of the archangels conceived of as a chain with links representing the innumerable grades of being:

God	—	pure act
angels	—	pure intellect
man	—	intellect
		sense
animals	—	sense
plants	—	growth
inanimate matter	—	mere unchanging existence[3]

It will be seen that the maintenance of order in Creation depends upon the subordination in Man of the sensual to the spiritual and that this is the weak link, the point at which Evil may concentrate its attack upon the Divine order. By inflaming

[1] Genesis iii. 1. I owe this suggestion to Mr. Edgar King, who played Becket in my production of the play. In the land of Eliot's birth, the spelling is not archaic, but by 1935 it may have acquired the Biblical overtone for him. Whether or not it had does not affect the main part of my argument.

[2] See p. 19 above.

[3] Readers interested in this element of the metaphysical tradition of Western Christianity are referred to E. M. W. Tillyard, *The Elizabethan World Picture* (Chatto and Windus, London, 1948) and, for an account of its origin and history, to A. O. Lovejoy, *The Great Chain of Being* (Cambridge, Mass., 1936).

the animal part of Man and causing it to dominate the angelic part, Evil turns the order topsy-turvy at its key-point. Man turns his back on God and becomes mere animal, for when he forgets the fatherhood of God, he has nothing left but his brotherhood with the beast:

> I have seen
> Rings of light coiling downwards, descending
> To the horror of the ape (p. 67).

The link between the animal creation and God is broken and disorder rules in the natural world. Thus the keynote of this chorus is:

> I have seen
> Trunk and horn, tusk and hoof, in odd places (p. 67).

This disorder persists in Man as Original Sin, but the Atonement provided the remedy for all men to avail themselves of and made possible the restoration of the order inherent in the Creation. As we have already observed, however, men tend to ignore the proffered remedy and must be reminded of it by martyrdom. And martyrdom, reproducing the pattern of the Atonement in miniature, reaffirms the natural order which has been menaced by the agents of martyrdom.

Thus, the particular threat to the natural order envisaged in the play stems from the four Knights, 'the death-bringers'. They are the agents through whom Evil is renewing its attack upon the Divine order. Mr. Grover Smith notes that when the Knights enter

'bawling, "Come down Daniel to the lions' den," in the manner of Lindsay's "Daniel Jazz," they make a jocular acknowledgment of the martyr's triumph, even while degrading themselves to beasts'.[1]

The First Priest speaks of them as 'men / Who would damn themselves to beasts' (p. 73) and in the last chorus of Part I,

[1] *Op. cit.*, p. 182. Compare especially 'Are you washed in the blood of the Lamb?' (p. 74) with Vachel Lindsay's 'General William Booth'. 'The mark of the beast' in the first of the three stanzas is, of course, from Revelation xiii. 17.

beasts are associated with the 'Lords of Hell', the Tempters.[1]
The Chorus feel themselves involved in this bestial degradation:

> What is woven in the councils of princes
> Is woven also in our veins, our brains,
> Is woven like a pattern of living worms
> In the guts of the women of Canterbury.[2]

In 'consenting' to the martyrdom, they share the disorder of evil
and are

> United to the spiritual flesh of nature,
> Mastered by the animal powers of spirit,
> Dominated by the lust of self-demolition,
> By the final utter uttermost death of spirit,
> By the final ecstasy of waste and shame.[3]

[1] This parallel between the four Tempters and the four Knights is one
justification for the doubling of these parts. The linking of Fourth Tempter
and Fourth Knight is particularly significant, and the silence of the Fourth
Knight throughout most of the time he is on-stage, his failure to join in all
but one of the lines spoken in unison (p. 66)—unless he joins in the group
speeches on pp. 74–5, where the triple form invites partial division among
the other three Knights—gives him an impressive isolation; it is almost as if
he were the motive behind the others, the personification of Evil. This silence
was Mr. Martin Browne's idea (see the Preface to the Second Edition, p. 7).

[2] p. 68. The community of sin is stressed in a parallel passage in Eliot's
introduction to *Nightwood* by Djuna Barnes (Faber and Faber, 1937): 'all of
us, so far as we attach outselves to created objects and surrender our wills to
temporal ends, are eaten by the same worm'.

[3] p. 68. Cf. Martz, reprinted Unger, *Critique*, p. 454:
'The agony of the Women here, as the sexual imagery shows, comes from
recognizing the degradation of humanity into the animal; and the echo of
Shakespeare's "The expense of spirit in a waste of shame" extends the horror.'
Mr. Martz's striking analysis of the 'death-bringers' chorus differs slightly in
emphasis from mine:
'Eliot is creating here the vision of a universe without order, a vision given
in the only way in which the "type of the common man" can realize it, by all
the "quickened senses." The order of time is abolished: the merry fluting of a
summer's afternoon is heard at night mingled with the owl's "hollow note of
death." Bats, with the huge scaly wings of Lucifer, slant over the noon sky. The
creative mind of God and Man is gone; the scavengers and the least sensitive,
least conscious forms of life take over. The threat of Death exists even in the
most delicate flowers. And with this disorder humanity feels its involvement: "I
have lain on the floor of the sea and breathed with the breathing of the sea-
anemone, swallowed with ingurgitation of the sponge." But, paradoxically,

77

At first the blood of Thomas seems to defile the land, their beasts, and themselves (p. 76). They see it as symptomatic of their guilt, linking them to the murderers: 'We are soiled by a filth that we cannot clean, united to supernatural vermin' (p. 77). Thomas, however, has 'fought the beast / And ... conquered' (p. 74) and the true relation of man to the animal creation, the true order of Nature, re-asserts itself with the spiritual renewal of his sacrifice, so that the beasts are secured in their proper places and the Chorus can say:

> all things affirm Thee in living; the bird in the air, both the
> hawk and the finch; the beast on the earth, both the wolf and
> the lamb; the worm in the soil and the worm in the belly.
> Therefore man, whom Thou hast made to be conscious of Thee,
> must consciously praise Thee, in thought and in word and
> in deed (p. 86).

It is only through man that Nature can become articulate in its praise of the Creator:

> Even in us the voices of seasons, the snuffle of winter, the song
> of spring, the drone of summer, the voices of beasts and of
> birds, praise Thee (p. 86).

In this last chorus the recurrent images of the play (the Waste Land, the seasons, beasts and birds, the everyday tasks, the blood of redemption) are gathered together and resolved in a significant pattern. They all fit together in the scheme of God's Providence: by the blood of redemption fertility is restored to the Waste Land so that the rhythm of the seasons can remain undisturbed, the natural order can be preserved, men can perform their seasonal tasks and give articulate praise not just for themselves, but for

---

the Women are saved, not lost, by such a vision, for here gradually emerges the human consciousness at highest intensity, recognizing all creation as part of a pattern which points to this moment, seeing themselves as "death-bringers," admitting Sin, crying for absolution. The disorder in the first two-thirds of this chorus, with its long irresolute lines, changes to a balanced order of versification, phrasing, and thought as the Chorus recognizes its responsibility' (pp. 457–8).

the beasts as well, and all creatures are secured in their ordained places, fulfilling their role in 'the eternal design'. As Miss Patricia Adair notes,

'The satisfaction we receive from this final pattern and resolution of the dominant images . . . is surely akin to our perception of a similar process in music.' [1]

By this kind of richness and fulness of implication, Eliot has restored the true values of poetic drama, the ramification of meaning on all the planes of awareness that man is capable of—intellectual, sensuous and spiritual. He has shown how drama can still be an instrument of community in the two senses corresponding to its original function as an extension of the liturgy and as an interpretation of God's word in terms of flesh and blood. For the purpose of his play, the audience becomes a congregation, having interpreted to it the significance of martyrdom and being invited to participate in the celebration of an act of martyrdom. Part II has something of the quality of liturgical celebration. It is not a plain representation of 'the historical fact' [2] but a ritual presentation of the act of martyrdom in its timeless significance, having a relationship to the historical fact which is like that of the Holy Communion to the Last Supper. Of course, it is much nearer in form to the historical martyrdom than the Eucharist is to the historical act of Our Lord. But in so far as it moves away from sheer representation, it moves in this direction. The audience is invited to participate in spirit, and through the act of watching and hearing to strengthen its link with the Communion of Saints.

It is important to notice, however, that while this kind of drama is an extension of, or a supplement to, worship, it is not in itself worship. As Eliot points out:

'a religious play, to be good, must not be purely religious. If it is, it is simply doing something that the liturgy does better; and the religious play is not a substitute for liturgical observance and

[1] Patricia Adair, 'Mr. Eliot's "Murder in the Cathedral"' *The Cambridge Journal*, Vol. IV, No. 2 (November, 1950), p. 93.

[2] p. 38. The whole play challenges the modern indifference to Thomas's sacrifice 'prophesied' by the Fourth Tempter.

ceremonial, but something different. It is a combination of
religious with ordinary dramatic interest.' [1]

Even when the play uses ritual, as in the procession of the Priests
at the beginning of Part II, it employs it for a dramatic purpose,
in this case to mark the passage of time and lead up to the entry
of the Knights in a way which will point the significance of
Thomas's observation in his Sermon: 'Is it an accident, do you
think, that the day of the first martyr follows immediately the
day of the Birth of Christ? By no means' (p. 49).

But Eliot's concern is not just with the Church, the body of
believers: it is with the whole of society, in which he diagnoses
the sickness of the Waste Land. In a lecture given in 1937, he
said:

'the creation of a living religious drama in our time is not to be
conceived as a problem entirely isolated from that of the secular
theatre. I would even ask you to look at it the other way about
from the usual, and say, that it is not so much that the Christian
Faith needs the drama (for its evangelising possibilities) but that
the drama needs the Christian Faith. . . .

'What I am opposing is not merely a division of religious and
secular drama into watertight compartments; what I am propos-
ing is not merely that we need to go to a religious play or to a
secular play in much the same spirit. It is an opposition to the
compartmentalisation of life in general, to the sharp division
between our religious and our ordinary life. . . . [In our present
society] we have to adapt ourselves, every day, to the compromise
of liberalism: to living among, and to maintaining common
sympathy and common action (as indeed is duty as well as
necessity) with, people who deny or ignore the fundamentals
of Christianity. On the one hand we must accept, and on the
other we must never accept as finality, this state of affairs. Merely
to conduct our own life among ourselves, as we think right,
and to abandon the task of evangelisation, would be abnegation
of an essential duty.

'So, in a small and more particular matter, there would be
something wrong about the aim of developing and maintain-

[1] 'Religious Drama: Mediaeval and Modern', *The University of Edinburgh
Journal*, Vol. IX, No. 1 (Autumn, 1937), p. 10.

ing a religious drama as something having nothing to do with the ordinary stage. If we became strict Puritans, and abstained from attending any but religious drama, we should be wrongly cutting ourselves off from the life of the world; if we determined merely to preserve in ourselves two attitudes, one for cathedral drama and the other for the West End, we should be dividing our own minds unjustifiably and with bad results. We need to strive towards a kind of *reintegration* of both kinds of drama, just as we need to strive towards a reintegration of life.' [1]

It is not surprising, therefore, that he should want next to portray a part of the contemporary scene in a religious play written for the theatre. But when he came to do so, he had to face the fact that *Murder in the Cathedral*, although it may be said to herald the revival of true poetic drama in England, was very much a special case and did not supply a generally applicable formula.

[1] *Ibid.*, pp. 10 and 13.

Chapter Four

Plays in a Contemporary Setting—I
'The Family Reunion' (1939)

'What we have to do is to bring poetry into the world in which the audience lives and to which it returns when it leaves the theatre; not to transport the audience into some imaginary world totally unlike its own, an unreal world in which poetry is tolerated. What I should hope might be achieved, by a generation of dramatists having the benefit of our experience, is that the audience should find, at the moment of awareness that it is hearing poetry, that it is saying to itself: "*I* could talk in poetry too!" Then we should not be transported into an artificial world; on the contrary, our own sordid, dreary daily world would be suddenly illuminated and transfigured.' [1]

THE only kind of poetic drama being written in any quantity when Eliot began to write for the theatre was a survival of Romanticism. The Georgian poetic drama—the plays of Lascelles Abercrombie, Laurence Binyon, Gordon Bottomley, John Drinkwater, James Elroy Flecker, and John Masefield—was, for the most part, cut off from contemporary life by its poetic diction and by its choice of remote subjects which would justify the use of exalted language. When Masefield or Drinkwater, for instance, wrote about times as recent as the nineteenth century, as they did in *Nan* and *Abraham Lincoln*, they resorted to prose. Eliot followed this tradition in *Murder in the Cathedral* to the extent that he relied upon a historical subject to justify his use of a more obvious kind of poetry. But he did not want to write merely for a coterie, as the Georgians

[1] *Poetry and Drama*, p. 27 (*On Poetry and Poets*, p. 82).

had done. He wanted to write for an audience of ordinary people about the kind of life they knew. Even though *Murder in the Cathedral* had been written for a festival, it was a religious festival rather than an artistic one, and the audience was essentially unsophisticated.[1]

A year or two before he began to devote his creative energies to drama, he said:

'Every poet would like, I fancy, to be able to think that he had some direct social utility. . . . He would like to convey the pleasures of poetry, not only to a larger audience, but to larger groups of people collectively; and the theatre is the best place in which to do it.' [2]

A little earlier in the same lecture, he had made a confession of his own aspirations which must have been something of a surprise at the time, coming as it did from one of the most erudite of modern poets, one who was already the object of a cult:

'I believe that the poet naturally prefers to write for as large and miscellaneous an audience as possible, and that it is the half-educated and ill-educated, rather than the uneducated, who stand in his way: I myself should like an audience which could neither read nor write. The most useful poetry, socially, would be one which cut across all the present stratifications of public taste—stratifications which are perhaps a sign of social disintegration. The ideal medium for poetry, to my mind, and the most direct means of social "usefulness" for poetry, is the theatre. In a play of Shakespeare you get several levels of significance. For the simplest auditors there is the plot, for the more thoughtful the character and conflict of character, for the more literary the words and phrasing, for the more musically sensitive the rhythm, and for auditors of greater sensitiveness and understanding a meaning which reveals itself gradually. And I do not believe that the classification of audience is so clear-cut as this; but rather that the sensitiveness of every auditor is acted upon by all these elements

---

[1] See Ashley Dukes, 'T. S. Eliot in the Theatre', in March's *Symposium*, p. 14.

[2] *The Use of Poetry and the Use of Criticism* (1933), p. 154. Cf. *The Sacred Wood*, ed. cit., p. 70: 'Possibly the majority of attempts to confect a poetic drama have begun at the wrong end; they have aimed at the small public which wants "poetry".'

at once, though in different degrees of consciousness. At none of these levels is the auditor bothered by the presence of that which he does not understand, or by the presence of that in which he is not interested.'[1]

But a problem had arisen with which Shakespeare had not been faced. He had been able to count upon an uninhibited response to poetry in his audience since poetry had always been the medium for serious theatre. But audiences accustomed to hearing nothing but naturalistic prose in contemporary plays had become conscious of poetry as allegedly 'unnatural'. As Eliot soon perceived, it was no longer possible to move from verse into prose, or from prose into verse as Shakespeare had done at need. Such a transition will nowadays make the audience 'aware, with a jolt, of the medium'.[2] Of course, the author may want to produce this jolt. Eliot himself planned such an effect in the second of the two passages of prose in *Murder in the Cathedral*—the apologia of the Knights, where the abrupt transition from verse is part of the shock treatment.[3] But this is a special case, as is the whole play. Eliot has come to believe that, in modern verse drama generally,

'prose should be used very sparingly indeed; that we should aim at a form of verse in which everything can be said that has to be said; and that when we find some situation which is intractable in verse, it is merely that our form of verse is inelastic. And if there prove to be scenes which we cannot put in verse, we must either develop our verse, or avoid having to introduce such scenes. For we have to accustom our audiences to verse to the point at which they will cease to be conscious of it; and to introduce prose dialogue, would only be to distract their attention from the play itself to the medium of its expression. But if our verse is to have so wide a range that it can say anything that has to be said, it follows that it will not be "poetry" all the time. It will only be "poetry" when the dramatic situation has reached such a

---

[1] *The Use of Poetry and the Use of Criticism* (1933), pp. 152-3.
[2] *Poetry and Drama*, p. 13 (*On Poetry and Poets*, p. 73).
[3] pp. 77 ff. The other passage is the sermon, of which Eliot says in *Poetry and Drama*, pp. 25-6 (*On Poetry and Poets*, p. 81): 'A sermon cast in verse is too unusual an experience for even the most regular churchgoer: nobody would have responded to it as a sermon at all.'

point of intensity that poetry becomes the natural utterance because then it is the only language in which the emotions can be expressed at all.'[1]

When he came to write his first full-length play in a modern setting, therefore, he excluded prose except for a short reading from a newspaper (pp. 95–6) and the reading of a telegram (p. 131), both of which would have sounded even stranger in verse than a sermon, and he evolved

'a rhythm close to contemporary speech, in which the stresses could be made to come wherever we should naturally put them, in uttering the particular phrase on the particular occasion'.[2]

Going back to the root principle of English prosody, organization by stress, he devised a line of varying length but a fixed number of stresses, normally three, with a caesura coming after the first or the second stress. This is the basic verse-form which he has used throughout his later plays, for, as Martin Browne points out, it proved

'capable of including every kind of contemporary speech, from the banal conversation of a drawing-room at tea-time to the revelations of the heart's depth and the terror of eternal things. . . . The form, . . . though appearing loose at first reading, is in reality closely knit, and should impose its discipline naturally on a sensitive actor. This verse is dramatic in the true sense, that the form of the verse heightens the tension and sharpens the

---

[1] *Poetry and Drama*, pp. 14–15 (*On Poetry and Poets*, pp. 74–5). Cf. with the corresponding passages in 'The Aims of Poetic Drama', *Adam*, No. 200 (November, 1949), p. 13, and in *The Aims of Poetic Drama*, the Presidential Address . . . p. 6. This conviction of the necessity for functional poetry in the theatre reinforced Eliot's own aspiration
'to write poetry which should be essentially poetry, with nothing poetic about it, poetry standing naked in its bare bones, or poetry so transparent that we should not see the poetry, but that which we are meant to see through the poetry'
—quoted by F. O. Matthiessen, *op. cit.*, p. 90, from an unpublished lecture on 'English Letter Writers' which was delivered in New Haven, Connecticut, during the winter of 1933. It is the Dantean style that he emulates. (See chapter V, page 154, note 3 below.)

[2] *Poetry and Drama*, p. 27 (*On Poetry and Poets*, p. 82). Cf. 'The Aims of Poetic Drama', *Adam*, 200 (November, 1949), p. 12.

characterization . . . . [Eliot] is able in this play to create individuals fully alive in their idiosyncrasies and consistent in their thoughts and feelings: yet to bind them into the greater whole which reveals them as types of human nature'.[1]

The degree of control that the verse gives over characterization and dramatic tension can be illustrated from the scene in which the uncles and aunts discuss 'the younger generation' (pp. 14-15). Here, the stiff, pompous, insensitive rhythm which characterizes Charles, especially in his more obtuse mood, gives way to an ampler, more relaxed, but still circumscribed movement as Gerald makes his kindly gesture. Mary's pent-up emotion reveals itself in a very jerky movement (the repetitions in 'information . . . generation' and 'I don't deserve . . . . I don't belong' are the more obvious means of achieving a kind of stumbling bitterness). The awkward silence which covers her exit is broken by Violet's sharp decisiveness. Gerald's reaction does not go deeper than bemusement; the rhythm has only a slight hesitancy. With his stolid complacency, Charles moves firmly in to put Mary's outburst into perspective, as he would think. And, finally, Amy with her characteristically domineering rhythm closes the incident. The tenacious rhythm of her monosyllabic half-line 'but life may still go right' prevents us from interpreting it as mere wish; she clearly intends to do what she can to make it go right. The scene demonstrates that poetic drama can have something of the precision of a musical score. Character and dramatic structure are here integrated in the verse rhythm, through which the tension of the awkward moment is built up and resolved.

Having taken a decisive step in the rehabilitation of verse, Eliot had also now to tackle the lack of moral and social conventions, which we have seen to be the other half of the problem of recreating poetic drama. In *Murder in the Cathedral* he had been writing for a special audience, an audience sharing his beliefs and assumptions. He could build his play upon the pattern of the Atonement, knowing that it would be recognized and that what he had new to say would be intelligible in the light of it. But in writing for a secular audience, he was faced with the problem of

[1] E. Martin Browne, 'The Dramatic Verse of T. S. Eliot', March's *Symposium*, pp. 203-4.

surmounting not only ignorance about Christianity but also prejudice against it.

In our society, which is essentially irreligious although it retains many vestiges of Christianity, people tend to dismiss the Christian view of life as outmoded without attempting to understand it fully. As Eliot said in a talk broadcast in 1932:

'It is so difficult to talk to people about things of which they have no knowledge, when they have been made sordidly familiar with the *names* for the things: when they have heard repeated so many words belonging to Christian theology, and have never heard anything of Christian theology itself!' [1]

He had, therefore, as Richard Findlater has put it, 'to find ways of expressing Christian values obliquely in secular terms'.[2] In general, he has followed the educational principle of starting with the known and working into the unknown. Thinking as yet perhaps only of the cultured audience which read his poetry, he began in *The Family Reunion* with a reworking of classical myth —the story of Orestes as treated in the *Oresteia* of Aeschylus— in which he made no attempt to hide his borrowings. The Eumenides, for example, are obviously the Aeschylean figures, but they are given a Christian dimension. It is as if Eliot is showing the way in which Christianity completes the intuitions of the Greek poet.

We see, then, why Eliot may have gone to a Greek play for the basis of *The Family Reunion*. But this does not explain why all his dramatic work has been, to a greater or lesser extent, modelled on Greek originals. Beginning with an Aristophanic melodrama, he went on in *Murder in the Cathedral*, as we have seen, to imitate the form of Greek tragedy, and with *The Family Reunion* he began to adapt classical material to naturalistic form. (Apart from an adherence to the Unities of Time and Place,[3] and an adaptation of

[1] 'Building up the Christian World', *The Listener*, Vol. VII, No. 169, 6 April, 1932, p. 502.
[2] Richard Findlater, *The Unholy Trade* (Victor Gollancz, London, 1952), p. 137.
[3] The time of the action is one day and the scene transfers merely from the drawing-room to the library at Wishwood. One of the interlocutors in the 'Dialogue on Dramatic Poetry' expresses what might have been Eliot's own view of the Unities at one time—that they 'make for intensity' (*Selected Essays*, p. 58).

the chorus, there is little indebtedness to classical form.) And although in his later plays he has gone to some trouble to disguise his borrowings, to transform the Greek elements into modern equivalents, he has continued to base his work upon the plots of Greek tragedy. Why is this?

Comparison with the modern French dramatists who have adapted classical plots takes us some way towards an explanation. Signor Melchiori observes that they

'deliberately gave a new twist to the ancient myths: keeping even the mythological names, they wanted to emphasize the connection, they wanted their audiences to assume from the very start that their characters were literary creations acquiring little by little new individual personalities. Eliot instead tried to follow the reverse process by starting from characters who were supposed to belong to ordinary life in modern times and making the audience realize that their plight was the same as that of Greek heroes. The result is that while in the first case we have abstract types gradually humanized, in Eliot we have everyday characters dehumanized.' [1]

If by 'dehumanized' Signor Melchiori means revealed as permanent types, I would agree with him in substance, though I am not happy about the overtones of the word. But his fundamental distinction seems to me to be revealing. For the modern French dramatists in question—notably Cocteau, Giraudoux, Anouilh and Sartre—the process ends in an image of modern man; for Eliot it ends in an image of permanent human nature being subsumed under the divine. His eclecticism leads towards universality and the fulfilment of the role of poetry in the theatre: 'What poetry should do in the theatre is a kind of humble shadow or analogy of the Incarnation, whereby the human is taken up into the divine.' [2]

Where surface poetry is in abeyance, Eliot attempts to make up for it by building upon a poetic foundation. In this he is developing a method which he distinguished in Joyce's *Ulysses*. In a review written in 1923 he suggested that

[1] Giorgio Melchiori, *The Tightrope Walkers* (Routledge and Kegan Paul, 1956), p. 136.

[2] 'The Aims of Poetic Drama', *Adam*, No. 200 (November, 1949), p. 12.

'In using the myth, in manipulating a continuous parallel between contemporaneity and antiquity, Mr. Joyce is pursuing a method which others must pursue after him. They will not be imitators, any more than the scientist who uses the discoveries of an Einstein in pursuing his own, independent, further investigations. It is simply a way of controlling, of ordering, of giving a shape and a significance to the immense panorama of futility and anarchy which is contemporary history. . . . It is . . . a step toward making the modern world possible for art.'[1]

Among Eliot's investigations has been the use of myth in his plays in a contemporary setting as an attempt to ensure that each play has a poetic heart, a vision of human life more profound than naturalism can give. As Ronald Peacock remarks,

'what he [Eliot] attempts to do is to portray a realistic scene—the family in the country house, the barrister with wife, mistress, and family circle—through which an underlying mythical pattern diffuses its meanings to the surface; so that the "real" becomes, without being negated or displaced, transparent, and through it the myth appears as the immanent meaning.'[2]

It is an attempt which is unlikely to succeed the first time, which, in fact, is likely to require many experiments in adjusting the ancient to the modern, and Eliot does not make his attempt any easier by choosing at the outset to rework the greatest extant example of classical drama, to adapt a design which in its profound integration has never been surpassed.

In *Agamemnon*, the first play in the great trilogy of Aeschylus, the hero returns from the Trojan war to be murdered by his wife Clytemnestra and her lover Aegisthus. In *Choephoroe* (The Libation Bearers), his son Orestes avenges his father's death by killing his mother. Thereafter, as murderer of his mother, he is pursued by the Erinyes or Furies. In the third play, *Eumenides*, he appeals to the Areopagus, the newly established court of justice in Athens, only to find the judges equally divided. At this point, the goddess Pallas Athene intervenes on his behalf and offers the Furies a new

---

[1] 'Ulysses, Order and Myth', *The Dial*, LXXV (November, 1923), p. 483.
[2] Ronald Peacock, 'Public and Private Problems in Modern Drama', *Bulletin of the John Rylands Library* (Manchester), Vol. 36 (1953–4), pp. 53–4.

role: if they will yield to persuasion and no longer stir up inter-
necine strife, they will be honoured as spirits of mercy. After
some hesitation, they accept and become the Eumenides or kindly
ones, figures of good will.

In this change of Erinyes into Eumenides, Aeschylus dramatized
the tremendous advance achieved when mankind gave up primitive blood-vengeance and submitted to orderly procedure in
courts of law, when 'humane statute purg'd the gentle weal', as
Shakespeare put it.[1] In the new world of Apollo and Athene,
patron deities of Athens, a more beneficent order had come into
being. As Aeschylus seems to see it, the change implies not merely
an improvement in human society, a great advance in civilization,
but a change also in divine justice, in deity itself. Such a change is
inconceivable in the Christian conception of Godhead; it is man's
view of God which has been changed through the Christian
revelation, changed from a conception of a just and wrathful God
to one of a merciful and loving God. The transformation of
Harry's attitude to the Eumenides implies an analogous change in
his conception of God, but the change does not, of course, extend
beyond the conversion of an individual. There is no corresponding
change in Orestes, for Aeschylean drama operates only intermittently upon the psychological level.

It will be seen from the summary of the *Oresteia* that the action
of *The Family Reunion* corresponds to the action of *Choephoroe*
more than to any other part of the trilogy; the one big addition is
the transformation of the Erinyes into the Eumenides from the
third play.[2] But even where the parallel is closest, the action is

---

[1] *Macbeth*, III. iv. 76.

[2] The only three verbal echoes I have noted are

(a) *Choephoroe*, 1051–2, already used as an epigraph to *Sweeney Agonistes*.
Cf. p. 25.

(b) *Choephoroe*, 277–80, which may be transformed into 'the cancer / That
eats away the self' (p. 31). Cf. also p. 67.

(c) *Eumenides*, 307–11, trans. George Thomson:

O come, let us dance in a ring and declare,
As our purpose is fixed,
To the tune of this terrible music
Those laws whereby
We determine the fortune of mortals.

Cf. *The Family Reunion*, p. 97:

transformed in the light of the Christian dispensation. There is no actual murder, it would seem, in Harry's case; there was certainly no murder in his father's case, although there was a plan. In both cases, however, the sinful wish has been felt, and in the Christian view the intention is as evil as the deed. Moreover, in whatever way Harry was to blame for his wife's death, his departure from Wishwood at the end of the play is certainly the direct cause of his mother's death. But the important qualification here is that his going is for her redemption, for her *eternal* life.[1]

Eliot has transferred much of the guilt from Clytemnestra-Amy. It is Harry's father who falls in love with another and plans to murder his legal partner. Amy, although she knows of his love for Agatha, keeps him. In doing this, perhaps, she may be thought to have killed the real man:

> Seven years I kept him,
> For the sake of the future, a discontented ghost,
> In his own house (p. 117).

Thus she too is involved in the tangle of sin. Not only does she use a person in this inhuman way and seek to impose her will upon all around her; she is also capable of willing someone else's death, or so Mary believes (p. 49).

This almost lethal hatred is the curse upon the House of Monchensey. It represents both less and more than the curse upon the House of Atreus; it no longer reveals itself as a primitive blood-feud, but it may well stand for the murderous impulse in humanity, the mark of Cain, and it certainly symbolizes the visitation of the sins of the fathers 'upon the children unto the third and fourth generation of them that hate me'. Likewise,

---

> And whether in Argos or England,
> There are certain inflexible laws,
> Unalterable, in the nature of music.

[1] See p. 136. It will be noted that Harry is pursued by the Furies for the 'murder' of his wife, not his mother. It may be that Clytemnestra has been diffracted, as some characters of Euripides are diffracted in *The Confidential Clerk*, and that Harry's wife is a mother-substitute, such as mother-dominated men are apt to marry. What evidence there is in the play seems, however, to point to a weak woman, the very opposite of Amy (see pp. 20–1 and 49). Harry's marriage would seem to have been a gesture of defiance, a rebellion against his mother's attempt to dominate him.

the Erinyes-Eumenides are both less and more than the Aeschylean figures; they are no longer primeval deities, daughters of Night, but instead they represent the promptings of conscience and are the instruments of Divine Grace—

love and terror

Of what waits and wants me, and will not let me fall (p. 115).

Whereas in his previous play, Eliot portrayed the fulfilment of a spiritual election in martyrdom, here he traces the way in which a man discovers in himself such an election. His Orestes figure, Harry, Lord Monchensey, returns to his ancestral home after an absence of eight years, haunted, in the literal sense, by a feeling of responsibility for his wife's death. He says he pushed her overboard in mid-Atlantic (p. 30); Downing's account of his behaviour seems to corroborate this (pp. 40-2); and Harry's attitude to Winchell, the local sergeant of police, is 'suspicious' (pp. 80-2). But the fact is that, for all his scruples of conscience, he does not give himself up to the police, and when he learns of his father's wish to kill his mother, he seems to recognize it as relevant to himself and discover in it the truth of his own situation:

> Perhaps my life has only been a dream
> Dreamt through me by the minds of others. Perhaps
> I only dreamt I pushed her.

AGATHA

> So I had supposed.   What of it? (p. 104).

It seems that Charles has an inkling of the truth when he says:

> I suspect it is simply that the wish to get rid of her
> Makes him believe he did (p. 33).

Having failed to evade his sense of guilt in travel, Harry has returned to the scene of his childhood, hoping to recapture something of childhood's innocence.[1] But his

---

[1] The name Wishwood is probably symbolic. Cf. Roy Battenhouse, 'Eliot's "The Family Reunion" as Christian Prophecy', *Christendom*, Vol. X, No. 3 (Summer, 1945), p. 317:
'I suspect that the very name Wishwood is intended by Eliot to stand for universal man's Dream House, located in a wood of wish and memory—turned to by man for refuge but discovered to be only an asylum for ghosts.'

instinct to return to the point of departure
And start again as if nothing had happened (p. 56)

proves to be 'all folly', just as Agatha, in her capacity as auxiliary
Chorus, has anticipated:

When the loop in time comes—and it does not come for everybody—
The hidden is revealed, and the spectres show themselves (p. 18).

It is the re-encounter with his old self, 'the boy who left', that
brings the horror into the open; here the spirits of guilt (the
Eumenides) become visible for the first time. He has sensed their
presence in many places; he has known that they were watching
him, but he has never before seen them. Why should they have
waited until now to show themselves (p. 25)? It is not until
much later in the play that he discovers

That the last apparent refuge, the safe shelter,
That is where one meets them. That is the way of spectres . . .
      (p. 113).

Most of the family assembled to greet him on his return have
no glimmering of understanding of his problem. His mother,
who seeks to dominate all around her, is herself dominated by a
fear of death, in which she can find no meaning (p. 16); this
spiritual paralysis prevents her from seeing that Harry's is a spiritual problem. The quartet of uncles and aunts who form a chorus
representing obtuse humanity recoil in fear from the unknown
and try to 'explain it away' (pp. 32–3). To none of these are the
Eumenides visible.

Only two of the family are alive enough spiritually to understand Harry's problem and to share his experience. They are
Mary, his childhood companion, and Agatha, the youngest of the
aunts, who are both helped towards understanding by their love
of him. With Mary he gets nearest to the boy that was and the
man that might have been, and it is then that the spirits of guilt
become most oppressive. 'You bring me news', he tells her,

      Of a door that opens at the end of a corridor,
      Sunlight and singing; when I had felt sure
      That every corridor only led to another,

> Or to a blank wall; that I kept moving
> Only so as not to stay still. Singing and light (pp. 60-61).

The sunlight and singing symbolize the warmth and harmony of the human love he might have shared with Mary. The Eumenides appear in order to make it clear that this is no longer possible for him, if it ever was. He remonstrates with them:

> When I knew her, I was not the same person.
> I was not any person. Nothing that I did
> Has to do with me. The accident of a dreaming moment,
> Of a dreaming age, when I was someone else
> Thinking of something else, puts me among you (p. 62).

Harry is here trying to dissociate himself from his past, which now seems unreal, and from the earlier self which 'knew her' (his wife) and which seems in retrospect to have had no spiritual definition ('I was not any person'). He is to come to see that he cannot cut himself off from the past or pretend that it was different from what it was. He must accept the past and its consequences in the present in order to build a future, for, as Agatha sees,

> the future can only be built
> Upon the real past (p. 17).

Only when the past is accepted is there hope of redeeming it by future action.[1] Thinking to help him, Mary pretends that the Eumenides are not there,[2] but this is not the way to help him, as Agatha, with her greater insight, is to perceive. At this stage Harry is still trying to fight them, and in his anger and frustration, he turns on her. It is only when he learns from Agatha the sad history of his parents and achieves a state of spiritual communion with her that he is enabled to accept the Eumenides as manifestations of Divine Love rather than Divine Wrath.[3]

[1] Cf. *The Cocktail Party*, p. 163.

[2] One must assume that she has seen because she says to Agatha later on: 'Oh! . . . so . . . *you* have seen them too!' (p. 121).

[3] In a letter to Mr. E. Martin Browne quoted by Matthiessen (pp. 167–8), Eliot himself outlines this aspect of the play's development:

'The scene with Mary is meant to bring out, as I am aware it fails to, the conflict inside him between . . . repulsion for Mary as a woman, and the attraction which the *normal* part of him that is left, feels toward her personally *for the first time*. This is the first time since his marriage ("there was no ecstasy")

From the moment of his arrival he knows that his sense of guilt
>goes a good deal deeper
>Than what people call their conscience.
>>. . . It is not my conscience,
>Not my mind. that is diseased, but the world
>>I have to live in (p. 31).

And later that day, looking back on the experience of the afternoon, he realizes that in the course of the years that he has had to live since he 'came home, a few hours ago, to Wishwood' (p. 91), he has gained a truer perspective. As he tells his uncles and aunts:

>You go on trying to think of each thing separately,
>Making small things important, so that everything
>May be unimportant, a slight deviation
>From some imaginary course that life ought to take,
>That you call normal. What you call the normal
>Is merely the unreal and the unimportant.
>I was like that in a way, so long as I could think
>Even of my own life as an isolated ruin,
>A casual bit of waste in an orderly universe.
>But it begins to seem just part of some huge disaster,
>Some monstrous mistake and aberration
>Of all men, of the world, which I cannot put in order.[1]

that he has been attracted towards any woman. The attraction glimmers for a moment in his mind, half-consciously as a possible "way of escape", and the Furies (for the Furies are *divine* instruments, not simple hell-hounds) come in the nick of time to warn him away from this evasion—though at that moment he misunderstands their function. Now, this attraction towards Mary has stirred him up, but, owing to his mental state, is incapable of developing; therefore he finds refuge in an ambiguous relation—the attraction half of a son, half of a lover, to Agatha, who reciprocates in somewhat the same way. And this gives the cue for the second appearance of the Furies, more patently in their role of divine messengers, to let him know clearly that the only way out is purgation and holiness. They become exactly "hounds of heaven". And Agatha understands this clearly, though Harry only understands it yet in flashes.'

[1] p. 91. Cf. Eliot's introduction to *Nightwood* by Djuna Barnes (Faber and Faber, 1937): 'The miseries that people suffer through their particular abnormalities of temperament are visible on the surface: the deeper design is that of the human misery and bondage which is universal.' Cf. also *The Cocktail Party*, p. 117.

This 'monstrous mistake and aberration / Of all men' is, of course, the Fall of Man, and its result is Original Sin, the guiltiness that we all share as members of a humanity which has fallen away from God, the guiltiness that we inherit as part of our birthright. It is indeed something which he cannot 'put in order', but he *can* share in the sufferings of Christ,[1] by which the Atonement and the re-ordering are effected for all men.

Within the world of the play, this universal sin is symbolized by the curse upon the Monchensey family, corresponding to the curse upon the house of Atreus in the *Oresteia*.[2] The coldness of Wishwood—'Wishwood was always a cold place, Amy' (p. 11)— has its counterpart in the lack of warmth in the human hearts there, the lovelessness.[3] Agatha remembers

> A summer day of unusual heat
> For this cold country[4]

when she and Harry's father fell in love, the outcome of which was his desire to kill Amy. When she tells Harry this, he perceives the sense in which, in his own case, the sins of the fathers are visited upon the children. He recognizes, moreover, that he shares the sin of his father in a particular way, for they have had an exactly similar sinful wish—to rid themselves of their wives by murder—a wish that by Christian standards is as evil as the deed itself. Agatha thus helps him to put his own sense of sin into perspective:

> It is possible that you have not known what sin
> You shall expiate, or whose, or why. It is certain

---

[1] In the words of Saint Paul, 'complete what is lacking in Christ's afflictions for the sake of his body, that is, the Church' (Colossians, i. 24, R.V.).

[2] The curse upon the house of Atreus began with the murder of his brother's children by Thyestes; the curse upon the house of Monchensey began with the wish to kill Amy while she was carrying Harry. Grover Smith tells us that 'The early drafts of the play take the curse back to a mad great-uncle Harry, a satanic Thyestes' (*T. S. Eliot's Poetry and Plays*, 1956, p. 202).

[3] Cf. pp. 46, 102, and Harry's statement that:
> Family affection
> Was a kind of formal obligation (p. 106).

[4] p. 102. Cf. Harry's use of the same expression on p. 77. This was, it would seem, the day on which Agatha 'only looked through the little door . . .' (p. 107). Cf. pp. 102–3.

That the knowledge of it must precede the expiation.
It is possible that sin may strain and struggle
In its dark instinctive birth, to come to consciousness
And so find expurgation. It is possible
You are the consciousness of your unhappy family,
Its bird sent flying through the purgatorial flame.
Indeed it is possible. You may learn hereafter,
Moving alone through flames of ice, chosen
To resolve the enchantment under which we suffer
(pp. 104-5).

Until now Agatha has carried the burden of guilt on behalf of the family because she alone has understood that guilt. Now it passes to Harry, her spiritual child, who has grown to a spiritual stature which allows him to assume the burden and to do something about it.[1]

In this moment of spiritual communion, they share the peace of the 'rose-garden' (pp. 107-8). In the scene with Mary, Harry has had a sense of the 'sunlight and singing' beyond 'a door that opens at the end of a corridor' (p. 60), and, years before with his father, Agatha has had a glimpse of the garden (p. 107). But now they both find themselves inside it. John Middleton Murry's comment on this passage is finely perceptive:

'Agatha, with Harry's father, "only looked through the little door When the sun was shining on the rose-garden". But when she has told her secret to Harry she "walks through the little door" and he "runs to meet her in the rose-garden". It is not pressing the poet's symbolism too hard to interpret passing through the little door as the attainment of love beyond desire, and looking through it as the vision of such love when it comes to one entangled in desire. Agatha's love for Harry and Harry's response to it are an instantaneous and eternal passing through the little door.'[2]

The 'tiny voices' which Agatha heard in the distance when she 'only looked through the little door' suggest the possible extension of love through children, and now that possibility is realized

---

[1] The sinful wish for someone's death is characteristic of the family. Amy seems to have felt it, too (p. 49), and Charles (p. 35).
[2] *Unprofessional Essays* (Cape, 1956), p. 168.

in the spirit. For Agatha sees Harry as the child who might have been hers, who *is* 'in some way' hers,[1] and in this moment he knows, for the first time, the happiness of a mother's undemanding love.

But the moment signifies more than the spiritual fulfilment of human love. The moment in the 'rose-garden'—a central symbol in Eliot's work[2]—seems to represent the moment of illumination which human love can give—the glimpse of the deepest reality, the refreshment of the spirit, which can come in the way of ordinary living. It is the worldly counterpart of the mystical illumination which is sought through abnegation of ordinary life —the way of ascetic contemplation and the aspiration to the peace at 'the still point of the turning world'—and though it is a less direct apprehension of the ultimate reality than the mystical identification with the divine, it too leads towards the fruition of love in beatitude. It is, in fact, the experience of Dante, for whom the process of salvation began in the moment in which he saw Beatrice.

But this is not to be Harry's path of redemption. More depends upon his choice than his personal salvation. So, once again, the Eumenides appear to remind him that he must not rest content in human love, and now, with his newly achieved spiritual maturity he is able to see them as they really are and to see what they re-quire of him:

This time, you are real, this time, you are outside me,
And just endurable. I know that you are ready,
Ready to leave Wishwood, and I am going with you (p. 109).

This recognition of the reality of the Eumenides and of their objective existence symbolizes, presumably, the clarification that comes from knowing that the guilt is not just his but that of the whole family. They are 'just endurable' now because they have acquired a meaning which defines the demands they are making

---

[1] See pp. 104 and 110.
[2] Cf. *Four Quartets*, pp. 7–8, 10, and *The Confidential Clerk*, pp. 51–4. For fuller discussion of the symbol, see Leonard Unger in the bibliography for this play, and Robert D. Wagner, 'The Meaning of T. S. Eliot's Rose-Garden', *PMLA*, LXIX (1954), pp. 22–33, and Louis L. Martz in Unger's *Critique*, pp. 447–54.

on him. Previously they have seemed neither inside nor outside:

> Were they simply outside,
> I might escape somewhere, perhaps. Were they simply inside
> I could cheat them perhaps with the aid of Dr. Warburton—
> Or any other doctor, . . .
> But this is too real for your words to alter (p. 93).

He can only alter the condition for himself, by recognizing the objective reality of the Eumenides and by facing up to what they require of him, instead of trying to escape.

In trying to evade the spirits of guilt, he has been trying to deny the demands made upon him by the unknown reality which they represent. But because this unknown reality is the final reality, there can be no personal reality which is not grounded in it, which does not spring from an acceptance of it. In accepting it, therefore, Harry finds personal integration.

One of the flaws in the play is that the early stages of Harry's spiritual development are left vague. They can be filled in, however, from the story of Sweeney's murderer-friend, who

> didn't know if he was alive
> and the girl was dead
> He didn't know if the girl was alive
> and he was dead. . . . [1]

This explains the origin of Harry's nightmarish suspension between two realities, natural and supernatural. In the scene in which Warburton chats with the family, we get a glimpse of the first stage of Harry's painful adjustment to the deeper reality:

> It is really harder to believe in murder
> Than to believe in cancer. Cancer is here:
> The lump, the dull pain, the occasional sickness:
> Murder a reversal of sleep and waking.
> Murder was there. Your ordinary murderer
> Regards himself as an innocent victim.
> To himself he is still what he used to be
> Or what he would be. He cannot realize
> That everything is irrevocable,
> The past unredeemable (p. 67).

[1] *Collected Poems*, p. 131.

Clearly, it is the recognition of the murderous impulse within himself which has been the origin of Harry's spiritual awakening. If it seems strange that a man's path to salvation should begin in an evil deed or evil impulse, the explanation is suggested by Eliot:

'So far as we are human, what we do must be either evil or good; so far as we do evil or good, we are human; and it is better, in a paradoxical way, to do evil than to do nothing: at least, we exist.' [1]

In the scene in which Winchell comes to tell him about John's accident, Harry's behaviour illustrates the dilemma of Sweeney's friend; only it's a policeman whose existence he doubts, instead of a milkman or rent-collector (pp. 80-1).

So far as we can piece it together, then, this has been Harry's story. Shocked by his wife's death into an awareness of the unreality of the natural world and doubting the reality of the supernatural world, he has lived a nightmare existence, not knowing dream from reality or reality from dream:

> What I see
> May be one dream or another; if there is nothing else
> The most real is what I fear (pp. 55-6).

It is the acceptance of the reality of what he fears that makes it possible for him to find a true perspective:

> The things I thought were real are shadows, and the real
> Are what I thought were private shadows. O that awful privacy
> Of the insane mind! Now I can live in public. [2]

Now his experience of the past year takes on a pattern and a meaning for him:

> Now I know that all my life has been a flight
> And phantoms fed upon me while I fled (p. 113).

Having turned and faced them, however, he has found the

---

[1] *Selected Essays*, p. 429.

[2] pp. 106-7. In the *Oresteia* Orestes is actually stricken by madness, and Ivy, at least, thinks that Harry is mad (p. 33). Harry himself, however, knows that his malady is more than psychological (p. 93).

creatures of terror transformed into 'bright angels' whom he must follow (p. 115):

> And now I know
> That my business is not to run away, but to pursue,
> Not to avoid being found, but to seek (p. 113).

His search will lead him to safety and away from Wishwood (pp. 113-14). Agatha explains as fully as can be explained:

> Here the danger, here the death, here, not elsewhere;
> Elsewhere no doubt is agony, renunciation,
> But birth and life. Harry has crossed the frontier
> Beyond which safety and danger have a different meaning.
> And he cannot return. That is his privilege.[1]

So he will go where the agents of the divine purpose lead, and to Amy's question 'Where are you going?' there can be no precise answer: [2]

> Where does one go from a world of insanity?
> Somewhere on the other side of despair.
> To the worship in the desert, the thirst and deprivation,
> A stony sanctuary and a primitive altar,

[1] pp. 120-1. Grover Smith (p. 211) points out the resemblance of Agatha's words to a passage in 'Eeldrop and Appleplex' quoted on p. 35 above.

[2] Of course, this hasn't stopped people from asking the question. Richard Findlater in his biography of *Michael Redgrave, Actor* (Heinemann, 1956), pp. 49-50, tells how, 'having worked for many days' in the initial production of the play 'trying to translate Eliot's intention into acting terms', Redgrave finally said to the author in rehearsal:

' "I'm awfully sorry to be so stupid, but would you mind telling me what *does* happen to this young man at the end of the play?"

' "Oh, yes," replied Mr. Eliot agreeably. "I think he and the chauffeur go off and get jobs in the East End."

' "It's a pity," suggested Redgrave diffidently, "that we couldn't have a line to suggest something of the sort."

'Eliot was surprised. "Do you really *need* one?"

'Plucking up courage, Redgrave explained his predicament, the poet said he would think it over, and arrived at rehearsals the following day with some twenty-five additional lines—exactly as required. (The play, however, had already been published, and these lines have never been added to any subsequent edition.)'

> The heat of the sun and the icy vigil,
> A care over lives of humble people.[1]

He only knows that the kind of normal life his mother has planned for him is impossible. He turns over his rights as eldest son to John:

> What would destroy me will be life for John,
> I am responsible for him. Why I have this election
> I do not understand. It must have been preparing always,
> And I see it was what I always wanted (p. 115).

He has accepted his election and he goes off to fulfil his part in the Divine Providence, one aspect of which, and the only aspect he yet knows, is expiation of the sin of his family:

'Conceived and brought forth in hatred not in love, he bears the sins of his parents, at once their victim and their perpetuator, for he has been himself incapable of love. Mary's "ordinary hopelessness", and his wife's wretchedness are fruits of this sin, his parents' and his own, the sin of failure in loving. He has to learn to love. He must go away into solitude and silence, like the scapegoat, laden with sin, driven out into the wilderness, so that years later, or months—we do not know how long it may be—he may find what ways of love are possible for him. What is impossible is that he should remain at Wishwood, where his mother does not want what he can give, and where Mary, who does not share his burden of knowledge, can be hurt by his presence and the gulf between them. He is sustained by the discovery that he is loved. There are not eyes spying and watching to find him out; there is a "single eye above the desert".' [2]

It is the Christian pattern of Atonement and involves the forsaking of family and all earthly attachments.[3] His going means

---

[1] pp. 114–15. Cf. *The Cocktail Party*, pp. 124–5.
[2] Helen Gardner, *The Art of T. S. Eliot* (1949), p. 154.
[3] Cf. St. Matthew, x. 35–8:
'For I am come to set a man at variance against his father, and the daughter against her mother, and the daughter in law against her mother in law. And a man's foes shall be they of his own household. He that loveth father or mother more than me is not worthy of me: and he that loveth son or daughter

the death of his mother, as he must know,[1] but his going is *for* her no less than the others. As Agatha says at the end of the play, in completing the ritual of blowing out the candles on Amy's birthday cake:

> This way the pilgrimage
> Of expiation. . .
> So the knot be unknotted . . .
> And the curse be ended . . .
> By those who depart
> In several directions
> For their own redemption
> And that of the departed (p. 136).

With the death of Amy the pattern of the Orestes story is completed, but it has been transformed in the light of the Christian revelation.

The play is built around Harry's discovery of spiritual election. The significance of the other characters depends upon their relationship to this central experience. They arrange themselves almost schematically in degrees of spiritual perception.

On the one hand there are those who are spiritually alive and see the Eumenides. Agatha has known one way of illumination in her love for Harry's father and has glimpsed the possibility of another:

There are hours when there seems to be no past or future,
Only a present moment of pointed light
When you want to burn. When you stretch out your hand
To the flames. They only come once,
Thank God, that kind. Perhaps there is another kind,
I believe, across a whole Thibet of broken stones
That lie, fang up, a lifetime's march. I have believed this (pp.
102–3).

more than me is not worthy of me. And he that taketh not his cross, and followeth after me, is not worthy of me,'
and the words of St. John of the Cross used as an epigraph to *Sweeney Agonistes*:
'Hence the soul cannot be possessed of the divine union, until it has divested itself of the love of created beings' (*The Ascent of Mount Carmel*, Bk. I, ch. iv).
[1] Doctor Warburton having told him:
A sudden shock
Might send her off at any moment (p. 78).

This insight makes it possible for her to become his spiritual mentor, as well as an interpreter of the action for the audience. As Violet comments on one occasion, underlining the significance of what Agatha has just said: 'Agatha's remarks are invariably pointed' (p. 92). In fact, Agatha 'acts as an auxiliary Chorus'.[1] Because the function of the main Chorus is to represent obtuse humanity, someone is necessary to interpret the action more perceptively, and Agatha is best suited to do that.

Mary, too, intuitively understands Harry and his problem, though less fully than Agatha. She and he shared their few happy moments of childhood, and she, it seems, has loved him, for all her disinclination to be ruled by Amy's desire for their marriage (p. 49). When Harry finds his direction, he unwittingly helps her to find hers (pp. 121–2). It is fittingly she and Agatha, the 'watchers and waiters' (p. 50), who perform the final ritual.

Agatha and Mary have an intellectual background.[2] As if to remind us that it is not a matter of intellectual but of spiritual awareness, the unintellectual Downing, Harry's servant and chauffeur, also sees 'them ghosts'—and sees them before Harry himself. He is one of the pure in heart who, like Eggerson, the old confidential clerk, sees a bit more and a bit further than any of the others:

> And I have a kind of feeling that his Lordship won't need me
> Very long now. I can't give you any reasons.
> But to show you what I mean, though you'd hardly credit it,
> I've always said, whatever happened to his Lordship
> Was just a kind of preparation for something else (p. 129).

Over against these three characters, there stand the spiritually dead, who cannot see the Eumenides. Stung by their insensitivity, Harry cries out:

> You are all people
> To whom nothing has happened, at most a continual impact
> Of external events. You have gone through life in sleep,
> Never woken to the nightmare (p. 28).

---

[1] Findlater, p. 140.

[2] Agatha is the principal of a women's college (p. 100). Mary has been one of her students, one whom she considered a suitable candidate for a fellowship (p. 48).

They are all dominated by sterile fear.

Amy dreads the passing of time and, above all, the stopping of time which is death:

O Sun, that was once so warm, O Light that was taken for granted
When I was young and strong, and sun and light unsought for
And the night unfeared and the day expected
And clocks could be trusted, tomorrow assured
And time would not stop in the dark!
Put on the lights.[1]

In this movement from the conventionalized expression of intimate fear to the naturalistic command, the root impulse of her being is revealed to us. Her imagination is keenly alive to the terror of death, but it remains a sterile terror which she tries to suppress:

> I do not want the clock to stop in the dark.
> If you want to know why I never leave Wishwood
> That is the reason. I keep Wishwood alive
> To keep the family alive, to keep them together,
> To keep me alive, and I live to keep them.
> You none of you understand how old you are
> And death will come to you as a mild surprise,
> A momentary shudder in a vacant room.
> Only Agatha seems to discover some meaning in death
> Which I cannot find (pp. 15–16).

So she tries to arrest change[2] and to perpetuate the Wishwood she has 'supported' and which has 'supported her'.[3] This is her defence against time. But when Harry refuses to accept the role she wishes to impose on him and Mary too breaks away from her domination, she glimpses the puniness of that defence:

> So you will all leave me!
> An old woman alone in a damned house . . . (p. 122).

[1] p. 11. Cf. *Four Quartets*, p. 26.
[2] See p. 21 ('Please behave only / As if nothing had happened in the last eight years'), pp. 26–7, 51–2. Her attempt to impose roles on others is part of her attempt to stop people and things from changing. Cf. pp. 53, 106.
[3] p. 102. Cf. p. 117.

And she dies with 'a momentary shudder in a vacant room', crying

> The clock has stopped in the dark! (p. 131)

But there has been the suggestion that she was capable of learning from experience:

> At my age, I only just begin to apprehend the truth
> About things too late to mend: and that is to be old.
> Nevertheless, I am glad if I can come to know them.
> I always wanted too much for my children,
> More than life can give. And now I am punished for it.[1]

Amy does not understand Harry's problem, though one has the impression that she could partly understand if she would. Her explanation to the others that he 'is going away—to become a missionary'[2] sounds very much like a sneer at something she is afraid of.

The quartet of uncles and aunts who compose the Chorus seem, with one partial exception, to be unable to understand what is happening; Charles alone has a glimmering of its significance:

> It's very odd,
> But I am beginning to feel, just beginning to feel
> That there is something I *could* understand, if I were told it.[3]

But most of the time he is, like the others, a representative of obtuse humanity. They are stock English types, slightly caricatured. From time to time they draw together, as if to find safety in numbers, and voice their fear of the unknown. As Matthiessen points out, 'They are unlike the usual Greek chorus in that their role is not to illuminate the action, but to express

---

[1] pp. 126–7. Cf. Eliot's comment on the *Vita Nuova*:
'There is . . . a practical sense of realities behind it, which is antiromantic: not to expect more from *life* than it can give or more from *human* beings than they can give; to look to *death* for what life cannot give' (*Selected Essays*, p. 275).
Amy's trouble is that she cannot look to death in this way, whereas, as she points out, Agatha can (p. 16).

[2] p. 124. Harry's reply is on p. 125.

[3] pp. 127–8. Cf. pp. 31 and 35, which suggest that he has almost been awakened from his spiritual torpor by a sinful wish.

their baffled inability to understand what is happening.'¹ Because, however, they express small, everyday fears, which members of the audience will recognize as akin to their own experience, they form a link between the audience and the action. The difficulty of the play for most audiences stems from the fact that Harry's experience is exceptional and remote. At a level of apprehension nearer that of the average member of an audience, the Chorus express the fear of spiritual reality which Harry comes to accept. By implication, therefore, they help to interpret the action, even though they do not understand it.

In Priestley's *I Have Been Here Before*, Dr. Gortler suggests that

'What seems to happen continually just outside the edge of our attention—the little fears and fancies, as you call them—may be all-important because they belong to a profounder reality, like the vague sounds of the city outside that we hear sometimes inside a theatre.'²

It is these 'little fears and fancies' to which the Chorus give expression. In the first chorus (pp. 22–3), just before Harry enters, they voice their unease at being assembled 'at Amy's command, to play an unread part in some monstrous farce', their fear of being 'ridiculous in some nightmare pantomime' (p. 23). When Harry has told them that he pushed his wife overboard and Downing seemed to corroborate this, they are assailed by fear of a public scandal and terror of the ugly reality that may be revealed, which they would prefer to ignore: it isn't nice to have a murderer in the family, but it's worse still to realize that the unknown has irrupted into the family circle and that you no longer recognize your nephew. For the Chorus,

> any explanation will satisfy:
> We only ask to be reassured
> About the noises in the cellar
> And the window that should not have been open.

¹ *Op. cit.*, p. 166.
² *The Plays of J. B. Priestley* (William Heinemann, London, 1948), Vol. I, p. 220. Cf. Harry's apprehension of the Furies 'Always flickering at the corner of my eye' (p. 57), and Eliot's reference in *Poetry and Drama*, p. 34 (*On Poetry and Poets*, p. 86) to the 'fringe' of feeling, 'which we can only detect, so to speak, out of the corner of the eye and can never completely focus'.

Why do we all behave as if the door might suddenly open, the
    curtains be drawn,
The cellar make some dreadful disclosure, the roof disappear,
And we should cease to be sure of what is real or unreal?
Hold tight, hold tight, we must insist that the world is what we
    have always taken it to be (pp. 44–5).

They dread being drawn into something different from ordinary
reality. They are afraid because their comfortable conception of
time as an orderly succession is threatened and their complacent
picture of family history as a series of innocent snapshots im-
perilled:

And the wings of the future darken the past, the beak and claws
    have desecrated
History. Shamed
The first cry in the bedroom, the noise in the nursery, mutilated
The family album, rendered ludicrous
The tenants' dinner, the family picnic on the moors (p. 69).

They are aware of the possibility of a curse on the house:

In an old house there is always listening, and more is heard than
    is spoken.
And what is spoken remains in the room, waiting for the future
    to hear it.
And whatever happens began in the past, and presses hard on the
    future.
The agony in the curtained bedroom, whether of birth or of
    dying,
Gathers in to itself all the voices of the past, and projects them
    into the future (p. 96).

But they evade the implications. They conclude that 'There is
nothing at all to be done about it' (p. 97) and turn their attention
to the weather and the 'international catastrophes', the distant
evils about which they *cannot* do anything. They recoil from what
they do not understand, from the great unanswered questions
about ultimate reality, and take refuge in the pseudo-realities of
social convention: 'we must adjust ourselves to the moment: we
must do the right thing' (p. 134).

They are like those 'philosophical persons' described by the wise old Lafeu in Shakespeare's play, who

'make modern and familiar things supernatural and causeless. Hence it is that we make trifles of terrors, ensconcing ourselves into seeming knowledge when we should submit ourselves to an unknown fear.' [1]

For, as Solomon tells us, 'The fear of the LORD is the beginning of knowledge.' [2] Perhaps the best final comment is the observation of Agatha, which almost forms an introduction to the first chorus:

> Thus with most careful devotion
> Thus with precise attention
> To detail, interfering preparation
> Of that which is already prepared
> Men tighten the knot of confusion
> Into perfect misunderstanding,
> Reflecting a pocket-torch of observation
> Upon each other's opacity
> Neglecting all the admonitions
> From the world around the corner (pp. 21–2).

This schematism or patterning of the characters makes for clarity, but has dangers which Eliot does not entirely avoid. It will be recalled that Eliot experimented with this kind of structure in *Sweeney Agonistes*, where, he says, his intention was 'to have one character whose sensibility and intelligence should be on the plane of the most sensitive and intelligent members of the audience' and to set him over against 'the other personages in the play . . . who were to be material, literal-minded and visionless'.[3] Since the fragments do little more than illustrate a state of being,

---

[1] *All's Well that Ends Well*, II. iii. 1–6. Cf. *The Rock*, p. 65:
'I'm afraid you've got that disease they call the modern mind. Which is as much as to say, you'll take no end of trouble to explain away what any man in 'is senses would just believe and take for granted.'

[2] Proverbs i. 7. Eliot would supplement this with the Christian message of love and mercy: 'We need to recover the sense of religious fear, so that it may be overcome by religious hope' (*The Idea of a Christian Society*, p. 62).

[3] *The Use of Poetry and the Use of Criticism* (1933), p. 153.

the weakness of this theory does not appear. But in a full-length play, where development is necessary, the fact that the central character exists in a world of his own, quite distinct from the world of most of the others in the play, is apt to hamper dramatic movement. Of course, the fact that the visionless characters remain stationary emphasizes the development of the central character. But the fact that he cannot communicate with them tends to lead to baffled inaction. Eliot solves this problem by having intermediary characters to whom Harry can talk effectively and who can help him to understand his predicament and thus to develop.

There is another danger, however, which Eliot does not, and perhaps does not want to, avoid. If the Chorus is meant to represent something like the ordinary level of insight—or rather lack of insight—and to be the means by which the average member of an audience is enabled to penetrate to the deeper level at which the essential action proceeds, then one must conclude that the gap between the two levels is too wide. Of course, no one will identify himself entirely with the slightly caricatured uncles and aunts, but even if one starts ahead of them the territory soon becomes too strange for most people. To some extent, Mary and Agatha act as guides for us as for Harry himself, but there is no clear line of advance and the sign-posts are few and far between. Only the rare person who has already made some exploration of the territory will find the play an intelligible experience. For this reason, *The Family Reunion* is not likely to appeal to an average audience. And if Eliot intended it merely for special audiences, there would be an end of the matter. There are indications, however, that he tried to cater for an audience comprehending various levels.

He attempts, up to a point, to impose the pattern of an ordinary thriller.[1] The uncles and aunts question Downing about the circumstances of the death of Harry's wife (pp. 38–43) and bring in Warburton and get him to sound Harry (pp. 34–5, 73–80). When Winchell pays his visit, he behaves most strangely (pp.

---

[1] Cf. Eliot's comment on the persistence of the popular appeal of the thriller through the ages (*Selected Essays*, p. 81), quoted in note 1, p. 37 above. We have already seen the slight exploitation of this appeal in *Sweeney Agonistes* and in the apologia of the Fourth Knight in *Murder in the Cathedral*.

80–82). But soon afterwards we get to the heart of the matter, and the thriller-like interest is abruptly dismissed:

> What we have written is not a story of detection,
> Of crime and punishment, but of sin and expiation (p. 104).

If, as seems not unlikely, Eliot was trying to provide something to suit each stratum of a normal audience,[1] was trying, like his burglar-poet, to provide 'a nice bit of meat for the house-dog',[2] then we can only say that his application of the principle is tantalizing. There is not quite enough sustenance here for the superficial observer; he is left 'promise-crammed' and very much aware of the presence of matter not suited to his palate or his digestion. To vary the metaphor, the weak swimmer suddenly finds that his air-belt has been deflated and he is quite out of his depth.

Eliot was at this time and for some time afterwards quite prepared to leave his audience feeling disturbed. In an interview given in 1949 he said: 'I should not like anyone seeing a play of mine to feel completely comfortable.'[3] But there is an important difference between feeling uncomfortable or disturbed and feeling dissatisfied or cheated. An ordinary member of the audience at a production of *The Family Reunion* has some right to protest that he has been led up the garden path.

Thus the play demonstrates the need for some continuity between levels of appeal in a play, at least in a play in which it is part of the author's intention to lead his audience to a deeper understanding of the significance of human behaviour. This intention is defeated if the gap between levels of meaning is too great. Even if each level of meaning is satisfactory entertainment and complete in itself, there is little point in labouring to evolve such a compendious form. The different strata in the audience may just as well go to different theatres, as they nowadays tend

[1] See the passage from *The Use of Poetry and the Use of Criticism*, p. 153, quoted above, pp. 83–4.

[2] *Ibid.*, p. 151. Cf. 'Five Points on Dramatic Writing' (A Letter to Ezra Pound), *Townsman*, Vol. I, No. 3 (July, 1938), p. 10:
'IF you can keep the bloody audience's attention engaged, then you can perform any monkey tricks you like when they ain't looking, and it's what you do behind the audience's back so to speak that makes your play IMMORTAL for a while.'

[3] *World Review*, November, 1949, p. 21.

to do anyway. The whole point is to lead the more superficial observers to the deeper understanding we spoke of. This would seem to be the main reason for Eliot's attempt to integrate the different levels of meaning in his later plays.

There are, in fact, two levels of meaning which come nearer to being satisfactorily integrated in the total pattern of *The Family Reunion* than does the superimposition of detective-story suspense we have been examining. These are what might be called the psychological and anthropological implications of the action. Downing suggests that Harry 'Suffered from what they call a kind of repression' (p. 40) and the play is full of 'hints and guesses' about the psychology of Harry's condition which will fascinate those who place great store by psycho-analysis.[1] Harry himself sees quite clearly that psychological medicine would be of no use to him (p. 93). But the limitations of psycho-analysis are not insisted on, as they are in *The Cocktail Party*, where it provides the main symbolism. The anthropological interest, on the other hand, is a kind of survival from one of Eliot's earlier preoccupations; it is less evident here than in *Murder in the Cathedral*. The coldness of Wishwood and its significance have already been commented upon. The action of the play takes place in late March. Amy is waiting for the clemency of summer. But the painful rebirth of spring must come first and, as Mary says,

> The spring is very late in this northern country,
> Late and uncertain.[2]

With the return of Harry and his acceptance of the sacrificial

[1] See, for example, pp. 52–5, 74–5, 100. Eliot refuses, however, to develop the psychological interest beyond a certain point. In this he may have been reacting against Eugene O'Neill's adaptation of the *Oresteia*, *Mourning Becomes Electra*, with its gloomy Freudianism. But, in any case, for him psychology can go only a short way towards explaining the human predicament.

[2] p. 46. Cf. C. L. Barber, *The Southern Review*, VI (1940–41), p. 410 fn. (Unger's *Critique*, p. 437):

'Mary is the "hyacinth girl" or *la figlia che piange*, in the play: the continuity of Eliot's key scenes and personages was underlined by Eliot himself when he had her enter on the London stage actually carrying hyacinths.'

As a counterpart to the 'hyacinth girl' of *The Waste Land*, ll. 35–41, Mary is marked out as someone with whom Harry might share the experience of the 'rose-garden'.

burden on behalf of his family, the spiritual renewal can take place:

> the season of birth
> Is the season of sacrifice
> For the tree and the beast, and the fish
> Thrashing itself upstream:
> And what of the terrified spirit
> Compelled to be reborn . . . ?[1]

But Harry's experience is not only seen as parallel to the processes of Nature. It is also seen as an epitome of the experience of the human race:

> the past experience revived in the meaning
> Is not the experience of one life only
> But of many generations—not forgetting
> Something that is probably quite ineffable:
> The backward look behind the assurance
> Of recorded history, the backward half-look
> Over the shoulder, towards the primitive terror.[2]

The preservation of the Eumenides in their Aeschylean form serves as a reminder of this 'primitive terror'. The *Oresteia* dramatized the controlling of the terror by civilized law and the new conception of deity. Eliot reminds us that it is still present in Man beneath the veneer of civilization, that it is part of his heritage. Man cannot deny it, for he must build the future upon 'the real past.' And when he accepts it, he discovers its purpose in the divine economy. The play is thus seen as a portrait of permanent human nature in its modern predicament.

[1] p. 60. The parallel between the painfulness of spiritual rebirth and the pain of seasonal renewal is also suggested in the opening lines of *The Waste Land* (*Collected Poems*, p. 61).

[2] *Four Quartets*, pp. 28-9. The 'backward look' is an experience vividly portrayed in Conrad's *Heart of Darkness*, where the primeval darkness is found to be preserved not only in the heart of the Dark Continent but also in the heart of civilized man. Eliot thought so highly of Conrad's story that he wanted to use a quotation from it as epigraph to *The Waste Land* but was dissuaded by Ezra Pound, and did use a quotation from it as epigraph to *The Hollow Men*. On his indebtedness to Conrad, see Leonard Unger, *The Man in the Name*, (1956), pp. 194-218.

Eliot himself now finds a number of flaws in the play. 'The deepest flaw of all', he says,

'was in a failure of adjustment between the Greek story and the modern situation. I should either have stuck closer to Aeschylus or else taken a great deal more liberty with his myth.' [1]

In following the pattern of the *Oresteia*, for example, to the extent of making Harry responsible for Amy's death, he has tipped the balance of sympathy against him. He himself now finds his hero 'an insufferable prig' and Amy, 'except perhaps for the chauffeur, the only complete human being in the play'.[2] Matthiessen suggests that

'Though Agatha may tell Harry that "Love compels cruelty/ To those who do not understand love", Eliot has not succeeded in persuading us that Harry has anything of the overmastering love of God that alone could give sanction to the mystic's terrible renunciation.' [3]

The lack of human warmth in Harry may be accounted for as part of the curse upon his family. And we notice that when

---

[1] *Poetry and Drama*, p. 30 (*On Poetry and Poets*, p. 84). He goes on to recommend that in future productions the Eumenides be imagined and not given physical embodiment. It would be a foolhardy director who ignored this advice; but it does mean that certain effects are blurred (see the stage directions on pp. 62-3, 109), though if the action is reinterpreted slightly the damage can be partly repaired.

[2] *Ibid.*, p. 31. It is possible to take a different view, as Mr. Leonard Unger's reaction to this passage shows:

'Whatever its weaknesses are, the ambiguity is not in the play, but in Eliot's recently developed attitude. Within the framework of the play, Harry is the most complete human being, for he becomes increasingly conscious of the deeper reality, while the mother is only the most forceful person and most fully realized persona in the world of the aunts and uncles, the world of appearances, "What we have always taken it to be ... the ordinary business of living." Eliot's mentioning the chauffeur is a hyperbole by which emphasis is given to his own newly developed attitude, for the chauffeur has no facet of "completeness," but is merely an ordinary person. He is a stock figure of literary convention, the lowly person and minor character who stands outside the dramatic complication while making a few simple but wise remarks from the sidelines.' —*The Man in the Name*, p. 221.

[3] *Op. cit.*, p. 171.

he has learned of the rift between his mother and father, he says:

> Now I see
> I might even become fonder of my mother—
> More compassionate at least—by understanding.
> But she would not like that (p. 106).

But what disturbs us is that, although his wife's death is the motive of his spiritual awakening, remorse or concern for her as a person never shows itself. Agatha remarks that 'it could not have been easy, / Living with Harry' (p. 49), but Harry himself shows no awareness of this.

In fact, the personal aspect of the guilt is played down, in order presumably to bring him nearer to the pattern of the guiltless one suffering for the guilty. I cannot entirely agree with Grover Smith that:

'Although Eliot at one stage of the writing planned that Harry should be expiating the crime of having desired to kill his wife, the play conveys nothing of the kind. Harry is expiating a family curse, of which he is simply the victim. . . . In Harry's case there is obviously no guilt for his father's sin. . . . Harry has inherited merely the curse, the retribution never visited upon the father. This, in the manner of retribution for the original sin of Adam, includes both Harry's particular, personal sin, that of willing his wife's death . . . and the rest of the suffering he has to endure in the play. But Harry is not guilty of his own sin, because it was determined by his father's. Harry is innocent. The play, as it issued from Eliot's hands, curiously asks the audience to sentimentalize Harry's own crime, for which he is not repentant, and to approve of Harry's expiating the curse in order to atone for his father's crime, for which he is not to blame. If he has been guilty of original sin, like the rest of the human race, that fact has nothing to do with the plot.' [1]

Nothing is said on the point in the play as we have it, but what connection is there between his wife's death and the spiritual torment which begins with it, if he felt no sense of guilt for having willed her death? Moreover, the inherited sin is none the

---

[1] *Op. cit.*, pp. 201-2.

less real for being inherited, especially when it reveals itself in the same disposition towards murderous hate. Finally, I see no evidence in the play for supposing that Harry is meant to be Christ-like to the extent of being free from Original Sin. On the contrary, a crucial passage [1] can only be explained, I suggest, as a reference to Original Sin and that has a great deal to do with the plot if the curse on the house is the curse on Adam's seed, as I have assumed. On the other hand, the passage following the revelation of his father's sin gives some support to Grover Smith's argument, though Agatha only says:

> *It is possible* that you have not known what sin
> You shall expiate, or whose, or why.[2]

Despite the under-pattern of Greek myth, the mode of the play is much nearer naturalism than is that of *Murder in the Cathedral*. In this sense Eliot is here entering into overt competition with prose drama, as he thought necessary.[3] In fact, superficially it reminds one of the kind of play Granville-Barker was writing in the first decade of the century; *The Voysey Inheritance* is a sort of secular counterpart. But it is far from being a naturalistic play, and it seems to me that Eliot does himself an injustice in criticizing it from something like a naturalistic standpoint.

By 1950, he had come to the conclusion that he had taken too long over the exposition, extending it even into the second part, and had scamped the climax.[4] Considered, however, as an Ibsenian exploration of the past embedded in the present, an unravelling of the situation and of its consequences,[5] the second part is not perhaps as untheatrical as he suggests. The flaws are inherent in the subject as matter for drama. The climax of the play is Harry's decision to 'follow the Furies'—a phrase which at one time Eliot thought to use as title—and leave Wishwood. But how can such a decision be made dramatic? Eliot tries to avoid anticlimax by a highly charged scene of recrimination between Amy and Agatha, but there is little more he can do

---

[1] p. 91 quoted on p. 95 above.   [2] p. 104. My italics.
[3] *Poetry and Drama*, p. 26 (*On Poetry and Poets*, p. 81).
[4] *Poetry and Drama*, pp. 29–30 (*On Poetry and Poets*, pp. 83–4).
[5] The powerful scene between Amy and Agatha (p. 116 ff.) reminds one of *John Gabriel Borkman*.

beyond introducing a certain amount of speculation about Harry's future, some comic (by the choric uncles and aunts) and some serious (by Downing), and creating a spurious sense of completeness by the death of Amy. But he rightly does not work up the departure of Harry into anything like a big scene; to have done so would have been to falsify the experience of the play.

Throughout, he uses what adventitious aids he can to create suspense and fulfil the normal expectations of an audience. We have already noticed how, up to a point, he attempts to impose the pattern of a thriller on his material. A much more successful device is one that had been used in *George and Margaret*, the popular comedy which was first produced in 1937 and ran in the West End for two years. In this the eponymous characters are prepared for throughout, but do not arrive until the very end. In *The Family Reunion* we hear repeatedly of Arthur and John, the younger brothers, who are also expected for the reunion. Early in the play we are led to believe that they will arive before Harry and his arrival is thus made even more of a surprise.[1] The reason for Arthur's delay in arriving is made the subject of excellent comic relief (pp. 93–5) and John's accident is made the motive for Winchell's visit, which is useful to the plot. Moreover, these unseen characters are justified by more than function. Their mother says 'I am only certain of Arthur and John' (p. 16). So their failure to arrive is ironic, pointing the uncertainty of human certainty. Thus, whereas the audience is liable to feel cheated in the matter of the thriller pattern, they do not feel cheated here because the delays are skilfully contrived and provide matter for concern and amusement. But these devices sit somewhat uneasily on a craggily difficult play. The experience Eliot has tried to make into drama resists any obvious dramatic shaping.

It is an experience analogous to that of the *Four Quartets*, and requires a number of conventions for its expression. Christopher Hassall remarks how Eliot experiments in the play

'with a variant of the soliloquy where "thinking aloud" becomes a form of communication whenever direct dialogue is found to be too much of a simplification. The prevalence of this device

---

[1] See pp. 16 and 23. Harry's entry dramatizes the sudden irruption of the unknown into the settled round of existence.

and the lack of what I must call external dialogue, though a big part of this play's fascination, is yet a danger. The eye (in which I include the mind's eye) can be kept waiting too long. We do not need to be looking continually at the bodies of characters after they have begun to seem mere fountains of uttered feeling, so consistently does the real drama move on the plane of the mind. In a sense, not only does speech go beyond external dialogue, but the whole play develops beyond external presentation.' [1]

This explains why *The Family Reunion* is an admirable play for broadcasting.

Eliot seems in many ways in this play to be trying to extend the range of dramatic expression. Ronald Peacock observes, for instance, that those sections of the choruses where the members speak as individuals and yet voice their secret thoughts, constitute 'a new form of the aside, a formalized extension of it'.[2] Eliot may here be profiting from the example of Eugene O'Neill's *Strange Interlude* (1928), but since these asides come either within the body of a choric speech or at the end of one, where the characters are emerging from their communal experience, they are made acceptable by the over-all stylization, and do not present the same technical difficulties as those in O'Neill's play.

The choruses as a whole perhaps are not so successful. Eliot had become aware that he had depended heavily on the chorus in *Murder in the Cathedral* and decided that next time he would 'try to integrate the chorus more closely into the play'.[3] Therefore he has reduced the number of his chorus to four and individualized its members, giving them functions and characteristics independent of their choric functions. But this involves a number of difficulties. He himself now considers the device unsatisfactory because of the problem it presents to the actor, the problem of transition 'from individual, characterized part to membership of a chorus'.[4] Moreover, by choosing to limit his chorus to the expression of sterile fear and baffled understanding, although he may have forged an interpretative link with his audience, as I

---

[1] *Notes on the Verse Drama, The Masque*, No. 6, 1948, p. 21.
[2] *The Poet in the Theatre*, p. 13.
[3] *Poetry and Drama*, p. 25 (*On Poetry and Poets*, p. 81).
[4] *Poetry and Drama*, p. 28 (*On Poetry and Poets*, p. 82).

have suggested, he has run the risk of lowering the dramatic temperature. Certainly, the choruses provide nothing like the tremendous emotional release of the choruses in *Murder in the Cathedral*.

The emotional release in this play occurs much more in the quasi-soliloquies and in what Eliot calls 'lyrical duets'. In two of the key scenes, the duologue between Harry and Mary and that between Harry and Agatha, the characters move into a state of communion in which they are sharing experience at the deepest level of being. Eliot is being unduly severe on himself when he speaks of these passages as

'too much like operatic arias. The member of the audience, if he enjoys this sort of thing, is putting up with a suspension of the action in order to enjoy a poetic fantasia.' [1]

It may appear foolhardy temerity to venture to disagree with this estimate, inviting the imputation of enjoying 'a poetic fantasia'. But these passages seem to me a bold experiment, an attempt to extend the range of drama and take in shared experience as part of its province. They are another example of the kind of sharing of experience that we find in the choruses of the play, but they are on an altogether higher level. If one views the interior action as the most important part of the play—and one obviously must— they form the climaxes of the First and Second Parts.

The runes are a different matter. They have a quality of the macabre which does not fit into the play when it is shorn of the visual representation of the Eumenides. These three passages of incantation[2] all have to do with the mechanism of the curse, which is only acceptable if thought of as a metaphor for Original Sin. Exorcism introduces connotations of witchcraft which jar a modern audience.[3] I agree with Matthiessen that when

'Agatha closes the play by reciting a rune to end the curse while she and Mary make a stylized dance around the birthday cake and blow out the candles, so that the "last words shall be spoken in

---

[1] *Poetry and Drama*, p. 28 (*On Poetry and Poets*, p. 83).

[2] pp. 70, 110, 134–6.

[3] Perhaps Eliot would not think of this as undesirable. The Chorus say 'And we know nothing of exorcism' (p. 97) and they make this a fatalistic excuse for inaction.

the dark", as in the service of *tenebrae*, the effect seems an unintentional parody of liturgy rather than a reinvigoration from it.' [1]

Some parts of the runes provide an important, even an indispensable, comment on the action; but one wishes they could have been incorporated in a less hieratic way.

Of these conventions, the runes are the farthest from the easy conversational style in which much of the play is written, but most of them create difficulties of transition. This was probably one of the chief problems in writing, as it is in acting the play. If your norm is a style not very far removed from naturalism, how are you to rise to the intensity of which poetry is capable? In writing *The Cocktail Party* Eliot discovered how to do it by long, smooth transitions of which the audience is not aware. In *The Family Reunion* for the most part he tried a frontal assault and jumped back and forth from something like naturalism into more conventionalized forms of speech. The quasi-soliloquy with which the play opens is an example of this. We have already noted how successfully Eliot there moves back to the level of naturalistic speech. In other quasi-soliloquies, he trusts the actor to do it for him.[2] Occasionally, he tries to effect a transition through laughter, as when Gerald caps Agatha's intense prophetic evocation of what Harry's return will mean to him by the comment—

> I don't in the least know what you're talking about.
> You seem to be wanting to give us all the hump (p. 18).

Like Violet's

>   I do not understand
> A single thing that's happened (p. 127)

and one or two other comments of this kind, this betrays an uneasiness of tone, as if the author was not sure of the way audiences would take his profundities and provided a kind of defence-mechanism in laughter. But the laughter may take on ironic overtones and destroy the atmosphere instead of reinforcing it.

---

[1] *Op. cit.*, p. 170.
[2] See, e.g., p. 16 ('Which I cannot find/—I am only certain of Arthur and John'), p. 25 (Harry).

As for the runes, Eliot isolates two of them—those ending the two halves of the play—so that a break in action coming immediately after the formalism of a chorus allows a stepping-up to the level of oracular speech. The middle rune occurs at the climax of the play, when Harry accepts the Eumenides as instruments of salvation, and here the transition is provided by business: 'Agatha goes to the window, in a somnambular fashion, and . . . steps into the place which the Eumenides had occupied' (p. 109). After making her sibylline pronouncement, 'She moves back into the room' and 'awakes' to ask:

> What have I been saying? I think I was saying
> That you have a long journey (p. 110),

so that we are returned to the moment before the Eumenides showed themselves to Harry (p. 108: 'You have a long journey'), the implication being that what has taken place in between has belonged to another dimension of experience—has been a moment out of time.

The transition to the level of group speech in the choruses is almost entirely left to the director, except for the first, where Agatha plays in to it by a passage of impersonal comment (p. 21). The transitions to and from the 'lyrical duets', however, are almost entirely achieved in the writing, and here Eliot's poetic mastery is apparent.[1]

The kind of effect achieved in these lyrical passages indicates that the play needs to be listened to in a special way, much as one would listen to a small-scale opera, with its arias, duets, quartets, and so on. It has, too, something of the retarded action of opera, together with the flexibility in time of film. As we have seen, Eliot himself notes the resemblance to opera with

---

[1] The modulation into the first 'lyrical duet' (pp. 58–9) is achieved with only the tiniest jolt in the movement into chant. The movement out of it (p. 60) is more abrupt, and is achieved by a device similar to that used at the end of the second rune (p. 110). Eliot does not provide such a long bridge-passage into the second duet (p. 107), but the emotional temperature of the scene should have reached a point at which the actor can move quite easily into the necessary 'trance-like state'. The movement out of this duet (p. 108) is superbly modulated.

disapproval.[1] In the greatest operas, however, the arias are not just 'lyrical interludes' during which the action is suspended; they are means by which the characters express their deepest and most intimate feelings. The action rises to them and is the justification for them, but, in the last resort, it is they which justify the whole opera. I am inclined to see the 'lyrical interludes' of *The Family Reunion* in this light.

Eliot's own strictures upon the play are made in the light of his ultimate objective, the 'mirage of the perfection of verse drama' that he has had before him for many years.[2] Considered in this light, it must appear a digression, being too obviously poetic. But considered in and for itself, it is one of the most remarkable products of his genius. It is of a richness and complexity comparable with the best of his non-dramatic poetry. In it he often writes at the height of his personal style, whereas in the later plays he has deliberately thinned out his style and abrogated part of his poetic power. Even if it is not a complete success as drama, it is a permanent addition to our literature, and if our theatre cannot find room from time to time to stage a failure as magnificent as this, it will be considerably the poorer. For my own part, I am far from pronouncing it an irretrievable failure theatrically. It may prove to be an important extension of drama that we have not yet fully understood.[3] One has the example of the long neglect of Claudel; and I can think of no English play which comes nearer to his kind of drama. As a profound exploration of a complex spiritual state, and an attempt to communicate with the audience on the level of spiritual experience, *The Family Reunion* is unique in our drama.

[1] *Poetry and Drama*, p. 28 (*On Poetry and Poets*, p. 83). See also 'The Aims of Poetic Drama', *Adam*, 200 (November, 1949), pp. 12–13, from which the phrase 'lyrical interlude' is taken.

[2] *Poetry and Drama*, p. 34 (*On Poetry and Poets*, p. 87).

[3] Cf. Sir Herbert Read's suggestion that 'the future may have in store for us a form of poetic drama that imitates not so much modes of action as states of sensibility' (*The True Voice of Feeling*, Faber and Faber, 1953, p. 150).

Chapter Five

Plays in a Contemporary Setting—II
'The Cocktail Party' (1949)

W HEN, in an interview, Eliot was asked, 'How would you, out of the bitter experience of the present time, wish mankind to develop?' he answered:

'I should speak of a greater spiritual consciousness, which is not asking that everybody should rise to the same conscious level, but that everybody should have some awareness of the depths of spiritual development and some appreciation and respect for those more exceptional people who can proceed further in spiritual knowledge than most of us can.'[1]

This statement reflects Eliot's great interest in, and desire for, an organic communal life—a healthy functioning of all parts of society based on mutual understanding; it is one aspect of his 'idea of a Christian society'. He is particularly interested in the way the ordinary man 'is helped to establish his life by the power of the saint's sacrifice to fertilize the lives of others'.[2] We saw that this was the basic significance of the relation between Becket and the chorus of ' poor women of Canterbury'. In Eliot's plays in a contemporary setting, as in the life they reflect, the saint

[1] J. P. Hodin, 'The Condition of Man Today. An Interview with T. S. Eliot', *Horizon*, Vol. XII, No. 68 (August, 1945), p. 88.
[2] D. E. S. Maxwell, p. 200.

becomes more and more remote and ordinary experience is brought into the foreground. In *The Family Reunion*, the exceptional person is still in the centre of the picture, but it is a family portrait and his spiritual election is made on behalf of the family. In *The Cocktail Party*, the exceptional person has been moved to one side of the composition and the social group is in the centre.[1]

Thus we see that Eliot is not concerned with the person of exceptional spiritual awareness, or the saint, in isolation, but always with his relationship to the community, to ordinary men and women. He wants therefore to reach ordinary people, to help them towards 'some awareness of the depths of spiritual development'. That, I would suggest, is why he has sought as wide an audience as possible, even to the extent of challenging West End comedy on its own ground. Beyond his artist's concern with the reintegration of poetry and drama, there lies, it seems to me, this social and spiritual concern. He wants to bring poetry back into the theatre because poetry alone can reveal the kind of pattern which gives significance to life.

The Cocktail Party, produced in 1949, ten years after *The Family Reunion*, was a decisive step in bringing poetic drama into 'overt competition' with naturalistic prose drama. Here Eliot tried to infiltrate rather than make a frontal attack. He sacrificed almost all obvious poetic devices and renounced his attempt to revive the conventions of the earlier poetic drama apart from the basic convention of the verse itself. There are no quasi-soliloquies, no 'lyrical duets'. The elements of ritual and choric speaking are reduced to a very short section, the libation at the end of Act II (pp. 132-3), and this is rather like a solemn form of the toast to absent friends. The symbolic figures (the Guardians) are given a naturalistic *raison d'être*; they are members of the Chamberlaynes' social circle. The spiritual adviser, a role fulfilled in a rather sibylline way by Agatha in *The Family Reunion*, is now more naturalistically the psychiatrist, the modern secular counterpart.

Most notable of all is the increased flexibility of the verse, which can now move easily from the small-talk of the opening of the play to the impassioned insight of Celia in the scene in the

---

[1] Cf. Foster Hailey, 'An Interview with T. S. Eliot', *The New York Times*, 16 April, 1950, Section 2, p. 1, col. 7: 'Mr. Eliot has said that he did not intend to portray one [character] as more important than the others.'

consulting room.[1] Moreover, it comes very near that transparent simplicity to which Eliot aspires. Mr. Raymond Williams very neatly sums up the difference between the verse of this play and that of the previous play. The verse of *The Cocktail Party*, he says, is

'always, at every level, *statement*, of a deliberate lucidity, and with the minimum of imagery and evocation. In *The Family Reunion* the speech of Harry and Agatha is full of the characteristic imagery of Eliot's general poetry: the corridor, the footfall, the door opening into the garden. The words:
—"have often a network of tentacular roots, reaching down to the deepest terrors and desires."

'In *The Cocktail Party*, the verse is never, or hardly ever, of that kind. It is verse of the surface, although not superficial. It is conscious, lucid statement, with a generality which is quite unlike the normal verse of *The Family Reunion*. . . . It is a very remarkable achievement, for it is both eminently speakable and also the instrument of complete precision in the expression of feeling. . . . However the play as a whole may be judged, this development of a flexible, lucid verse manner, based very closely on speech and yet capable of the greatest precision and distinction, is unquestionably a major achievement.'[2]

It is a manner which can assimilate the hesitancy of someone seeking the exact words to express his experience (e.g. pp. 57-8, 118-21) or the sudden shifts of thought and feeling in a quarrel (pp. 82-3, 104-5). It is, in fact, so deft that it seems able to do anything required by the dramatic situation.

As we have seen, Eliot was early aware of the contemporary self-consciousness about poetry as a hampering factor. A tendency to think of it as something pleasant to listen to but having little to do with real life, an artificial form of speech which disguised reality rather than revealed it, an excuse for a pretty fantastication of behaviour on the stage rather than a laying bare of the living processes of the mind and heart—this tendency was inherited from the minor Romantic poetry which was for long the staple diet in schools and thus determined the average expectancy from, and

[1] Cf. *Poetry and Drama*, p. 31 (*On Poetry and Poets*, pp. 84-5).
[2] *Drama from Ibsen to Eliot*, pp. 239-40.

response to, poetry until the thirties at least. It was a taste that was largely gratified by the Georgian poet-dramatists and made verse-drama a matter of special festivals and arty-crafty cults. This cultivation of the language beautiful was alien to Eliot with his fierce concern for truth. He wanted to make his hearers forget about poetry as a special organization of language in order that they might respond to it as a special mode of awareness. He has, therefore, systematically eliminated everything in his style that might remind the audience that they are listening to poetry, and deliberately brought it near to prose so that they shall not be aware of the medium, but instead let it work upon them at moments of intensity as only poetry can. It does not matter if they think it prose as long as that prevents the setting up of the barrier of a special attitude.[1] Eliot has even been prepared to run the risk of losing the distinctive qualities of poetry for the most part, provided that he could at key points achieve the heightened awareness of which it alone is capable.[2] In this way, he countered the

[1] Critics have delighted in setting out passages from the later plays as prose and implying that it makes no difference. But in doing so, they usually do just two things: they demonstrate, on the one hand, that Eliot has succeeded in reproducing ordinary speech rhythms as he set out to do, and, on the other hand, they reveal the subtle differences that the verse-form makes as a means of conveying the dramatist's intention to the actor. To mention only the most obvious of these differences, the subtle stresses at the end of a line or the run-on into the next line help to shape the music of the speech and give it its dramatic pattern. In any case, as Eliot has said, 'To have the virtues of good prose is the first and minimum requirement of good poetry'—'Johnson's "London" and "The Vanity of Human Wishes" ', 1930, reprinted in *English Critical Essays, Twentieth Century*, selected by Phyllis M. Jones, O.U.P., World's Classics, 1933, p. 305.

[2] Cf. *Poetry and Drama*, p. 32 (*On Poetry and Poets*, p. 85), Eliot has been so successful in following his 'ascetic rule' that he can indulge in a little joke about poetry:

REILLY
Do you mind if I quote poetry, Mrs. Chamberlayne?
LAVINIA
Oh no, I should love to hear you speaking poetry . . .
JULIA
She has made a point, Henry.
LAVINIA
. . . if it answers my question.
(*The Cocktail Party*, p. 160.)
All references are to the Fourth Impression (Revised).

prejudice against modern verse-drama in the commercial theatre. The long run of *The Cocktail Party* in London and New York was a landmark in the revival of poetic drama.

For some time after the curtain goes up on the burst of laughter which marks Julia's failure to see the joke, we might be watching an ordinary West End comedy, if it were not for the unmistakable distinction of style, which catches the circular movement of this kind of pseudo-wit made popular by Noel Coward[1] and uses it to indicate the narrow circle of understanding of this social clique. The kind of patterning that we find here—'obvious in print, but in speech . . . virtually unconscious, since the repetitions on which the rhythm depends are normal elements of conversation'[2]—is necessary in fast-moving comic style, as the 'bouncing' of lines from comedian to 'feeder' in the older-style music-hall act amply demonstrates, and is especially helpful at the beginning of a play where clarity of exposition is needed as well as speed. It is used here also to parody empty small-talk. As Miss M. C. Bradbrook observes, this 'bright' conversation

'might sound as if it were being merely too faithful to the banalities of social chatter were it not for this extremely ominous rhythm, which sounds its echoing chime all round the circle of the symmetrically grouped characters.'[3]

[1] An example which catches this characteristic of Coward's pseudo-wit, as well as speed of repartee and its almost mechanical precision, is on p. 34: 'But it's more the cinema that interests both of us . . .'

[2] Raymond Williams, *Drama from Ibsen to Eliot*, p. 239.

[3] *T. S. Eliot*, Supplement to British Book News Published for the British Council by Longmans Green & Co. (Rev. ed., 1955), p. 42. Cf. the interesting analysis by A. L. Pattisson:

'At curtain-rise we plunge into a painfully unsuccessful party, where well-bred guests, to cover up an awkward situation, are valiantly struggling to keep the ball of vapid party-talk rolling. Their highly mannered, over-emphatic speech, helped in the second line by a couple of italicized words, starts to hammer a metre into our heads. The number of syllables per line may vary considerably, but three heavy stresses are persistently there, and soon the omission or increase of one would cause us as much disquiet as a sudden irregularity of our heartbeat. As we settle to the rhythm the over-emphasis becomes unnecessary and the affectation of the party manners is allowed to give way a little to unobtrusive sincerity, still couched in the most everyday terms.'
—'Which is the Opposite of Prose?', *Drama*, New Series, No. 33 (Summer, 1954), p. 32.

Miss Bradbrook also points out the resemblance to the style of *Sweeney Agonistes*.[1] In fact, with its party atmosphere and its telephone conversations, *The Cocktail Party* seems almost to take up where *Sweeney* left off, though of course on a higher social level and with a great deal more subtlety in the development of character.

Eliot was by this time acquiring professional skill in the mechanics of playwriting, in the techniques of suspense and surprise.[2] Thus in the opening scene a sense of mystery is created around the Unidentified Guest, who knows none of the people Julia mentions and thus is set apart from the clique, while Julia's curiosity about Lavinia's aunt arouses the audience's suspicion that there is more here than meets the eye. Interest is engaged, suspense aroused. Later in the Act, suspense is built up by the delayed telephone call (pp. 42–4). Act II starts off well, if not with surprise at finding out who the Unidentified Guest is, at least with confirmation of suspicion, which is always satisfying; and no sooner has one mystery been cleared up than our curiosity is engaged by the mysteriousness of the arrangements in the consulting room. And before long we are being drawn yet further into a strange, secretive world, where Alex and Julia appear in a very different light: the sudden revelation of the real selves beneath the social masks would be startling if we hadn't been prepared for it by this atmosphere. The last Act is an altogether simpler structure—so much so that, as Eliot himself is aware,[3] it runs the risk of seeming just an epilogue. Even so, there is an attempt to create suspense: Alex's story is delayed but kept in the audience's mind.[4]

The shaping is that of the customary three-act play, as opposed to the less usual two-part form he has previously used. He contrives a neat circular structure, with the Chamberlaynes about to embark at the end of the play on a cocktail party similar to the one which opened the play, with the significant difference that

---

[1] Cf. especially pp. 30–1 with *Collected Poems*, pp. 129–30. Giorgio Melchiori, *The Tightrope Walkers*, p. 146, points out the recurrence of the cannibals and missionaries (*Collected Poems*, p. 126).

[2] Cf. *Poetry and Drama*, p. 32 (*On Poetry and Poets*, p. 85).

[3] *Ibid.*

[4] See pp. 147 and 148.

Lavinia and Edward are giving it together:[1]

> EDWARD
>
> And now for the party.
>
> LAVINIA
>
>> Now for the party.
>
> EDWARD
>
> It will soon be over.
>
> LAVINIA
>
>> I wish it would begin.
>
> EDWARD
>
> There's the doorbell.
>
> LAVINIA
>
>> Oh, I'm glad. It's begun (pp. 166-7).

In lightness of touch we are almost back to the beginning, but now the 'echoing chime' has a restful completion, as of 'calm of mind, all passion spent'. And it is not just a 'clever' ending; it suggests the notion of circularity with which readers of the *Four Quartets* are familiar.[2] Edward and Lavinia, moreover, are now aware that 'every moment is a fresh beginning' (p. 165).

Between the two parties, there has been a smooth progression to the climax in Act II, where the verse, having heightened its intensity imperceptibly by stages, probes the heart of the matter without declaring itself as poetry. At this point we have our one piece of ritualistic convention, and it has been so carefully led up to that there is the minimum of dislocation. Both parts of *The Family Reunion* end with such a piece of ritualistic incantation, though it is there more exorcism than prayer. In the later play the corresponding passage is followed by a modulation to a curtain-line laugh:

> REILLY
>
> There is one for whom the words cannot be spoken.

.   .   .   .

[1] The sameness and the difference are pointed. Edward and Lavinia refer to the earlier party (p. 136); the first guests are all the same people who were present at the earlier party—a dramatic contrivance to round off the story of this group of people—; Reilly refers twice to his earlier visit (pp. 160, 166); and Julia again assumes tigers where there are none (p. 141; cf. p. 7).

[2] See *Four Quartets*, pp. 15, 23, 42, 43-4.

ALEX
Others, perhaps, will speak them.
You know, I have connections—even in California (p. 133).

The improvement in poise is very noticeable. Eliot can now
touch upon profundities with featherweight lightness:

JULIA
Edward! Don't you realize how lucky you are
To have *two* Good Samaritans? I never heard of that before.
EDWARD
The man who fell among thieves was luckier than I:
He was left at an inn (p. 49).

It is only when we see or read the play a second time that we
know that Julia is a Good Samaritan in the spiritual sense.[1]
   The movement from church to theatre, the movement into
the picture-frame stage of the naturalistic era, is here almost complete. The play is, on the surface, a comedy of manners in the
modern style. There are plenty of touches of the pseudo-wit made
fashionable by Coward, and Julia is a minor masterpiece of comic
characterization, popping in throughout the first Act to give
relief to the serious discussion. Alex backs her up in this, but is not
quite so successful a creation: his tiresome knowingness *is* a little
tiresome. Moreover, there is plot enough to keep the audience
happy while the burglar-poet goes silently to work. As the neat
combination of two closely interlinked triangles is discovered
piecemeal—Peter in love with Celia, Celia in love with Edward
and so on—enough possibilities are opened up to gain and retain
the interest of most audiences. But gradually we are led into an
exploration of the situation very much more serious than is usual
in this kind of play. We discover that although Eliot seems to have
left the church far behind, the emergent pattern has a family
likeness to that of his earlier plays.
   The exceptional individual is no longer in the foreground or in
the centre of the design. He, or in this case she, is still a part of the
design and a very important part, but the poet's attention has

[1] Other instances where Eliot deals lightly with the essentially serious are
on pp. 32 (St. Anthony), and 144 ('one can't dine out on eating Christians—
/ Even among pagans!').

shifted to the mass of unexceptional people. Celia's death, the gruesome details of which momentarily cloud the domestic atmosphere of the Third Act, is remote from that setting, but relevant to it. The emphasis is upon the salvation of a group and not an individual—upon the salvation of the group centred on Edward and Lavinia Chamberlayne, who give the cocktail party.

It is the shock of finding that his wife has left him which sets Edward on the path of self-exploration under the guidance of the Unidentified Guest. Like all of us, he finds 'it's easier to talk to a person you don't know' (p. 21). But, as the mysterious guest warns him,

> to approach the stranger
> Is to invite the unexpected. . . .
> It is to start a train of events
> Beyond your control (pp. 24-5).

The unknown is irrupting into the settled round of his life, destroying his comfortable assumptions. He knows that he has taken his wife for granted. What he now learns is that he has taken himself for granted, too. He finds that he has 'lost touch with the person' he thought he was, as the Unidentified Guest puts it (p. 26). This has given him a 'jolt', but it will lead, the stranger continues,

> To finding out
> What you really are. What you really feel.
> What you really are among other people.
> Most of the time we take ourselves for granted,
> As we have to, and live on a little knowledge
> About ourselves as we were (p. 27).

We are here approaching one of the basic concepts of the play.

Eliot extends the Heraclitean conception of ubiquitous physical change into the realm of psychology. We cannot step twice into the same river, not merely because the water has flowed on, but because we have become different persons in the meantime: [1]

[1] The three fragments of Heraclitus which have to do with the river are 12, 49a, and 91 (Hermann Diels, *Die Fragmente der Vorsokratiker*, I). Seneca's comment on the second fragment curiously anticipates Eliot:

'None of us is the same man in old age that he was in youth; nor the same on the morrow as on the day preceding. Our bodies are hurried along like

You cannot face it steadily, but this thing is sure,
That time is no healer: the patient is no longer here.
When the train starts, and the passengers are settled
To fruit, periodicals and business letters
(And those who saw them off have left the platform)
Their faces relax from grief into relief,
To the sleepy rhythm of a hundred hours.
Fare forward, travellers! not escaping from the past
Into different lives, or into any future;
You are not the same people who left the station
Or who will arrive at any terminus. . . .[1]

We 'cannot face it steadily' because this is not a comfortable knowledge to live with, especially in its implications for our relations with other people. Even if we come to know a person intimately at one moment—and there are of course very narrow limits to our real knowledge of others in the first place—we must not assume that we know that person the next moment, because he will have changed. As the Unidentified Guest puts it:

we die to each other daily.
What we know of other people
Is only our memory of the moments
During which we knew them. And they have changed
To pretend that they and we are the same   [since then.
Is a useful and convenient social convention

flowing waters; every visible object accompanies time in its flight; of the things which we see, nothing is fixed. Even I myself as I comment on this change, am changed myself. This is just what Heraclitus says: "We go down twice into the same river, and yet into a different river." For the stream still keeps the same name, but the water has already flowed past. Of course this is much more evident in rivers than in human beings. Still, we mortals are also carried past in no less speedy a course; and this prompts me to marvel at our madness in cleaving with great affection to such a fleeting thing as the body, and in fearing lest some day we may die, when every instant means the death of our previous condition. Will you not stop fearing lest that may happen once which really happens every day?'
—Seneca ad Lucilium Epistulae Morales with an English translation by Richard M. Gummere, The Loeb Classical Library, Vol. I, p. 401, Ep. LVIII, sections 22–3. The idea of daily death has already been developed in Ep. XXIV, 19–21, pp. 176–8. Cf. *The Cocktail Party*, p. 63, quoted on pp. 132–3.
[1] *Four Quartets*, p. 30. Cf. Appendix II.

Which must sometimes be broken. We must also remember
That at every meeting we are meeting a stranger.[1]

The remedy here proposed is one of expediency,[2] but the first
line hints at the creative remedy of the Christian religion.[3] By
constant spiritual rebirth or renewal, we are preserved in the
mystical body of Christ, through which a permanent communion
or fellowship is possible. In that greater Faith, moreover, the
faith in one another by which alone we can live—*knowing* so
little of one another as we do—is strengthened. The expedient
remedy of the Unidentified Guest is difficult to maintain. Because it is impossible to have any permanent knowledge of others,
we tend to create our own image of them.[4] The danger for ourselves in doing this is that we shall accept the image as reality and
lose what contact we may once have had with the real person; the
danger for others is that we shall try to impose it on them. As
Eliot himself says:

'It is human, when we do not understand another human being,
and cannot ignore him, to exert an unconscious pressure on that
person to turn him into something that we *can* understand: many
husbands and wives exert this pressure on each other. The effect
on the person so influenced is liable to be the repression and
distortion, rather than the improvement, of the personality; and
no man is good enough to have the right to make another over
in his own image.[5]

His wife's departure makes Edward aware that he doesn't really
know her and doesn't know himself without her:

I *must* get her back, to find out what has happened
During the five years that we've been married.
I must find out who she is, to find out who I am (p. 28).

[1] p. 63. Cf. Djuna Barnes, *Nightwood* (Harcourt, Brace and Co., New York,
1937), p. 122: ' "To our friends", he [Dr. O'Connor] answered, "we die
every day, but to ourselves we die only at the end." '
[2] See pp. 64-6 for the expansion of this proposal.
[3] Cf. I Corinthians xv. 31: 'I protest by your rejoicing which I have in
Christ Jesus our Lord, I die daily.'
[4] Cf. pp. 122 head, 158 head.
[5] *Notes towards the Definition of Culture* (Faber and Faber, 1948), pp. 64-5. Cf.
The Cocktail Party, p. 99, quoted on p. 135.

He begins to understand how much he has depended on her, not just in the superficial sense, but in the sense that his existence was bound up with hers. In a way, her presence has concealed him from himself and now he is brought hard up against his own deficiency of being. Without her he is nothing. Eliot illuminates the cliché and gives it a new force.

Lavinia's motive in leaving Edward was the desire to administer just such a shock, she tells him when, twenty-four hours later, she has been brought back to him by the stranger, as Alcestis was brought back from the dead by Heracles in the play by Euripides from which Eliot has taken the nucleus of his plot. She has died on his behalf no less than Alcestis for Admetus, though in a different sense:

> I thought that if I died
> To you, I who had been only a ghost to you,
> You might be able to find the road back
> To a time when you were real (p. 87).

And indeed this is what has happened. In the scene in which he renounces his mistress, he begins to come to terms with himself, and this means recognizing himself not merely as a middle-aged man (p. 57) but also as one possessing 'the indomitable spirit of mediocrity':

> I see that my life was determined long ago
> And that the struggle to escape from it
> Is only a make-believe, a pretence
> That what is, is not, or could be changed (p. 58).

He is at last being honest with himself and his real self has a chance to emerge, as Celia sees (p. 58).

In the scene of reunion, where the verse is perfectly geared to the rapid changes of tempo in the quarrel that lays bare the radical contention between them, Lavinia reveals herself to him as the gravest threat to the existence of his new self:

> Must I become after all what you would make me? (p. 89).

She reinforces his sense of isolation ('Hell is oneself...') by interpreting his torment on a secular level:

I think you're on the edge of a nervous breakdown! (pp. 87-8).

In a mood not far from hysteria, he sees her as a torturer, 'The angel of destruction'.[1] Nevertheless, he follows her 'practical' suggestion (p. 88), and sees a doctor.

In the consulting room he describes his dilemma:

> We had not been alone again for fifteen minutes
> Before I felt, and still more acutely—
> Indeed, acutely, perhaps for the first time,
> The whole oppression, the unreality
> Of the role she had always imposed upon me
> With the obstinate, unconscious, sub-human strength
> That some women have. Without her, it was vacancy.
> When I thought she had left me, I began to dissolve,
> To cease to exist. That was what she had done to me!
> I cannot live with her—that is now intolerable;
> I cannot live without her, for she has made me incapable
> Of having any existence of my own (p. 99).

He diagnoses his own sickness as the 'death of the spirit' (p. 100). But he sees his problem in isolation. Reilly's task is to make him see that it is part of a 'total situation':

> The single patient
> Who is ill by himself, is rather the exception (p. 101).

He brings him face to face with Lavinia to the consternation of husband and wife, strips them of their last pretences,[2] and proceeds to show them 'how much [they] have in common'—

---

[1] p. 89. Mr. Kenneth Tynan points out the likeness of the passage from which this phrase is taken to the style of nineteenth-century melodrama ('Prose and the Playwright', *The Atlantic Monthly*, December, 1954, p. 76). He does not seem to have observed that Edward is here over-dramatizing his predicament and thus being melodramatic.

[2] As Julia reassures Reilly, he had to take the risk of what Edward and Lavinia would do once stripped of pretences:

> All we could do was to give them the chance.
> And now, when they are stripped naked to their souls
> And can choose, whether to put on proper costumes
> Or huddle quickly into new disguises,
> They have, for the first time, somewhere to start from (pp. 129-130).

> The same isolation.
> A man who finds himself incapable of loving
> And a woman who finds that no man can love her.
>
> .   .   .   .
>
> While still in a state of unenlightenment,
> *You* could always say: 'he could not love any woman;'
> *You* could always say: 'no man could love her.'
> You could accuse each other of your own faults,
> And so could avoid understanding each other.
> Now, you have only to reverse the propositions
> And put them together (pp. 110-11).

Edward and Lavinia choose to 'make the best of a bad job'—
to accept their inadequacies, which counterbalance one another,
so to speak—and Sir Henry dismisses them with the admonition:

'Go in peace. And work out your salvation with diligence.' [1]

Theirs is the one choice of the two that he has to offer; he has
reconciled them to 'the human condition':

> They may remember
> The vision they have had, but they cease to regret it,
> Maintain themselves by the common routine,
> Learn to avoid excessive expectation,
> Become tolerant of themselves and others,
> Giving and taking, in the usual actions
> What there is to give and take. They do not repine;
> Are contented with the morning that separates
> And with the evening that brings together

[1] p. 114. He says the same to Celia (p. 128). But he admits to Julia (p. 131)
that he doesn't understand what he is saying when he says it 'to one like her'.
The words are the dying Buddha's exhortation to his disciples, as translated
by Henry Clarke Warren in *Buddhism in Translations* (Harvard Oriental Series,
Vol. 3, 7th Issue, Cambridge, 1922), p. 109. Eliot knew the book, for he refers
to it in his notes to *The Waste Land* (l. 308). He may have used this saying of
the Buddha rather than the parallel exhortation of St. Paul ('work out your
own salvation with fear and trembling', Philippians, ii. 12) because he did not
want his Christianity to obtrude. On Eliot's debt to Buddhism in the play
see the article by R. Baird Shuman listed in the bibliography, and on his
affiliations to Buddhism generally see Harold E. McCarthy's article on 'T. S.
Eliot and Buddhism' in *Philosophy East and West*, Vol. II, No. 1 (April, 1952),
pp. 31-55.

For casual talk before the fire
Two people who know they do not understand each other,
Breeding children whom they do not understand
And who will never understand them.

.   .   .   .

In a world of lunacy,
Violence, stupidity, greed . . . it is a good life.[1]

The last Act shows Edward and Lavinia living this life. As
Julia points out,

the consequence of the Chamberlaynes' choice
Is a cocktail party (p. 164).

Critics have remarked with disappointment that the new-found
companionship of Edward and Lavinia reveals itself in a series of
clichés—concern for the comfort of the other, obvious compli-
ments, and so on.[2] But apart from the difficulty of making domestic smoothness interesting and the problem of making the necessary points clearly in the short time available there is the possibility
that Eliot is here seeking to illuminate the clichés, as he obviously
is elsewhere in the play. He is implying, perhaps, that for people
like Edward and Lavinia such little things constitute 'a good life'.
He is certainly not making a statement about marriage in general.
In an interview he remarked:

'Some people want to get a general statement on marriage
out of the relations of Edward and Lavinia. You can't depict all
your views about life. You are limited by time.'[3]

And in the play itself he makes a point of emphasizing, perhaps with
an eye to the ages-old bias in the Catholic tradition in favour of the

[1] pp. 123–4. Cf. Eliot's observation in 'The Aims of Poetic Drama', *Adam*,
200 (November, 1949), p. 16:
'Only God understands the creature; in human creation humanity is only
an instrument. Men and women do not necessarily understand their own
children, merely because they have begotten and borne them; they have to
try to learn to understand what they have created.'
[2] A subtler point is the contrast between the well-stocked and orderly
kitchen (p. 135) and the kitchen Alex had almost despaired over in Act I
(remarked by John Lawlor, *Virginia Quarterly Review*, Vol. 30, 1954, p. 443).
[3] Foster Hailey, p. 3, cols. 4–5.

celibate life wholly devoted to God's service, that ordinary life is not intrinsically inferior:

> Neither way is better.
> Both ways are necessary. It is also necessary
> To make a choice between them (p. 125).

Celia Coplestone, who has been Edward's mistress, chooses the second way. The shock of losing him destroys her illusions about herself and her way of life. Her first reaction is the realization that she has been living in an essentially unreal world—a dream, though it seemed real enough while it lasted. But her awakening has made her aware of the unreality of ordinary existence too: 'if this is reality, it is very like a dream' (p. 55). Moreover, the emergence of the new Edward makes her understand that the unreality of their love was partly due to her having made him a substitute for a very different sort of lover. In a sense, she has created a god in man's image and the real man could never have lived up to it:

> I see you as a person whom I never saw before.
> The man I saw before, he was only a projection—
> I see that now—of something that I wanted—
> No, not *wanted*—something I aspired to—
> Something that I desperately wanted to exist.
> It must happen somewhere—but what, and where is it?
> Edward, I see that I was simply making use of you.
> And I ask you to forgive me (p. 59).

By the time she reaches the consulting room, her experience has taken on a new meaning:

> what has happened has made me aware
> That I've always been alone. That one always is alone.
> Not simply the ending of one relationship,
> Not even simply finding that it never existed—
> But a revelation about my relationship
> With *everybody* (p. 118).

The first symptom of her 'illness' is this 'awareness of solitude' (p. 117). The second symptom is 'a sense of sin' (p. 119) which is strong in her, despite the fact that she has 'always been taught to disbelieve in sin'.[1] But the sense of sin that oppresses her is not 'sin in the ordinary sense . . . being immoral' (p. 119); it goes deeper than the sense of personal wrong-doing. Thinking 'over and over' about her affair with Edward, she has decided that

> it was all a mistake:
> But I don't see why mistakes should make one feel sinful!
> And yet I can't find any other word for it.
> It must be some kind of hallucination;
> Yet, at the same time, I'm frightened by the fear
> That it is more real than anything I believed in.
>
> . . . .
>
> It's not the feeling of anything I've ever *done*,
> Which I might get away from, or of anything in me
> I could get rid of—but of emptiness, of failure
> Towards someone, or something, outside of myself;
> And I feel I must . . . *atone*—is that the word?
> Can you treat a patient for such a state of mind? (pp. 120-1).

'Canst thou not minister to a mind diseas'd?' The answer might be that of Lady Macbeth's doctor:

> More needs she the divine than the physician.[2]

But the disease is not in Celia except as a member of sinful humanity and Eliot's physician is also, to some extent, a divine. At least he can help her to find her way towards the reality she craves and which she could not find in her affair with Edward:

> we had merely made use of each other
> Each for his purpose. That's horrible. Can we only love
> Something created by our own imagination?
> Are we all in fact unloving and unlovable?
> Then one *is* alone, and if one is alone
> Then lover and belovèd are equally unreal
> And the dreamer is no more real than his dreams (p. 122).

Not for her the reconciliation of unloving and unlovable that Edward and Lavinia will try to achieve. She has had glimpses of a

---

[1] p. 120. We recall that in his essay on Baudelaire Eliot said, 'the recognition of the reality of Sin is a New Life' (*Selected Essays*, p. 427).

[2] *Macbeth* V. iii. 40 and V. i. 72.

deeper reality, has dreamt a dream which is more real than ordinary reality, a dream in which the solitude is transcended by a love that bestows reality upon the dreamer:

> I have thought at moments that the ecstasy is real
> Although those who experience it may have no reality.
> For what happened is remembered like a dream
> In which one is exalted by intensity of loving
> In the spirit, a vibration of delight
> Without desire, for desire is fulfilled
> In the delight of loving. A state one does not know
> When awake. But what, or whom I loved,
> Or what in me was loving, I do not know.
> And if that is all meaningless, I want to be cured
> Of a craving for something I cannot find
> And of the shame of never finding it (p. 123).

Her choice, therefore, is for the second way offered by Sir Henry, the way which

> leads towards possession
> Of what you have sought for in the wrong place (p. 125).

Having distinguished as far as possible between the two ways, the ordinary man's way and the saint's way,[1] Reilly offers Celia her choice, and in order not to influence that choice he insists that 'Neither way is better./ Both ways are necessary'. Between them, society is renewed physically and spiritually. Both ways are valid spiritually in that they

> avoid the final desolation
> Of solitude in the phantasmal world
> Of imagination, shuffling memories and desires (p. 126).

But the ordinary way is no longer possible for Celia:

> I think it would really be dishonest
> For me, now, to try to make a life with *any*body!

---

[1] Of course, Reilly does not refer to it as the saint's way in describing it for Celia, but in talking to the Chamberlaynes he identifies the saints with those who go to the sanatorium (p. 112) and he sends Celia to the sanatorium (p. 126).

> I couldn't give anyone the kind of love—
> I wish I could—which belongs to that life.

So she chooses the second way, which leads to a painful death
(p. 124).

The paths chosen by Celia and the Chamberlaynes seem to be
diverging widely, but in the Third Act their choices are seen to
be different parts of a single pattern. Celia's choice, we learn there,
has led to crucifixion; the Chamberlaynes' choice has led to a
party at which the news of her death reaches them. One might
almost call the news 'good news', a 'gospel'. In reporting her
death, Reilly calls it 'a happy death', by which he does not mean,
he affirms, that she suffered less than an ordinary person would
have done:

> I'd say she suffered more, because more conscious
> Than the rest of us. She paid the highest price
> In suffering. That is part of the design (p. 161).

It is part of the design also in that it makes others identify themselves sympathetically with the sufferer and makes them keenly
aware of her sacrifice. This is the reason for the horror which
disturbs Act III.[1]

This final Act shows us the repercussions of Celia's choice in
the lives of others; in other words, it shows 'the power of the
saint's sacrifice to fertilize the lives of others'.[2] The immediate
efficacy of her death can only be hinted at:

> Who knows, Mrs. Chamberlayne,
> The difference that made to the natives who were dying
> Or the state of mind in which they died? (p. 159).

More definite is the effect on Peter Quilpe, the part it plays in
his development. Lavinia suggests that he, like Celia in her affair

[1] There was a more detailed description of the horrors of Celia's death in
the original version, but Eliot was persuaded at Edinburgh to trim it. In an
interview in which this matter was raised, Martin Browne 'described Eliot as
resenting deeply the soft interpretation of the Crucifixion and all martyrdom'
(Geoffrey Parsons, 'Solving Some of Eliot's Riddles', *New York Herald Tribune*,
12 February, 1950, Section 5, p. 2).

[2] D. E. S. Maxwell, p. 200.

with Edward, has loved 'something created by [his] imagination' (p. 122):

> What you've been living on is an image of Celia
> Which you made for yourself, to meet your own needs.[1]

He recognizes this as the truth, and, while Lavinia and Edward go on to explain that they understand because it has been their experience too, he comes to realize

> That I've only been interested in myself:
> And that isn't good enough for Celia (p. 158).

Celia has set a standard by which others will try to live. She has also borne witness to a deeper reality than that of ordinary life. The witness of her suffering is necessary because of the sin of the world, just as Becket's was, and in their way the Chamberlaynes acknowledge that 'the blood of the martyrs and the agony of the saints / Is upon our heads'. Edward suggests that:

> if this was right—if this was right for Celia—
> There must be something else that is terribly wrong,
> And the rest of us are somehow involved in the wrong.[2]

Lavinia agrees; she recalls her own spitefulness towards Celia and her failure to understand her. And Reilly tells them:

> You will have to live with these memories and make them
> Into something new. Only by acceptance
> Of the past will you alter its meaning (p. 163).

The Chamberlaynes are, in fact, accepting their past in this way,

---

[1] p. 158. The earlier history of Peter's relationship with Celia is traceable in the scene with Edward (pp. 33–43, especially pp. 38–9, 40). It was his 'first experience of reality' (p. 41), even though it seemed to him to exist 'between two unreal people' (p. 42). It is more than likely that, under the tutelage of Bela Szogody (the name is one of Eliot's jokes), he has moved on from this position in his discovery of reality, but as far as the Guardians of the play are concerned, at the end of Act II, 'He has not yet come to where the words are valid' (p. 133).

[2] p. 162. Cf. *The Idea of a Christian Society*, p. 73:
'The notion of communal responsibility, of the responsibility of every individual for the sins of the society to which he belongs, is one that needs to be more firmly apprehended.'

and as a symbol of this acceptance giving just such another cocktail party as they were holding at the beginning of the play. But because their own relationship is altered, the meaning of the party is altered. Celia's death has brought them closer together, as it has tied them to Peter (p. 164). The life of the spirit is invigorated and the bonds of society are strengthened. Before the party itself begins, a crucifixion has been recalled and a vicarious atonement recognized. The cocktail party can be the secular counterpart of the Communion Service if given in the right spirit, the titbits and the short drinks the equivalent of the bread and wine. The play is almost a piece of Metaphysical wit in its discovery of analogy in unlikely places.

The more explicit symbolism of spiritual death and rebirth derives from the *Alcestis* of Euripides, to which Eliot has gone 'as a point of departure'.[1] The Greek play begins with a prologue in which Apollo tells how, having been banished from Olympus and condemned for a time to serve a mortal, he became a herdsman of Admetus, King of Pherae, and found him a just and hospitable man. Apollo has persuaded the Fates to prolong the life of Admetus as a reward for his righteousness, provided that he can find someone who will die in his stead. The King has appealed to all his kinsmen to die for him, but none is willing. However, his wife, Alcestis, has agreed and at the beginning of the play is preparing for her death. Immediately after her death, and before the body has been buried, Heracles, son of Zeus, arrives at the palace on his way to fulfil yet another of his heroic labours. Despite his grief, Admetus carries out the sacred duties of hospitality and conceals the fact of his wife's death. Left to entertain himself during the funeral, Heracles makes merry to such an extent that one of the servants can endure it no longer and discloses the true situation. Heracles, touched by the fact that Admetus has given him hospitality in such circumstances, resolves to wrestle with Death and restore Alcestis to her home. He brings her back, a veiled figure, and persuades Admetus to take into his house this woman whom he says he has won as a prize at a nearby games. Having also persuaded Admetus himself to lead her into the house—the play everywhere heavily underlines the weakness of masculine nature by contrast with the fortitude of feminine

[1] *Poetry and Drama*, pp. 31–2 (*On Poetry and Poets*, p. 85).

nature represented by Alcestis herself—Heracles raises her veil and reveals the resurrected wife. Admetus is allowed to speak to her as much as he wishes, but she will not be able to answer him for three days, the length of time necessary for her to be 'unconsecrated' to the Gods beneath the earth (ll. 1144 ff.).

The play is a tragi-comedy with elements of satyr drama. It stands last among the group of four tragedies performed on one day and seems to have been designed to replace the ordinary satyr play. A gluttonous, drink-loving Heracles was a favourite character in the satyr plays proper, and something of this satyric character is carried over into *Alcestis*.

Most of the derivations from Euripides' play are completely ustified of themselves in *The Cocktail Party* by the interpretation Eliot puts upon them. Reilly's proneness to drink and song in the house of 'death' is one. Unlike Heracles, he is told by his host that his wife has 'departed'. But since he knows she can be brought back, he feels no need to restrain himself. The concealment of his wife's departure from the other guests, which is another derivation, is of course justified by Edward's pride. A borrowing which is not perhaps entirely justified of itself is the injunction of silence. In Euripides, where Admetus can question but Alcestis cannot reply, it has a sacred reason, as we have seen, and possibly a practical one—the need to restrict the number of speaking parts. In Eliot, where Lavinia can speak but Edward must not ask questions about where she has been (p. 29), the practical reasons seem paramount; it is necessary to the plot—Edward probably would not consult Reilly if he knew that Lavinia had been to his 'retreat' —and it serves perhaps as a safeguard against the deflation of the symbolism.[1]

In most cases, however, Eliot transforms his borrowings from Euripides into significant elements in a new entity. As Robert B. Heilman notes,

'Edward and Lavinia Chamberlayne are both treated like Admetus in being compelled to undergo moral introspection;

[1] Robert B. Heilman suggests that 'The ritual requirement is translated into a psychiatric strategem' (p. 109 fn.) but the purpose of the stratagem is not very clear. If, however, Edward were allowed to ask where Lavinia has been, he would be inclined to require greater exactitude than the symbolism would bear.

indeed, theirs is very much more severe and penetrating than his.' [1]

Moreover,

'In granting to Lavinia an element of unselfishness . . . Eliot retains the center of Alcestis's character, but at the same time he alters the proportions. In Alcestis the over-all emphasis is on the spirit of sacrifice. . . . In Lavinia we have only a glimpse of generosity. . . .' [2]

Finally,

'In the fine paradox of the "ghost" who can "die" [p. 87] Eliot has amplified the Euripides story, just as he has subtly varied it by the minute change of *die for* to *die to*.' [3]

It is this last which is the subtlest transformation. It brings the symbolism of Lavinia's return from the dead into touch with our everyday lives. The Heracles figure becomes a saviour from spiritual death:

> UNIDENTIFIED GUEST
>   it is a serious matter
> To bring someone back from the dead.
>   EDWARD
>   From the dead?
> That figure of speech is somewhat . . . dramatic,
> As it was only yesterday that my wife left me.
>   UNIDENTIFIED GUEST
> Ah, but we die to each other daily (p. 63).

The symbolism created by an amalgam of classical sources with Christianity merges with symbolism from the modern scene, from the new science of psychiatry. In a talk broadcast in 1932, Eliot discussed the uses and limitations of psychology:

'Psychology has very great utility in two ways. It can revive and has already to some extent revived, truths long since known to Christianity, but mostly forgotten and ignored, and it can put them in a form and a language understandable by modern people

---

[1] Heilman, p. 106.   [2] *Ibid.*, p. 110.   [3] *Ibid.*, p. 109.

to whom the language of Christianity is not only dead but un-decipherable.' [1]

This suggests one reason why Eliot uses the organization of psychiatric medicine in the play. The psychiatrist is the 'scientific' modern equivalent of the father confessor, and carries the 'authority' of science.

But psychology is not a satisfactory substitute for theology. As Eliot puts it, 'Psychology is an indispensable handmaid to theology; but, I think, a very poor housekeeper.' [2] He goes on to distinguish its limitations. One is that it gives people a sense of being 'absolved from all responsibility' and flatters their sense of self-importance. Another is that it

'seems to me for the most part to ignore the more intense, profound and satisfying emotions of religion. It must ignore their value because its function is merely to describe and not to express preference. But if this is true, it can never take the place of religion, though it can be an important accessory.' [3]

Psychiatry is, then, an inadequate substitute for the ministrations of the Church. It must give way to ritual at the climax of Act II (the libation) and it breaks down entirely over the death of Celia. Psychology has no adequate explanation of martyrdom.

It seems that by the very inadequacy of the symbolism Eliot means to suggest the limitations of medical science:

> It would need someone greater than the greatest doctor
> To cure *this* illness,

says Edward.[4] And the form of his consultation with Reilly is almost a parody of the accepted pattern of psycho-analysis:

EDWARD
I remember, in my childhood . . .

[1] 'The Search for Moral Sanction', *The Listener*, Vol. VII, No. 108, 30 March, 1932, p. 446.
[2] *Ibid.*   [3] *Ibid.*
[4] p. 54. The doctor himself (p. 97) objects to the term 'nervous breakdown' used by Celia (p. 53) and Lavinia (p. 88).

REILLY

I always begin from the immediate situation
And then go back as far as I find necessary.
You see, your memories of childhood—
I mean, in your present state of mind—
Would be largely fictitious; and as for your dreams,
You would produce amazing dreams, to oblige me.
I could make you dream any kind of dream I suggested,
And it would only go to flatter your vanity
With the temporary stimulus of feeling interesting (p. 98).

In the original production, which, we may be sure, was entirely in tune with Eliot's conception, the only person to lie on the customary couch in the psychiatrist's consulting room was the psychiatrist himself—an ironic reversal of the customary behaviour that American, if not British, audiences noted with amusement.[1]

Celia suggests the limitations of her 'pretty conventional' upbringing:

I had always been taught to disbelieve in sin.
Oh, I don't mean that it was never mentioned!
But anything wrong, from our point of view,
Was either bad form, or was psychological.
And bad form always led to disaster
Because the people one knew disapproved of it.
I don't worry much about form, myself—
But when everything's bad form, or mental kinks,
You either become bad form, and cease to care,
Or else, if you care, you must be kinky (p. 120).

But now she has acquired a sense of something wrong which is certainly not 'bad form' and which seems not to be 'psychological', though she wishes it were:

I should really *like* to think there's something wrong with me—
Because, if there isn't, then there's something wrong,
Or at least, very different from what it seemed to be,

[1] Maurice Zolotow, 'Psychoanalyzing the Doctor', *The New York Times*, 26 February, 1950, sec. 2, p. 3.

> With the world itself—and that's much more frightening!
> That would be terrible. So I'd rather believe
> There is something wrong with me, that could be put right.
> I'd do anything you told me to get back to normality.
>
> REILLY
>
> We must find out about you, before we decide
> What *is* normality.[1]

Probably the best comment upon this is the passage that Eliot quoted with approval, in a lecture given in 1956, from a comparison made by Aldous Huxley between Western psychiatry and the discipline of the East as found in Tao and Zen:

'The aim of Western psychiatry is to help the troubled individual to adjust himself to the society of less troubled individuals—individuals who are observed to be well adjusted to one another and the local institutions, but about whose adjustment to the fundamental Order of Things no enquiry is made. . . . But there is another kind of normality—a normality of perfect functioning . . . . Even a man who is perfectly adjusted to a deranged society can prepare himself, if he so desires, to become adjusted to the Nature of Things.'[2]

It is to this other kind of normality that Celia really aspires, and she gives her life to help reconcile a 'deranged society' with the 'fundamental Order of Things'.

In his capacity as psychiatrist, Reilly is the fashionable modern substitute for the priest, and his psychiatrist's couch is the substitute for the confessional box. But he is a poor substitute, unable to understand the advice he gives; he asks Julia about Celia's experience on the journey in which 'the human is Transhumanised'[3] and admits that

[1] p. 117. Cf. *The Family Reunion*, p. 91, and the passage from Eliot's introduction to *Nightwood* by Djuna Barnes quoted in note 1, p. 95.

[2] *On Poetry and Poets*, p. 105.

[3] pp. 130–1. I agree with W. K. Wimsatt that here Julia and Reilly 'speak of Celia in terms which slip over, though by ever so little, from the spiritual to the neo-Platonic or mysterious. "You and I don't know the process by which the human is Transhumanised . . . . Will she be frightened by the first appearance of projected spirits?" This is a little in the manner of the glosses to *The Ancient Mariner*, from Iamblichus, *De Mysteriis*' (*Sewanee Review*, LVIII, p. 675).

> when I say to one like her
'Work out your salvation with diligence', I do not understand
What I myself am saying.

Julia replies, 'You must accept your limitations' (p. 131). The psychiatrist has to be complemented by the Guardian.

The Guardians are perhaps the Christian counterparts of the rulers of Plato's ideal Republic.[1] We get a hint of a special symbolism in Edward's description of his two selves:

> The self that can say 'I want this—or want that'—
> The self that wills—he is a feeble creature;
> He has to come to terms in the end
> With the obstinate, the tougher self; who does not speak,
> Who never talks, who cannot argue;
> And who in some men may be the *guardian* (p. 58).

But at the end of this scene Celia shifts the meaning to other characters in the play when she proposes a toast:

> To the Guardians. It was you who spoke of guardians.
> *[They drink]*
> It may be that even Julia is a guardian.
> Perhaps she is *my* guardian (p. 61).

It becomes clear from the machinations of Act II that Julia is indeed her guardian and that Alex is Edward's. Does this mean that in some sense Julia is Celia's other self and that Alex is Edward's? This possible inference is not substantiated by the play, though, as William Arrowsmith points out,

> 'Eliot may . . . intend an analogy [between the guardian image in Edward's speech and the Guardians of the play] : what the personal "guardian" is in the individual the Christian "Guardian" is in the world.'[2]

---

[1] Grover Smith observes that
'The concept of guardianship, though indeed of diverse provenance, from the legal use of the term to the Stoic-Christian idea of guardian angels, recalls the Guardians in Plato's *Republic*, especially in view of the outline for the social role of the Community of Christians in Eliot's *The Idea of a Christian Society*, (1939)' (*op. cit.*, p. 220).
[2] *The Hudson Review*, III, p. 415, fn.

The Guardians seem to be members of the select group which Eliot calls the Community of Christians. Even in a Christian society he says:

'it is only from the much smaller number of conscious human beings, the Community of Christians, that one would expect a conscious Christian life on its highest social level'.[1]

He goes on to explain that the Community of Christians is not an organization,

'but a body of indefinite outline; composed of both clergy and laity, of the more conscious, more spiritually and intellectually developed of both. It will be their identity of belief and aspiration, their background of a common system of education and common culture, which will enable them to influence and be influenced by each other, and collectively to form the conscious mind and the conscience of the nation.'[2]

The members of this group are not necessarily highly gifted, either intellectually or spiritually:

'the possession of intellectual or spiritual gifts does not necessarily confer that intellectual understanding of spiritual issues which is the qualification for exerting the kind of influence here required. Nor is the person who possesses this qualification necessarily a "better Christian" in his private life than the man whose insight is less profound.'[3]

It would seem that such people can be as deceptive in their manner as the feathery-minded Julia and the overhelpful Alex of the play.[4] This gives Eliot good warrant for making excellent comedy out of them.

[1] *The Idea of a Christian Society* (Faber and Faber, 1939), p. 28.
[2] *Ibid.*, p. 42.   [3] *Ibid.*, p. 74.
[4] There is not, however, a complete split between social appearance and real self. Julia's curiosity, for instance, sets going the terrible snowball of truth (see pp. 79-80). And, of course, there are many hints of a deeper seriousness in her, such as her willingness to believe the man who said he could hear the cry of bats (p. 11), not to speak of her almost pathetic plea:

> I know you think I'm a silly old woman
> But I'm really very serious (p. 14).

And of course Alex is genuinely helpful to Peter as well as to Edward.

William Arrowsmith suggests that 'the guardians of the Christian idea are "the one-eyed in the kingdom of the blind"; nothing more exalted than that.'[1] And D. W. Harding points out that Reilly and Julia

'are both metaphorically one-eyed and need each other to give a whole vision. Julia, inquiring for her spectacles, says one lens is missing and Reilly then sings of himself as the One-Eyed Riley. Reilly says to Julia:

> When I express confidence in anything
> You always raise doubts; when I am apprehensive
> Then you see no reason for anything but confidence.

> JULIA
> That's one way in which I am so useful to you.

And at the end Edward says,

> Oh, it isn't much
> That I understand yet! But Sir Henry has been saying,
> I think, that every moment is a fresh beginning;
> And Julia, that life is only keeping on;
> And somehow, the two ideas seem to fit together.'[2]

It is as if, in our stunted society, we can achieve width of outlook only by spiritual co-operation.

In *The Idea of a Christian Society* Eliot said:

'a society has not ceased to be Christian until it has become positively something else. It is my contention that we have to-day a culture which is mainly negative, but which, so far as it is positive, is still Christian. I do not think that it can remain negative, because a negative culture has ceased to be efficient in a world where economic as well as spiritual forces are proving the efficiency of cultures which, even when pagan, are positive; and I believe that the choice before us is between the formation of a new Christian culture, and the acceptance of a pagan one' (p. 13).

The Cocktail Party seems to depict a stage in the creation of such a new Christian culture—
'a society in which the natural end of man—virtue and well-being

---

[1] *The Hudson Review*, III, p. 419.
[2] *The Kenyon Review*, XVIII (1956), pp. 346–7.

in community—is acknowledged for all, and the supernatural end —beatitude—for those who have eyes to see it'.[1]

William Arrowsmith suggests that it is

'a society which, dramatically, is being made before our eyes. The Christian conspiracy begins at the Chamberlaynes' but as the play ends, Alex and Julia and Reilly are off "to the Gunnings". And so the society comes to include those who, like Edward, may not *consciously* hold Christian beliefs.' [2]

The description 'Christian conspiracy' is unfortunately justi-fied. As we have observed, Eliot expressly says that his Com-munity of Christians, to which I am assuming Reilly, Julia, and Alex belong, is not an organization. Yet in the play they seem to belong to a mysterious religious organization, to move almost in the atmosphere of a secret society, and they certainly indulge in ritual somewhat resembling an esoteric cult. This kind of thing alienates most people, if only because they feel excluded. Eliot probably did not intend any such effect. Clearly the Community of Christians would share a special spiritual fellowship and would work together with intuitive understanding, but they would not set themselves apart in this way. The explanation probably lies in the necessity for dramatic heightening and for the creation of dramatic machinery. In the concrete dramatic situation, the 'body of very nebulous outline' [3] has been rather too sharply defined. As for the libation, any portrayal of the Community of Christians would be incomplete without some indication of the place of ritual in their lives. Yet it cannot be Christian ritual, since speci-fically Christian references are to be omitted. Eliot has therefore created, as background to the ritual, an indeterminate kind of religion with a trace of Nature mysticism in it:

> Let them build the hearth
> Under the protection of the stars . . . (p. 132).

Guardianship is, so to speak, the machinery of the plot. As instruments of a higher power, the Guardians contrive a good deal of the action of the play. In this way symbolism becomes highly

[1] *The Idea of a Christian Society*, p. 34.
[2] *The Hudson Review*, III, p. 420.
[3] *The Idea of a Christian Society*, p. 37.

functional, and, contrariwise, their manipulation of the plot assumes a metaphysical significance and suggests the way Divine Providence works in society. The highly amusing assemblage of the characters in the third scene of Act One—they all come running to Edward's flat in response to telegrams (pp. 66-78)—illustrates this aspect of the structure of the play. This ruse of the Guardians has served a useful purpose in the plot. As Lavinia says later about this visit of Celia and Peter,

> They had to tell us, themselves, that they had made their decision (p. 113)

Lavinia's reaction to the ruse of the telegrams is the feeling of being caught in a trap. At first the Divine Providence looks to her and Edward and Celia like the 'infernal machine' of M. Cocteau's imagination.[1] Edward suddenly finds himself in Hell (p. 87). Both Lavinia and Celia speak of the Divine agents as devils.[2] But it was the voluntary acts of Lavinia and Edward which started the machine running and seemed to rob them of their freedom. They have to learn the true meaning of freedom. Reilly is the agent who will reveal it to them, or, at least, put them in the way to discovering it for themselves.

As Father McLaughlin points out:

'In the volitional order, just as no one can sin except by an exercise of his free will, so no one can desire the fulfillment of his capacity save by a *personal* choice. To ensure such a free and personal decision, Reilly eliminated all outside influence over Edward by suggesting arguments for the opposite choice, a permanent separation from his wife, which, though suasive, were nevertheless sophistic and served, as Reilly had hoped, only to educe from Edward the deeply personal conviction to reunite himself to her.'[3]

Edward has not the insight, however, to see at first that he has made a deliberate choice; 'It seems to me that I might as well go home' (p. 112) is the nearest he comes to admission of choice in the consulting room. Celia, on the other hand, is able to say: 'I

---

[1] See pp. 46-7 (trap), 77, 85-6 (trap . . . cage), 95-6.
[2] Lavinia, pp. 79. 104; Celia, 51, 53.
[3] John J. McLaughlin, S. J., *Renascence*, III, p. 21.

know it is I who have made the decision' (p. 128). All three of them are on the way to discovering according to their capacity the truth of the sublime paradox of the Collect for Peace: '[His] service is perfect freedom.' Only in so far as men elect to do the will of God are they exercising their free will; in doing evil they are merely yielding to the subtle pressures of the World, the Flesh and the Devil.

Thus we see that there are certain ambiguities in the use of symbolism in the play and certain places where it deliberately breaks down. Eliot's next move is to be towards a closer integration of symbolism with naturalistic action, so that something more like seven-eighths of the iceberg of symbolism is submerged. But *The Cocktail Party* makes a great step towards creating a continuous surface of theatrical interest. It achieves a much happier balance between weight of meaning and immediate theatrical intelligibility than *The Family Reunion;* it is not too difficult to follow at a first seeing, yet capable of yielding greater wealth of meaning on further acquaintance.

There is a certain mellowness about *The Cocktail Party.* Eliot has moved beyond the necessity for tragedy into the realm of eternal comedy. Under the Christian dispensation, all endings can be happy. Eliot has devised a kind of comedy generically like Dante's *Divine Comedy,* the portrait of a world in which the characters, 'Nel mezzo del cammin di nostra vita',[1] come to themselves in a dark wood where the straight way is lost, and are set on the right path towards the fulfilment ordained for them in the Divine Providence.[2] *The Cocktail Party* is in part the fruition of a long devotion to the greatest of religious poets.[3]

---

[1] *In the middle of the journey of our life* (*The Inferno* I. i, trans. John D. Sinclair).
[2] Cf. Celia's reference to a forest on p. 122.
[3] 'I still, after forty years, regard his poetry as the most persistent and deepest influence upon my own verse'—Eliot, 'Talk on Dante', *The Adelphi,* New Series, Vol. 27, No. 2 (First Quarter, 1951), p. 106. Cf. *Selected Essays,* p. 252:
'For the science or art of writing verse, one has learned from the *Inferno* that the greatest poetry can be written with the greatest economy of words, and with the greatest austerity in the use of metaphor, simile, verbal beauty, and elegance.'
The relevance of this to the style of *The Cocktail Party* is evident.

Chapter Six

Plays in a Contemporary Setting—III
'The Confidential Clerk' (1953)

I
F one wanted to say something serious nowadays it was easier
to say it in comedy,' Eliot is reported as having said at a press
conference held in Edinburgh after the first night of *The Confidential Clerk*.[1] And, indeed, until his latest play, the trend
of his work was away from tragedy. In *The Family Reunion* the
pattern of Greek tragedy remained; though transfigured by the
Christian revelation, the borrowings from the *Oresteia* obtruded
upon the contemporary setting. For the bases of the plots of his
next two plays, Eliot turned to the tragi-comedies of Euripides
and, taking pains to 'conceal the origins',[2] transformed them into
modern comedy. In *The Cocktail Party* he achieved a beautifully
poised comedy of manners; in *The Confidential Clerk* he achieved
something nearer high farce. It is a play in the central tradition of
European comedy, which first flowered in Greek New Comedy,
was transplanted to the Rome of Plautus and Terence and thence
shed its seeds in all the countries of Europe, springing up early and
late, for instance, in Shakespeare's nursery. The strain grew sickly
until Oscar Wilde cross-fertilized it with the comedy of manners
and developed a brilliant new species in his hothouse. Yet the
characteristics of lost children, searching parents, and mistaken

---

[1] Edinburgh *Evening Dispatch*, 26 August, 1953.
[2] *Poetry and Drama*, p. 31 (*On Poetry and Poets*, p. 85).

identity, persisted all this while. Eliot's work shows likenesses to most of these species, not least to Wilde's in the bloom of mannered comedy. But for the nucleus of its plot it goes back beyond them all to the play in which the characteristics first appear in European drama, the *Ion* of Euripides.

In a prologue spoken by Hermes we are told that, years before, the god Apollo ravished Creusa, princess of Athens, and that she bore and abandoned a son. Found and reared by a priestess of the Delphic shrine, the child, Ion, has become an officer in the temple. Meanwhile, his mother has married Xuthus, a neighbouring chieftain. But the marriage has produced no children, and husband and wife are now coming to the Delphic oracle to ask a remedy. Apollo plans to let Xuthus think he has found a son in Ion so that the young man shall not be cheated of his birthright, the kingdom of Athens. He therefore declares through the oracle that the first person Xuthus meets on leaving the temple will be his son—an eventuality made possible by an escapade with a slave-girl. This turns out to be Ion, of course, and Xuthus, overjoyed, plans to take him home to succeed him in power and wealth (ll. 577-81). Ion points out that it is likely to grieve the childless Creusa to have to accept her husband's child into her home (607-20). In any case, he is loath to leave the calm of his life at Delphos for the busy life of the Athenian court; the prospect of wealth is no inducement (621-47). To the second objection, Xuthus replies simply: 'Learn to put up with your lot' (650); the first he proposes to deal with by keeping the relationship secret until such time as he can bring the queen round to accepting Ion as his successor (655-9). However, the Chorus defeats his plan by revealing all to Creusa. Her old servant imagines a sordid intrigue. Xuthus must have put out his bastard son to a foster mother in Delphos and deliberately brought Creusa there in order to retrieve his son as if by the god's will. The old man offers to take revenge for her by poisoning Ion. But this plot also goes awry, and Creusa has to take refuge on the altar of the god. At this point the priestess who found Ion intervenes, bringing the cradle, wrappings and trinkets which she found with him. By these tokens, Creusa recognizes her son, is reconciled to him, and reveals that his father was Apollo. Ion is inclined to believe this a fiction devised to lessen her shame. He appeals to the god himself and Pallas Athene appears on behalf of Apollo to confirm Creusa's claim. Ion then accepts his 'fine inheritance'.[1]

The parallels with Eliot's play are clear, much clearer than the parallels between *The Cocktail Party* and *Alcestis* and somewhat clearer than those between *The Family Reunion* and the *Oresteia*, even though the translation into modern terms is more complete than in the latter case. But if the main parallels are clear, they are not simple. Just as Shakespeare doubled the Plautine twins in order to increase the comic complication in *The Comedy of Errors*, so Eliot has split up the Euripidean foundling and invented a bastard daughter into the bargain. Ion is diffracted into Colby Simpkins and B. Kaghan. Their fathers are a musician and a poet respectively, music and poetry both being skills of Apollo. The play's theme of Divine Fatherhood also originates here. Whereas Ion discovers that he is the son of a god, Colby discovers that he is a son of God. Other parallels are simpler. Like Xuthus, Sir Claude jumps to a conclusion about his paternity (p. 127). Like Xuthus, again, he wants his supposed son to inherit his position and wealth, and proposes to conceal the relationship from his wife (p. 12). Like Ion, though for a different reason, Colby is reluctant to join his father (p. 38). Like Creusa, Lady Elizabeth yearns for motherhood (p. 12), but her 'pilgrimages' to spiritual specialists are the fashionable modern substitute for religion. The Old Servant's notion that Xuthus has put his son out to a foster-mother is realized in the plot of Eliot's play, and the foster-mother, Mrs. Guzzard, assumes the functions of the priestess of the temple *and* the *dea ex machina*, Pallas Athene.[2]

---

[1] l. 1618. Cf. *The Confidential Clerk*, p. 130: 'You knew your inheritance. Now I know mine.'

[2] It is interesting to note that Eliot brings the device of the *dea ex machina* into line with a general misconception. It is frequently said that Euripides and other ancient dramatists relied upon the *dea ex machina* to cut, if not to unravel, the Gordian knot of the complication. In fact, the device was employed in classical drama primarily not to bring about the solution of the plot but to foretell the future of the characters or point out the relationship between the events of the play and some feature of Athenian life, for this could be done only by someone possessing supernatural foresight. The device might also be used to put the seal of divine approval upon the solution arrived at in the play. And this is just what happens in the *Ion*. The *gnorismata* or birth-tokens have already proved that Ion is Creusa's child. Athene confirms that his father is Apollo, but it is primarily to 'pronounce his oracles' that she has come (1569–70). It

Being doubtless aware that Greek New Comedy was much akin to the *Ion*, Eliot seems to have gone for at least one detail to Menander. Agnoia or Misapprehension, the Prologue of *The Girl Who Gets her Hair Cut Short* (*Periceiromene*), tells the audience that she has caused Moschion to fall in love with Glycera so that their true relation as brother and sister may be revealed: 'For by the help of God the evil turns into good, even while it is coming to pass' (ll. 49–50). Similarly, it is the growth of love between Colby and Lucasta that brings to light the fact that they are apparently related, though of course in the end they prove not to be. Moreover, in Menander's plays, as Mrs. Katherine Lever points out,

'The recognition of long-lost relatives is only the obvious form of enlightenment. Far more significant is the recognition of self-knowledge. When Charisius [in *Epitrepontes* or *The Arbitrants*] recognizes the foundling baby as his, he recognizes that he has been as dishonourable as the wife he has been treating with such scorn. He is guilty of the same offence as she is, and he has added unkindness whereas his wife is forgiving. Through this self-knowledge justice is achieved—the same forgiveness for the same act. . . . The person like Smicrines, who refuses to admit his own responsibility, who blames Necessity for his actions, who does not see that his own character (*tropos*) is determining the action, is ridiculous in his blindness and must be brought to enlightenment before the play can end happily.' [1]

It is perhaps not too much to say that Eliot adapts the *Ion* in the light of Greek New Comedy.[2]

The original Greek pattern is elaborated to the point of farce. The piling up of complication in the Second Act as each of the young people is revealed to be either bastard or foundling is in fact a kind of spiritual farce; it is just that they are suddenly caught

must be made clear that Ion is the father of the Ionian race (1570–88). Eliot makes use of the popular misconception of the *dea ex machina* in order to spring a series of surprises at the end of the play. It is Eggerson who predicts Colby's future (p. 132).

[1] Katherine Lever, *The Art of Greek Comedy* (Methuen, 1956), pp. 198–9.
[2] Francis Fergusson suggests that the scheme of the vicissitudes of several generations—separations and reunions—'fits our time of dim displaced persons as well as it did late antiquity, also a time of exiles groping in the confusion of several demoralized cultural traditions' (*Sewanee Review*, LXIV, p. 566).

with their defences down, having doffed some of the armour of sophistication or removed their social masks, instead of being caught in their underwear like characters in the more usual type of farce. Despite a first impression of something like frivolity, the underpattern of serious meaning is almost completely integrated with the pattern of events. Behind the casual and almost callous interchange of parents and children lies the profound intuition that all earthly relationships are swallowed up in our relation to the heavenly Father, that, as Lady Elizabeth puts it, 'we are nearer to God than to anyone' (p. 72).

The meaning of that ultimate relationship is adumbrated in the complex of relationships in the play. At the centre of the design is Colby's search for a way of integrating the outer world of action with the inner world of spiritual being (the two kinds of reality). He finds that the way leads through fulfilment of relationship to others, in his case to his dead father, and, it is implied, to God. In the last resort, it is the discovery of a religious vocation, but this is merely hinted at.[1]

The theme is stated in the scene between Sir Claude Mulhammer and Colby in the First Act. Colby confesses that his new life is making a different person of him—a person he is not sure he likes. In moments of relaxation, however, the person he used to be, 'the disappointed organist', returns 'to take possession', and the attraction of the art he has forsaken becomes so powerful that he has to 'fight that person' (p. 38). What Sir Claude does in effect is to advise him how to fight strategically, to allow that person a limited place in his life, to develop, in fact, a secret life.

---

[1] Although the emphasis is different, *The Confidential Clerk* takes up and elaborates several minor themes of *The Cocktail Party*:
  (1) the discovery that one has a vocation to do something second-rate (cf. *The Cocktail Party*, p. 157, with *The Confidential Clerk*, pp. 40–41, 90);
  (2) the tendency to protect oneself by wearing a social mask (*The Cocktail Party*, pp. 129–30, *The Confidential Clerk*, p. 49);
  (3) the danger of imposing roles on others (*The Cocktail Party*, p. 99, *The Confidential Clerk*, p. 100. Cf. *The Family Reunion*, pp. 53, 106);
  (4) the need to accept the consequences of choice (*The Cocktail Party*, p. 163, *The Confidential Clerk*, p. 134).
Moreover, the relation of Colby and Lucasta seems to be a fuller treatment of the relationship between Peter and Celia. (Cf. *The Cocktail Party*, pp. 38–9, with *The Confidential Clerk*, pp. 46–7.)

He sees in Colby's experience a repetition of his own, for he wanted to be a potter, and became a financier only at the insistence of his father. In an effort to help Colby, he tells him about himself.

For him, the finer products of the potter's art are not for 'use' or 'decoration':

> For me, they are life itself. To be among such things,
> If it is an escape, is escape into living,
> Escape from a sordid world to a pure one.
>
> .   .   .   .
>
> I want a world where the form is the reality,
> Of which the substantial is only a shadow (p. 39).

For him, clearly, art is the doorway into the world of spiritual reality. But he was turned aside from his pursuit of this reality by 'family pressure' and went into his father's business:

> I loathed this occupation
> Until I began to feel my power in it.
> The life changed me, as it is changing you:
> It begins as a kind of make-believe
> And the make-believing makes it real (p. 40).

But it has never become fully satisfying to him, which is an indication of its lack of reality. He has had to engineer a secret life for himself, divorced from the ordinary business of living.

As a substitute for the creativity of which he has come to believe himself incapable,[1] he has assembled a collection of porcelain which he keeps in a private room:

> when I am alone, and look at one thing long enough,
> I sometimes have that sense of identification
> With the maker, of which I spoke—an agonising ecstasy
> Which makes life bearable. It's all I have.
> I suppose it takes the place of religion. . . .
> I dare say truly religious people—

[1] p. 41. Miss M. C. Bradbrook points out (*T. S. Eliot*, Writers and Their Work Series, rev. ed., 1955, p. 55) that these lines bear a resemblance to the passage in Eliot's lecture 'The Three Voices of Poetry', where he describes the 'moment of exhaustion . . .' that follows artistic creation (*On Poetry and Poets*, p. 98. Cf. pp. 99–100).

I've never known any—can find some unity.
Then there are also the men of genius.
There are others, it seems to me, who have at best to live
In two worlds—each a kind of make-believe (p. 42).

But in the offer to show his collection to Colby and his hint
that he would like to be admitted to Colby's private world of
music, there is a delicate suggestion that Sir Claude doesn't find
the arrangement of his life entirely satisfactory, that he is aware of
the unnatural divorce between its two parts and wants to create a
link between them by sharing the experience of 'the real world'
behind 'the private door' with someone from the world of ordinary living. Without that link, both worlds are make-believe.

Colby's innate honesty, his instinctive sense of reality, will not
allow him to accept the dichotomy of Sir Claude's life. Earlier in
the scene, he has expressed his uneasiness about the kind of pretence Sir Claude proposes as a means of keeping his son by him.
For 'a foolish reason', as he later admits to his wife (p. 79,) Sir
Claude has not wanted to confess to her that he had an illegiti-
mate son; so he proposes what he thinks is a harmless deception.
Colby, however, feels uneasy about 'building [his] life upon a
deception'. And, in any case, will Lady Elizabeth be taken in? Sir
Claude reassures him:

> She has always lived in a world of make-believe,
> And the best one can do is to guide her delusions
> In the right direction.
> ### COLBY
> It doesn't seem quite honest.
> If we all have to live in a world of make-believe,
> Is that good for us? Or a kindness to her?
> ### SIR CLAUDE
> If you haven't the strength to impose your own terms
> Upon life, you must accept the terms it offers you (pp. 36-7).

And when Sir Claude has explained what he means by this,
Colby is nearer to understanding, but no nearer to accepting, the
make-believe:

> something in me
> Rebels against accepting such conditions . . . (p. 42).

Sir Claude begins to see his mistake and is stunned by it. Colby hastens to reassure him that he is interested in his work and keen to do it well:

> I don't want my position
> To be, in any way, a make-believe (p. 44).

But the reassurance is disturbing in its implications and Sir Claude's impulse is to take refuge in his philosophy, a kind of stoic resignation, and in his private world of make-believe:

> Meanwhile, we must simply wait to learn
> What new conditions life will impose on us.
> Just when we think we have settled our account
> Life presents a new one, more difficult to pay.
> —I shall go now, and sit for a while with my china (p. 44).

Colby's reminder of business to be dealt with underlines the unsatisfactoriness of a refuge which is circumscribed by the pressure of external events. And, of course, he comes to feel by the end of the play that Sir Claude's pattern of make-believe will not do for him. He cannot accept the terms life imposes in the way Sir Claude has tried to do. He cannot rest content in the unreality of a divided life; there must be continuity between the inner and outer life, between the private and the public worlds, even if it means failure by the standards of the public world, means being a second-rate musician.

The unsatisfactoriness of the compromise proposed by Sir Claude emerges more clearly in the scene between Colby and Lucasta which opens Act Two. The insight which comes to Lucasta through her love for him illuminates his predicament. In giving up his career as a musician, she tells him:

> it's only the outer world that you've lost:
> You've still got your inner world—a world that's more real.
> That's why you're different from the rest of us:
> You have your secret garden; to which you can retire
> And lock the gate behind you.[1]

---

[1] p. 51. We have already noted the symbolism of the garden in *The Family Reunion*. In the present play, it has taken on a somewhat different orientation. The garden now clearly represents a propensity for withdrawal into oneself,

But this compensation is not satisfactory. This 'secret garden', he tells her, is

> not quite real to me—
> Although it's as real to me as . . . this world.
> But that's just the trouble. They seem so unrelated.
> I turn the key, and walk through the gate,
> And there I am . . . alone, in my 'garden'.
> Alone, that's the thing. That's why it's not real (p. 52).

Eggerson's garden, he suggests, is real because he retires to it physically as well as spiritually. What is more, he is not alone there—this is not explained, but presumably it is because God walks in his garden—and his withdrawal is productive; he has vegetables to bring back to Mrs. Eggerson.[1] Lucasta thinks he is

and this may derive from a conception in Henry James's *The Portrait of a Lady*:

'Her [Isabel's] nature had, in her conceit, a certain garden-like quality, a suggestion of perfume and murmuring boughs, of shady bowers and lengthening vistas, which made her feel that introspection was, after all, an exercise in the open air, and that a visit to the recesses of one's spirit was harmless when one returned from it with a lapful of roses. But she was often reminded that there were other gardens in the world than those of her remarkable soul, and that there were, moreover, a great many places which were not gardens at all—only dusky pestiferous tracts, planted thick with ugliness and misery.'
—Charles Scribner's Sons, N.Y., 1908, Vol. I, Ch. vi, p. 72. Isabel's emergence from her garden with a lapful of roses becomes Eggerson's provision of vegetables. The places which are 'not gardens at all . . .' are illustrated in Lucasta's sad description of her 'only garden' (p. 52). The character of Lady Elizabeth may owe something to Mrs. Touchett in the same novel. James's character is an eccentric who goes her own way independently of her husband, travels much and sends cryptic messages home, returns unexpectedly, takes people up and manages them, is unconventional and forthright in her speech, tending to tell people exactly what she thinks of them, and speaking pithily, almost epigrammatically, though a little vacuously, which detracts from the quality of the epigrams, but makes them the more amusing.

[1] There is a curious anticipation of Eggerson in one of the characters in Eliot's sketch 'Eeldrop and Appleplex', *The Little Review*, Vol. IV, No. 1 (May, 1917), p. 11:
'[Eeldrop:] "I am, I confess to you, in private life, a bank clerk. . . ." "And should, according to your theory, have a wife, three children, and a vegetable garden in a suburb," said Appleplex.
' "Such is precisely the case," returned Eeldrop, "but I had not thought it necessary to mention this biographical detail. As it is Saturday night, I shall return to my suburb. Tomorrow will be spent in that garden." '

joking, but he assures her that he is serious:

> What I mean is, my garden's no less unreal to me
> Than the world outside it. If you have two lives
> Which have nothing whatever to do with each other—
> Well, they're both unreal. But for Eggerson
> His garden is a part of one single world.

> LUCASTA
> But what do you want?
> COLBY
> Not to be alone there.
> If I were religious, God would walk in my garden
> And that would make the world outside it real
> And acceptable, I think (p. 53).

There is, he goes on to suggest, one other way in which both the garden and the outside world can be made real; this is by the penetration of another human being into the garden in the communion of love.

Thus we see that the gap between the two worlds, the public and the private, can only be bridged by love. The love may originate in the ordinary world (the love of parent and child, which is what Sir Claude has divined, or the love between man and woman, which we see developing between Colby and Lucasta in this scene) and extend into the other world, or it may originate in the other world, the world of creative love—which is why the love of creation may give admission to it—(the love of God for his creature, which is answered by the love of the creature for his Maker) and extend into the ordinary world. Without the bond of love, neither aspect of life is fruitful, neither world is truly real.

Lucasta is right in her intuition that Colby doesn't need anybody, any *human* person, that is (p. 54). For him, the garden and the outside world are to be made real by the presence of God. But this is not a realization that will come easily. The first step towards it is the desolation that comes from losing Lucasta and with her the hope that the garden will be made real by the presence of a loved *human* person's spirit there. He is to lose also his father and his mother and all other earthly attachments. But Lady Elizabeth obliquely suggests what the solution is to be in his case:

> Of course, there's something in us,
> In all of us, which isn't just heredity,
> But something unique. Something we have been
> From eternity. Something . . . straight from God.
> That means that we are nearer to God than to anyone.
> —Where did you live, as a child? (p. 72).

It is this question, coming at this significant moment, which starts the train of investigation that robs Colby of his supposed father and leads him to the Father.

Lady Elizabeth's intuition is possible because she refuses to believe in facts (p. 87) or to accept the terms that life imposes. Her apparent folly has its wisdom. Sir Claude has chosen 'obedience to the facts', but he comes to doubt whether he has been wise:

> I might have been truer to my father's inspiration
> If I had done what I wanted to do (p. 88).

Colby is free to be true to that inspiration when he finds it, because he distinguishes fact from fact, distinguishes between the dead and the living facts (p. 82). He is free also in the sense that the circumstances of his upbringing have left him detached from normal family relationships. When Sir Claude and Lady Elizabeth debate their claims to him, he finds himself 'simply indifferent' (p. 81). He finds himself free to create his own image of the father he would like to have:

> I should like a father
> Whom I had never known and couldn't know now,
> Because he would have died before I was born
> Or before I could remember; whom I could get to know
> Only by report, by documents—
> The story of his life, of his success or failure . . .
> Perhaps his failure more than his success—
>
> . . . .
>
> Whose image I could create in my own mind,
> To live with that image. An ordinary man
> Whose life I could in some way perpetuate . . . (p. 125).

When he is granted his wish by Mrs. Guzzard and discovers that his father was a disappointed musician, he finds that this completes his freedom (p. 128). He sees now that success doesn't matter, for his father was not a success (p. 129).

Sir Claude appeals to him to remain; but that is impossible for him now:

> As long as I believed that you were my father
> I was content to have had the same ambitions
> And in the same way to accept their failure.
> You had your father before you, as a model;
> You knew your inheritance. Now I know mine (p. 130).

As he emphasizes, he must follow his father.[1] In effect, his answer is that of Christ—'I must be about my father's business'—and the father he will follow is God as revealed in Christ, whom he *could* 'get to know / Only by report, by documents', that is, by the gospels; who was, by worldly standards, a failure; and whose life the Christian does try to imitate and perpetuate. Sir Claude has spent his life atoning to a dead father, but for a failure to understand him which is a product of Original Sin (p. 40). Colby is innocent of personal sin. If he suffers it will be as Christ suffered —on behalf of others. The implications are only faintly adumbrated:

> If there's agony, it's part of a total agony
> Which I can't begin to feel yet (p. 81).

But we are given a glimpse of the pattern underlying the action of the play. Behind the worldly quest of fathers for sons and sons for fathers lies the movement of the Divine Love, seeking response in the heart of man and revealing the way of reconciliation in Christ.

As in *The Family Reunion* and *The Cocktail Party*, a choice is made between a normal family life and a dedicated life leading away from the family. But in *The Confidential Clerk* the exceptional person is much more closely integrated in the pattern of ordinary life. Colby is only just beginning to discover his true vocation. He has even less awareness than Harry and Celia of the 'precise direction'. It is shrewd old Eggerson who sees the implications of his choice: 'You'll be thinking of reading for orders' (p. 132). Even outside the play, therefore, his destiny is to be less

[1] The phrase 'follow my father' occurs twice on p. 129.

unusual than Harry's or Celia's.[1] And within the play, his presence has served as a leaven, helping others to understand themselves, particularly their own inadequacies and limitations, and to understand others by accepting their different limitations. In other words, he has made possible a more fruitful communal life.

Although the characters exist on different levels of spiritual perception as in the previous plays, there is less schematism and much more intercommunication. Colby is not the only character who functions as a spiritual leaven. He inherits a quality possessed by Eggerson, his predecessor. As Mr. Spencer Brown observes, 'we catch the aura of a pun on the word *clerk*'.[2] Eliot himself has said that 'Eggerson is the only *developed* Christian in the play'.[3] He seems, in fact, to be one of the Community of Christians.[4] Everyone looks to him in a difficult situation.[5] Colby instinctively perceives that he has a special kind of integrity, as his allusion to Eggerson's 'garden' shows (pp. 52-3). He recognizes Eggerson as one of the pure in heart (p. 27). The 'very soul of tact and discretion' (p. 107), Eggerson is, as Sir Claude perceives, just the man to preside at the delicate enquiry into the circumstances of Colby's birth. Throughout the play, his shrewd insight has directed attention to Colby as an exceptional person. From tiny hints like his

[1] B. Kaghan, however, with what Colby calls 'a pretty shrewd insight' perceives that:

> He's the sort of fellow who might chuck it all
> And go to live on a desert island (p. 65).

[2] *Commentary*, Vol. 17, p. 368. Both the *Shorter Oxford English Dictionary* and *Webster's New International* still give clergyman or ecclesiastic as the primary meaning of the word, though it is little used in this way nowadays. The more obvious meaning Eliot puts upon it is also old-fashioned; a more normal modern designation would have been private secretary, which suggests that the pun is intended. We note that all the titles of Eliot's plays have some degree of irony.

[3] Mr. Martin Browne is reported as saying:

'Eliot . . . said to me "Eggerson is the only *developed* Christian in the play." I think to Eliot Eggerson is the catalyst. He is the man who cultivates his own garden, who is at peace with himself and his God. Everything else becomes soluble in his warmth. And Colby becomes his son in spirit in the end.'
—Burke Wilkinson, *The New York Times*, 7 February 1954, Section 2, p. 1, col. 7—p. 3, col. 4.

[4] See pp. 150-52 above.

[5] See p. 97 (Lucasta: 'Oh, I'm glad you're here, Eggy! You're such a support') and pp. 113-14.

assurance that, if anybody will find wild birds in London, Colby will (p. 9) to his foresight that Colby will 'be thinking of reading for orders' (p. 132), Eggerson, more than anyone else, understands, and helps us to understand, him.

Mrs. Guzzard too has some understanding of the design. This stems partly from her experience, but more from her function as the *dea ex machina* who unravels the entanglement. As Grover Smith points out, she is 'a kind of fairy godmother'[1] who would 'like to gratify everyone's wishes' (p. 123). But she knows that

> We all of us have to adapt ourselves
> To the wish that is granted. That can be a painful process
> (p. 123).

In other words—and Mrs. Guzzard herself uses the phrase (p. 125)—we have to 'come to terms' with the wish that is granted. For all his talk about accepting the terms life imposes, Sir Claude has not seen its implication. Mrs. Guzzard points out that

> You and I, Sir Claude,
> Had *our* wishes twenty-five years ago;
> But we failed to observe, when we had our wishes,
> That there was a time-limit clause in the contract (p. 134).

Sir Claude is still stunned by the discovery when the curtain falls.

Mrs. Guzzard singles out Lucasta as 'Perhaps . . . the wisest wisher here' (p. 124). But she has not come to this wisdom easily. It is Colby who has helped her to it. Sensing her insecurity, he has pierced the mask she presents to the world in self-defence (pp. 49-50). Lucasta envies *his* sense of security and the 'secret garden' to which he can retire and emerge refreshed, ready to face the world:

> I've no garden.
> I hardly feel that I'm even a person (p. 52).

Colby tries to reassure her that she is 'very much a person' and their growth in mutual understanding is delicately illustrated by the vestige of a lyrical duet (pp. 55-6). Colby's acceptance of her as she is, is helping her to establish herself as a person, so that she may eventually be able to dispense with her social mask, which

[1] *Op. cit.*, p. 228.

has merely hidden her essential nonentity. Therefore, his reaction to the news that she is Sir Claude's daughter, his apparent refusal to go on accepting her as she is, is a profound shock to her:

> I thought you'd come to see me as the real kind of person
> That I want to be. That I know I am.
> That was new to me. I suppose I was flattered.
> And I thought, now, perhaps, if someone else sees me
> As I really am, I might become myself (p. 59).

Now this hope seems to have been shattered and she knows at last that 'there's no escape' (p. 60).

In this moment of bitter disappointment she sees clearly that her previous wishes have been unreasonable, and this 'desolation does begin to make / A better life'.[1] She has already told Colby that B. Kaghan has been able to help her by fostering the impression she tries to create; in fact, he 'half believes in it', in spite of knowing all about her (p. 57). When he enters, most opportunely, she recognizes him as her 'guardian angel' (p. 61), though only with bitter flippancy as yet. Later, when the bitterness has passed away, she sees that, by the contrast of his personality, Colby has helped her 'to appreciate B.' (p. 97) and made her recognize that B. can give her the kind of security she needs (p. 99). Her interpretation of Colby's reaction and the re-adjustment it forced upon her have made her see Colby more clearly as

> something so different from the rest of us
> That we can't judge you (p. 102).

She has been forced also into the recognition of the limits of understanding which is necessary to a satisfactory relationship with anybody (p. 103).

The problem of understanding others is touched upon at many points in the play and a new emphasis is given to the need for trying to understand, which means recognizing the limits of understanding on both sides and making allowances for them. As Lucasta says:

> What's so difficult
> Is to recognise the limits of one's understanding (p. 103).

---

[1] *Antony and Cleopatra*, V. ii. 1–2.

But the effort to understand must be made, and made continuously because

> there's no end to understanding a person.
> All one can do is to understand them better,
> To keep up with them; so that as the other changes
> You can understand the change as soon as it happens,
> Though you couldn't have predicted it (p. 55).

And this effort to understand others, Colby and Lucasta suggest in their vestigial duet, induces change in oneself:

> COLBY
> perhaps what we call change . . .
> LUCASTA
> Is understanding better what one really is.
> And the reason why that comes about, perhaps . . .
> COLBY
> Is, beginning to understand another person (pp. 55-6).

The emphasis is new. In *The Family Reunion*, the gulf between the spiritually dead and the spiritually alive seemed unbridgeable; the emphasis was upon the impossibility of communication between them. In *The Cocktail Party*, the emphasis was still upon the need to accept the limits of understanding. In *The Confidential Clerk* it is upon the need to try to understand, while never assuming that one has succeeded.[1]

Sir Claude observes to Eggerson near the beginning of the play:

> There's always something one's ignorant of
> About anyone, however well one knows them;
> And that may be something of the greatest importance.
> It's when you're sure you understand a person
> That you're liable to make the worst mistake about him
> (pp. 14-15).

But it is one thing to see this and another thing to live by it. Ironically, it is about Colby, whom he is sure he understands

---

[1] This change in emphasis does not necessarily imply a change in Eliot's outlook. On the other hand, the fact that by 1950 he had come to think the hero of *The Family Reunion* 'an insufferable prig' and the mother 'except perhaps for the chauffeur, the only complete human being in the play' (*Poetry and Drama*, p. 31) does suggest a change. See, moreover, pp. 193-5 below.

because he thinks he recognizes in him a repetition of his own experience, that he makes his most painful mistake. The shock of finding out how very little he really understands Colby and the discovery which it leads to of how he has misunderstood his father makes him turn to his wife with a new need and a new sympathy (p. 88). He even begins to share his secret life with her —at least, his telling her of his early ambition to be a potter would seem to be a prelude to this—and the gap between the two parts of his life may be bridged in consequence.

The lesson they both learn from their experience in the play is that 'It's a great mistake . . . / For married people to take anything for granted' (p. 89). Lady Elizabeth in her turn reveals her secret ambition and disillusionment. She tells him how she had wanted 'to inspire an artist' or a poet, and how she had 'thought Tony was a poet':

> I thought I was escaping from a world that I loathed
> In Tony—and then, too late, I discovered
> He belonged to the world I wanted to escape from.[1]

They discover a new sympathy for each other, which may well prove the basis of a fuller married life:

> you and I, Claude, can understand each other,
> No matter how late. And perhaps that will help us
> To understand other people. I hope so (p. 100).

This is a new humility in Lady Elizabeth, who has hitherto tried to impose upon people the role she would prefer them to play. Lucasta tells her:

B. knows you think him common. And so he pretends
To be very common, because he knows you think so.
You gave us our parts. And we've shown that we can play them.[2]

[1] p. 90. Lady Elizabeth seems to have spent her life trying to escape from facts. As a child she tried to escape from the facts of her parentage by making believe that she was 'a foundling—or do I mean "changeling"?' (p. 72). Later she found a rationalization of this wish in the doctrine of reincarnation. After her disillusionment about Tony she believed that she was trying to obey the facts (p. 90). But her constant travel and her temporary enthusiasms for different kinds of esoteric wisdom hardly imply that. Certainly, she seems to have arrived at the convenient conclusion that facts don't matter (cf. p. 87).

[2] p. 100. Lady Elizabeth is like Amy in *The Family Reunion* in this desire to dictate what part everyone shall play. Cf. *The Family Reunion*, pp. 53, 106.

Her new desire to understand them and to accept them as they are will release them from the need to disguise their true selves beneath masks.

Because of the attempt at understanding which his presence has stimulated, Colby's going does not split the family as Harry's does; on the contrary, it reinforces the family solidarity, as was beautifully underlined by the drawing together of the characters at the end of Mr. Martin Browne's production:

> LADY ELIZABETH
> Claude, we've got to try to understand our children.
> KAGHAN
> And we should like to understand *you* . . .
>
> . . . .
>
> You know, Claude, both Lucasta and I
> Would like to mean something to you . . . if you'd let us;
> And we'd take the responsibility of meaning it.[1]

In *The Cocktail Party* Celia's death causes the Chamberlaynes and Peter Quilpe to feel a new bond of fellowship, but the implications are not illustrated in the play itself so well as here.

Perhaps because the exceptional person is not so exceptional as in the previous plays, his influence is more immediately and obviously fruitful. His destiny is not so unusual as, and therefore more intelligible than, that of Thomas or Harry or Celia and because there is greater understanding of it, its immediate efficacy is greater. The immediate efficacy of Harry's sacrifice is limited by the fact that most of the others completely fail to understand him and even though he departs to expiate the sin of his family, the immediate consequence is so destructive that it throws this out of perspective. In *The Confidential Clerk* the blow is softened in many ways. Colby is not really a member of this family at all, we discover, and as for his mother, it is she who has renounced the relationship and holds fast to her decision (p. 126).

In any case, Mrs. Guzzard is a somewhat depersonalized figure whose strength of character repels our sympathy. Sir Claude says that she is always punctual and that, if he was not punctual in his

---

[1] p. 135. B., lately revealed as Barnabas, 'the son of consolation', is living up to his name.

visits to her house, she always mentioned it (p. 105). Lucasta says that she 'looks rather formidable' (p. 105). She seems to be snobbish:

> I understood the child was very well connected:
> Otherwise, I should not have taken him (p. 111).

She has stifled her motherly feelings for the good of her child and, with tragic irony, become less than human in doing so. Eliot is careful not to upset the balance of sympathy, as he thinks he did in *The Family Reunion*.

Similarly, in the construction of the play we see Eliot learning from what he has come to consider mistakes in his earlier plays. He has come to feel that the last Act of *The Cocktail Party* is in danger of having the effect of an epilogue and he is 'determined to do something different . . . in this respect'.[1] In *The Confidential Clerk*, the increased skill in construction is marked. He begins cautiously and ekes out his material. Whereas in *The Cocktail Party* the curtain rises on an assemblage of most of the characters, he reverts here to the time-honoured practice of a preliminary duologue, in which the situation is explained. Apart from the last Act, in fact, most of the play is duologue. Moreover, the characters are introduced slowly, one at a time. For the most part the contrivance goes unnoticed in the theatre, and it is, indeed, an acceptable part of theatrical technique so long as it does not draw attention to itself. Seven lines after Colby enters, Sir Claude goes out, thus enabling him to talk more freely with Eggerson and elicit more information about Lady Elizabeth. This exit, however, has been prepared before Colby's entrance by talk of a telephone call (p. 15). B. Kaghan's panache allows him to introduce himself with a theatrical flourish—'Enter B. Kaghan' (p. 18) —but he has really come on ahead of Lucasta to prepare her entrance. Lady Elizabeth's entrance is probably one of the most carefully prepared in the history of drama. Sir Claude has talked about her to Eggerson: Eggerson has talked about her to Colby: Lucasta has talked about her—all of them arousing our curiosity— and when she arrives unexpectedly, she causes consternation. Even now, she doesn't enter immediately and her 'words off stage are not intended to be heard distinctly by an audience in the

---

[1] *Poetry and Drama*, p. 32 (*On Poetry and Poets*, p. 85).

theatre', which further intensifies curiosity. There is a running commentary on her actions and as she enters she is greeted simultaneously by Eggerson and Sir Claude. She quickly proceeds to outstrip all expectations by 'recognizing' Colby as 'the young man [she] interviewed' and recommended to Sir Claude (pp. 30–3). The comedy is further enhanced by her criticizing Sir Claude for his bad memory (p. 33). Eliot has skilfully built up his first climax and when Lady Elizabeth's short scene is over he feels he can afford to settle down to a duologue for the rest of Act One, a duologue in which he begins to explore the profounder implications of the situation.

Act Two begins with another profoundly exploratory duologue, in which we get nearer the level of intensity usually associated with poetry. Gradually, the other characters are drawn into the complication which begins with the revelation that Lucasta is Sir Claude's daughter, and the entanglement reaches its climax when Lady Elizabeth comes to believe that Colby is *her* son.[1] Thus Act Three begins with a great deal to unravel, and it is not unravelled without a good deal of further complication, as in some of the comedies of Terence. The re-allocation of parents and children is farcical in its complexity. There is no danger that Act Three will seem an epilogue. The mounting entanglement reaches its peak here. But this has not been achieved without a certain thinness in the opening scenes of the play. The beginning of the play is much flatter than the beginning of *The Cocktail Party*, which has tremendous comic verve.

The same combination of technical smoothness and thinness of substance is to be seen in several aspects of the play. Mr. Martin Browne considers it a better play than *The Cocktail Party*

'because the things he [Eliot] sets out to say are all said *in* the lives of the characters, characters involved in dramatic action. There are no onlookers—no Alex or Julia or Reilly. Even Eggerson, the clerk himself, is involved by his final curtain acquisition of Colby as his spiritual son.' [2]

[1] As in the last Act of *The Cocktail Party*, Eliot uses a delayed revelation in working up to his climax (pp. 75–6).

[2] Burke Wilkinson, *The New York Times*, 7 February, 1954, Section 2, p. 1, col. 6.

Moreover, there is no schematism such as we noticed in the earlier plays. As Miss Helen Gardner pointed out in a review so penetrating that I cannot forbear to quote at length from it:

'*The Confidential Clerk* has a unity which Mr. Eliot has not achieved before in a play. No single one of the characters has a monopoly of wisdom or virtue, and no character exists simply to be despised or guyed. Each in his or her own way has glimpses of the truth and each is capable of suffering, because capable of love . . . .

'[The] gulf that in Mr. Eliot's earlier plays separated the heroes from their fellows does not yawn in *The Confidential Clerk*. In *The Family Reunion* Harry and Agatha hardly seemed to belong to the same species as the uncles and aunts of the chorus. Even in *The Cocktail Party*, where different ways of salvation were shown, the death of Celia and the domestic felicity of Edward and Lavinia were too far apart for either to seem true; each infected the other with a kind of unreality. The obscurely faithful Eggerson is a better touchstone in the world of comedy than the romantically conceived Celia, presenting, quite unconsciously, a stronger challenge to our conception of the good life.' [1]

But the obverse of this quality of unity is the absence of any compelling experience. Miss Gardner makes this point also:

'In *The Cocktail Party* the divine broke into the pattern of human lives in the form of the heroic, and the heroic is, as Von Hügel said, the most easily recognisable manifestation of the supernatural. It is not difficult to respond with admiration to the mystic's search for union and the martyr's absolute rejection of what this life has to offer. But to be asked to find a test of the values by which we live in Mr. Eggerson, pottering about in his garden in Joshua Park, performing commissions for Mrs. E. at the draper's, and finding everyone has a heart of gold, is another matter. Mr. Eggerson never opens his mouth without a cliché. . . . .

'For a poet to place such a character at the centre of his play is the strongest possible indication that "the poetry does not matter".

[1] Helen Gardner, *The New Statesman and Nation*, 20 March, 1954, p. 373, col. 2, and p. 374, col. 1.

What the author has to say here is said in the whole design of his plot, in the behaviour of all the characters to each other. The play stands or falls by our acceptance of the characters and not by any particular scenes or passages of deep significance or high poetic beauty. This is not to say that the play is not finely written and that those characters who properly can do so do not express themselves with an exquisite precision. But whatever message the play holds is diffused over the whole.

'As I see the play, judgment of Mr. Eliot's achievement must depend on our judgment of his characterisation, on whether we believe in his characters and whether we care about them. The queer family party we are left with at the end, Sir Claude, Lady Elizabeth, Lucasta, and B. Kaghan, both convince the imagination, I think, and touch the heart. The difficulty lies in Colby and Mr. Eggerson. For Colby has very little character and Mr. Eggerson perhaps too much. . . . The theatre exaggerates, and in the glare of the footlights Eggerson may come out as too little a person and too much a character part. In these two roles Mr. Eliot has asked a great deal of his actors.'[1]

Without agreeing that 'judgment of Mr. Eliot's achievement must depend on our judgment of his characterisation'—for characterization is, in poetic drama, but one aspect of the poetic vision—I would agree that the play is weakened by the tameness of the key characters, 'the only *developed* Christian in the play' and the spiritually elect.

In the character of Eggerson, Eliot seems to be making the minimal claim for the influence of the Christian in the contemporary world, which may be good moral strategy, but is hardly good dramatic strategy. In Colby, as William Arrowsmith observes, he faces the difficult task of creating 'a character who must stand for the incipiently perfect Christian life', who is, as Mr. Arrowsmith puts it, a 'blueprint' of a Christian.[2] His only spiritual reaction in the play is a negative one, a reaction against the kind of compromise proposed by Sir Claude. He drifts until the chance of fulfilment is offered. It is a deeply truthful portrait

[1] Helen Gardner, *The New Statesman and Nation*, 20 March, 1954, pp. 373–4.
[2] *The Hudson Review*, VII (1954), p. 294.

of a sensitive nature, but hardly a compelling dramatic figure.[1] His experience lacks the urgency of Harry's or Celia's.

With this diminution of the intensity of religious experience, poetry tends also to disappear. But Eliot has allowed for this. He is here sacrificing poetry of the parts in an attempt to discover what poetry of the whole is. His path of exploration seems to have been towards the lowest common multiple of poetry and drama. It is as if he has sought, by reducing poetry to a minimum, to discover the essential and distinctive quality it can bring to drama, to find, so to speak, the level of union between poetry and drama.

The poetry is now at its most easily conversational, serving for the most part just to give a certain elegance and precision, and deepening only occasionally to the expression of innermost thoughts and feelings. The play has a poetic centre—the Euripidean plot transfigured by the Christian revelation of the Divine Father—but it has an almost completely naturalistic surface, apart from the intrusion of the *dea ex machina* in the person of Mrs. Guzzard, whose ability to grant the wishes of the other characters, although it has a naturalistic basis, is oracular in tone.[2] And it is probably necessary that some part of the symbolic core shall obtrude above the surface if the deeper significance is not to go completely unregarded. But even here there is no deliberate puzzlement, no disruption of the surface meaning. The final effect of a performance is, as a reviewer of the book said, that the audience

'may be left wondering what it is all really about, but this uncertainty evidently is of the kind that teases without irritating the mind. There are possible meanings that might become clearer on a second viewing. Meanwhile, the comedy on the stage arouses at every turn a curiosity which it satisfies with neat comic dexterity.'[3]

[1] Cf. C. L. Barber in the third edition of F. O. Matthiessen's *The Achievement of T. S. Eliot*, p. 223:
'It is a triumph to have been able to create him [Colby] in the negating role he has to play without his being priggish; Eliot has done it by creating a young man who has the diffidence, not of weakness, but of exceptional power that has not yet found itself, that is incommensurate with his situation.'

[2] For the rest, there is the merest suggestion of a 'lyrical duet' (pp. 55–6) and the concept of guardianship is reduced to something like a fashionable figure of speech (p. 61).

[3] *The Times Literary Supplement*, 19 March, 1954, p. 180.

By a deliberate thinning of his material, Eliot has achieved mechanical smoothness. Emphasis has been put upon the development of the plot and the experience of the group rather than upon the experience of the individual and his spiritual evolution. Towards the end of the second act Colby goes numb (p. 81), and remains so for most of the remainder of the play. To some extent, he merges into a total pattern of the kind which distinguishes poetic drama, but that pattern does not emerge with the clarity which we observed in *Murder in the Cathedral* and *The Cocktail Party*. It remains shadowy. *The Confidential Clerk* does belong to the realm of poetic drama, if only by the fineness with which it delineates feeling, but perhaps it is only just across the border from prose.

Chapter Seven

Plays in a Contemporary Setting—IV
'The Elder Statesman' (1958)

EVERY new work by Eliot makes it necessary for us to adjust our view of the totality of his work. Themes and situations and images in the earlier work are apt to take on a new significance, and the relationship between the works often becomes clearer. So, with the addition of *The Elder Statesman*, the plays fall into a new pattern. The sense of the un-heroic dimensions of our age which has been strong in Eliot from the time of *Prufrock* led him away from tragedy for a time; yet he has come back, in his latest play, to the borders of the tragic realm, has come back, in fact, to the region of melodrama, into which he made a foray in *Sweeney Agonistes*, and, as in that first dramatic essay, the melodrama is tempered with an admixture of comedy. The first major play was a tragedy, though a Christian tragedy, which, in the larger pattern of Providence, may be seen as a Divine Comedy. The first of the plays in a contemporary setting was, in effect, an attempt to modernize a Greek tragedy without softening the tragic outlines. In *The Cocktail Party*, however, he turned tragi-comedy into something much nearer comedy; the tragic element which he introduced—the death of Celia—is merely reported and takes its place within the comic pattern. He went on, in *The Confidential Clerk*, to render melo-drama, a lower form of tragedy, into something very like farce, a lower form of comedy. With *The Elder Statesman* he returns to the sterner form of Greek tragedy—from Aeschylus he jumped to Euripides, and now he turns back to Sophocles, the middle member of the great triad of Greek tragic writers—but he reduces it to something much nearer melodrama. And just as the almost farcical *The Confidential Clerk* forms a pendant to the comic *The Cocktail Party*, so the melodramatic *The Elder Statesman* forms a pendant to the tragic *The Family Reunion*.

'Harry's career needs to be completed by an *Orestes* or an *Oedipus at Colonos*,' wrote Eliot in a letter to Mr. E. Martin Browne about *The Family Reunion*.[1] And it is to the final play of Sophocles that he has turned for the basic pattern of his latest play. Clearly, however, Lord Claverton is not Harry grown old, doubtful though Harry's fate may be. Indeed, Lord Claverton has yet to turn and face his ghosts when the play begins. His is an experience that parallels Harry's—it is in the place where he might least expect to encounter them that the ghosts assail him—but does not complement it.

In *Oedipus the King*, the earlier of the two plays by Sophocles dealing with Oedipus, the hero, having years before struck down and killed, without knowing that it was his father and the King of Thebes, an old man who tried to push him off the road, and having gone on in his ignorance to marry his mother and become ruler of Thebes, now seeks to rid the land of a plague sent by the gods. The Delphic Oracle reveals that the affliction will only be lifted when the slayer of the previous king has been driven from the land. Oedipus undertakes to track down the guilty man and is gradually forced to realize that it is he. Jocasta, his wife and mother, glimpses the truth before he does, goes indoors and hangs herself. When he in turn perceives the terrible chain of events, he blinds himself in passionate acknowledgment of his failure to see truly. At the end of the play he goes off into the exile he has ordained for himself.

In *Oedipus at Colonus*, the exiled king, now grown old, comes to Colonus near Athens, to a grove sacred to the Erinyes or Furies, where they are worshipped under the propitiatory title of Eumenides or Kindly Ones. (It will be recalled that their transformation is dramatized at the end of the *Oresteia*, upon which *The Family Reunion* is based.) Led by his daughter Antigone,

[1] Quoted by F. O. Matthiessen, Third Edition, p. 168.

Oedipus takes refuge in the grove and appeals to Theseus, King of Athens, for protection. From a prophecy made by Apollo, Oedipus has recognized the region in which he is to die and upon which his death will bring a blessing. However, the Oracle has also pronounced that, to ensure the welfare of Thebes, Oedipus must be buried in Theban soil. A deputation from Thebes soon comes to persuade him to return to his homeland and eventually resorts to force, but with the help of Theseus and the Athenians he is successful in his resistance. Next, his son Polyneices, who, having quarrelled with his brother and been driven into exile, is now about to attack Thebes, comes to ask his father's blessing on the venture. Bitterly alienated by his son's past treatment of him, Oedipus curses him instead. No sooner has Polyneices left than thunder from Olympus announces to Oedipus the hour of his death, and, needing guidance no longer, he leads the way to the place where, having dismissed all but Theseus, he suddenly disappears, leaving behind only his blessing on the land. His final word to his daughters might serve as an epigraph to Eliot's play:

> one word
> Makes all those difficulties disappear:
> That word is love.[1]

Like Oedipus, the exiled king, Lord Claverton, the retired statesman of Eliot's play, reaches the place which he comes to recognize as his last resting place. In Sophocles, as we have seen, the recognition springs from supernatural knowledge. In Eliot the explicitly supernatural is reduced to the more naturalistic level of the intuitive.[2] Like Oedipus too, Lord Claverton is attended by a daughter and visited by a son who is in trouble and wants his help and with whom he has a scene of bitter recrimination.[3] Unlike Oedipus, however, he is haunted by ghosts of the past.

---

[1] Sophocles, *Oedipus at Colonus*, An English Version by Robert Fitzgerald (Harcourt, Brace and Co., New York, 1941), p. 130 (ll. 1615 ff. in the Greek).

[2] *The Elder Statesman* (Faber and Faber, London, 1959), pp. 82, 108.

[3] As in Sophocles, his sister makes a plea for him. Eliot's transformation of Polyneices is reminiscent of Anouilh's in *Antigone*, where Creon describes him as a ne'er-do-well, gambling, driving fast cars, spending money as fast as he can get his hands on it, and generally causing his father great pain (Editions de la Table Ronde, Paris, 1946, p. 90). But, granted the pattern of Eliot's reworking of the story, Polyneices would have to become this sort of character.

The Erinyes of Sophocles are easily propitiated; Eliot's avenging Furies seem almost implacable. Sophocles clearly considers Oedipus innocent of guilt in having killed his father and married his mother. Indeed, he seems to have written this play to make his own view clear. Oedipus repeatedly justifies himself as having erred in ignorance, and the approval of the gods is manifested in his apotheosis.[1] Eliot's play has a different ethos. Man has free will and does not sin 'by a divine thrusting on'.[2] The sins of Oedipus are so reduced as to be hardly recognizable. Instead of killing his father for refusing to yield the right of way at a crossroads, Lord Claverton has run over an old man who was already dead. Instead of marrying his mother, he has taken a woman as his mistress and then refused to marry her.[3] Yet he is nagged by guilt, whereas Oedipus is not, because he interprets these incidents as examples of moral cowardice in himself, of refusal to face the consequences of his actions. When he finally brings himself to accept the responsibility for his influence on others, he is able to go serenely to his death, as Oedipus does, and achieve his own kind of apotheosis, leaving a blessing upon his daughter and her husband-to-be.

There is a more general likeness to *Oedipus at Colonus*. Just as Sophocles takes up again one of his greatest subjects, so in *The Elder Statesman* Eliot resumes many of the themes and a few of the situations of his earlier work. The parallel with *The Family Reunion*—a man fleeing from ghosts and the spiritual reality they represent has to turn and face them and accept that reality before he can find peace[4]—has already been noted. We have already remarked also on the resemblance to *Sweeney Agonistes* in the mixture of melodrama and comedy. It is not, however, the mix-

---

[1] *Oedipus at Colonus*, ll. 270-88, 437-9, 521—48, 962-1002, 1565-7.

[2] *King Lear*, I. ii. 118.

[3] A closer reminiscence of Sophocles is Lord Claverton's account of his marriage:

> We never understood each other.
> And so we lived, with a deep silence between us,
> And she died silently. She had nothing to say (p. 85).

This translates into terms of normal life the tremendous poignancy of the death of Jocasta, who, when she anticipates Oedipus in the realization of the truth, leaves the stage without telling him of her discovery and hangs herself.

[4] Ghosts: pp. 22, 85-6, 89. Flight from reality: pp. 70, 79.

ture as before. The extravagant humour and the social satire are tempered to the more elegant level of society and the melodrama no longer leans to the grotesque; in short, it is not an Aristophanic melodrama. Turning to the other plays, we detect a faint anticipation in *Murder in the Cathedral*, where in the days before his death a man reviews his past and finds spiritual wholeness. The links with the more recent plays are firmer and more numerous. The danger of imposing one's will on others, demonstrated in Amy, Sir Claude and Lady Elizabeth, is seen again in Lord Claverton.[1] Moreover, like Edward and Lavinia, like Lucasta and B. Kaghan, he has been hiding his true self beneath a mask.[2] The problem of change, which bulked so large in *The Cocktail Party*, is given a new dimension (pp. 13, 29). But, as one would expect, the strongest links are with the play nearest in time, *The Confidential Clerk*. The problem of living in two worlds is referred to early in the play,[3] and the central theme of the earlier play is taken up and developed in a new way; the question of inheritance is focused upon the repetition by a son of the father's mistakes.[4] Finally, Mrs Carghill seems to have a trick or two of Lady Elizabeth's speech. The feathery-minded humour of

> I actually *liked* to believe
> That I was a foundling—or do I mean 'changeling'?

becomes keenly pointed in

> 'That man is hollow'. That's what she [Effie] said.
> Or did she say 'yellow'? [5]

There are many links with the poems too, principally with those

---

[1] See particularly pp. 68, 105. Cf. *The Family Reunion*, pp. 53, 106; *The Cocktail Party*, p. 99; and *The Confidential Clerk*, p. 100.

[2] pp. 16, 34, 35, 56, 83–4, and 29 (Gomez). The idea of the social mask is found early in Eliot's work, e.g. *The Love Song of J. Alfred Prufrock*:
> There will be time, there will be time
> To prepare a face to meet the faces that you meet
> *(Collected Poems*, p. 12)*
and 'the masquerades / That time resumes' of *Preludes*, II (ibid., p. 21) and the 'deliberate disguises' of *The Hollow Men* (ibid., p. 88).

[3] pp. 13–14, 16–17.

[4] Inheritance: pp. 68–71, 72–3. Repetition of mistakes: 34, 60–1, 69–70, 73, 94, 96–7.

[5] *The Confidential Clerk*, p. 72; *The Elder Statesman*, p. 51.

which dramatize or contemplate old age. Throughout his career, Eliot has been 'much possessed' with age. In the early poems old men are frequent *personae*, serving in *Gerontion* and *The Waste Land* as convenient symbols of the culture of Western Europe grown old and decrepit and in *The Journey of the Magi* and *A Song for Simeon* as convenient illustrations of the pain involved in the death of the 'old man' and the birth of the 'new' of Christian metaphor as well as of the particular difficulty in old age of the adjustment demanded by spiritual awakening. The relevance of the latter predicament to *The Elder Statesman* is self-evident. It is, however, the meditations on old age in the later poems that point most directly to the play. The 'familiar compound ghost' whom Eliot meets in the firewatching episode of *Little Gidding* discloses 'the gifts reserved for age / To set a crown upon your lifetime's effort', the last of them being

> the rending pain of re-enactment
> Of all that you have done, and been; the shame
> Of motives late revealed, and the awareness
> Of things ill done and done to others' harm
> Which once you took for exercise of virtue.
> Then fools' approval stings, and honour stains.
> From wrong to wrong the exasperated spirit
> Proceeds, unless restored by that refining fire
> Where you must move in measure, like a dancer.[1]

Something very much like this is the experience of 'the elder statesman'. He has to undergo 'the rending pain of re-enactment' and he proceeds 'From wrong to wrong'—

> The mistaken attempts to correct mistakes
> By methods which proved to be equally mistaken (p. 99)—

until he is 'restored by that refining fire', which is the fire of Purgatory, the fire of the Divine Love.

The 'awareness / Of things ill done' is forced upon Lord Claverton by the visit of Gomez and the chance meeting with Mrs. Carghill. He comes to recognize that he has corrupted the one and betrayed the other. He is responsible for the thwarting of a prime natural instinct in Gomez. 'I have a gift for friendship,'

---

[1] *Four Quartets*, pp. 39–40. Cf. pp. 17–18, 22–3.

Gomez tells him (p. 33), and Dick Ferry was the friend that the soul of Fred Culverwell, in Hamlet's phrase, 'seal'd . . . for herself.' The reference to Polonius' precept about friendship—

> Those friends thou hast, and their adoption tried,
> Grapple them to thy soul with hoops of steel[1]—

makes this clear (p. 31). Where feeling is strong, the sophisticate can express it only obliquely, and a half-mocking use of second-hand rhetoric serves the purpose. With Gomez, of course, there is, too, an overtone of bitter cynicism born of betrayal, but this does not detract from—if anything it poignantly reinforces—the sincerity of the original emotion. For him, the 'bond' has been constricted as it has twisted; what he sees as betrayal draws him closer to his 'friend' even while it distorts the emotion of friendship. This friendship has indirectly robbed him of all other friendships; it made him the man on whom all his other friends and acquaintance turned their backs. He has made a new life in another country and has taken another name, this change of name being the outward symbol of an attempt to create a new self.[2] But this new self is not real because it has no connection with his earlier self; it is built on no foundation. To become a real person again, he needs to establish contact with someone who can serve as a link between the two selves, and no one can do this more effectively than the man who was responsible for this division of selves in the first place: 'I need you, Dick, to give me reality!' (p. 30). Fred Culverwell has, in this sense, died and become a ghost. At first, Lord Claverton disclaims all responsibility: 'You were a free moral agent . . .'[3] But he discovers eventually that this is not the way to escape his ghosts.

Another claim from the past soon comes to reinforce the claim of Fred Culverwell. Mrs. Carghill, who, as Maisie Montjoy, was once his mistress, returns to haunt him:

> you touched my soul—
> Pawed it, perhaps, and the touch still lingers.
> And I've touched yours.
> It's frightening to think that we're still together
> And more frightening to think that we may *always* be together
> (p. 57).

[1] *Hamlet*, I. iii. 62-3.   [2] p. 29. Cf. pp. 52, 68, 96.   [3] p. 39. Cf. p. 32

Mrs. Carghill has what for Lord Claverton is the uncomfortable Christian conception of man and woman becoming the inseparable unity of 'one flesh' which persists beyond the grave. Again he denies the claim: 'We'd settled our account. / What harm was done?' (p. 53). His conscience is clear, he affirms (p. 55). But we soon gather that it is not quite at ease. When Monica tells him that Michael has been in trouble again, he immediately suspects a repetition of his own misdeeds.[1]

The healing of his conscience, however, will be a complicated process. He cannot make reparation to these people, because he cannot turn back the clock and make them what they were. He can find absolution only in a roundabout way. He is to find it eventually in confessing to his daughter, but there is a barrier to be overcome first. His suppression of the sense of guilt has corrupted him and made his relations with his family a sham.

In evading his guilt, Lord Claverton has abnegated his real self, the sinning self. Pointing the contrast between them, Gomez observes:

> You've changed your name twice—by easy stages,
> And each step was merely a step up the ladder,
> So you weren't aware of becoming a different person:
> But where *I* changed my name, there was no social ladder.
> It was jumping a gap—and you can't jump back again.
> I parted from myself by a sudden effort,
> You, so slowly and sweetly, that you've never woken up
> To the fact that Dick Ferry died long ago (p. 29).

Consciously or unconsciously, Lord Claverton has become a 'hollow man', a mere façade, a mask without a face (pp. 16–17). Unless the innermost self has communion with another spirit, it will atrophy. Lord Claverton's mask has cut off all genuine communication with his wife and children. He has found himself 'at home' only in the public world, the world of politics, where everyone else wears a mask and will be less liable to notice his and where genuine communication is so rare as not to be missed. In the last resort, however, his attempt to compensate for failure in his private world by success in the public world has proved

---

[1] pp. 60–1. Cf. pp. 69–70.

abortive (pp. 21, 35). He has been thrown back upon himself
and the terrible isolation of his private world (pp. 15–16), where
all is sham except the love of and for his daughter, and even
this relationship is blighted by his fundamental evasion. Having
failed to get into touch with his children in the frank interchange
of love, he has attempted to dominate them, to impose his own
pattern upon them.

The Eliot of *East Coker* (1940) enjoins:

> Do not let me hear
> Of the wisdom of old men, but rather of their folly,
> Their fear of fear and frenzy, their fear of possession,
> Of belonging to another, or to others, or to God.[1]

Fearing to be possessed by others, because self-surrender means
the giving of all, the telling of all, Lord Claverton has distorted
the impulse of love in himself into possessiveness. The less we give
to others, the more we demand of them. When, near the end of
the play, Lord Claverton has 'had the illumination / Of knowing
what love is', he comes to understand the motive of his possessiveness:

> Why did I always want to dominate my children?
> Why did I mark out a narrow path for Michael?
> Because I wanted to perpetuate myself in him.
> Why did I want to keep you to myself, Monica?
> Because I wanted you to give your life to adoring
> The man that I pretended to myself that I was,
> So that I could believe in my own pretences.[2]

Monica's strength of character and her own experience of love
for Charles have allowed her to withstand the dangers of this
domination, but Michael's weaker character has been under-
mined. Even if Lord Claverton has been conscious before this
of the motive of his treatment of Michael, the irony of the outcome has been lost on him. He has merely succeeded in making

---

[1] *Four Quartets*, p. 18. This fear of losing one's self-possession is not peculiar
to old men, of course; it is the motivation of the young man's behaviour in
Portrait of a Lady. (Cf. *Collected Poems*, pp. 18, 19.)

[2] p. 105. Earlier testimony to his possessiveness occurs on pp. 11 and 14.

Michael repeat his own mistakes. Gomez points out to his old friend that

> He's followed your undergraduate career
> Without the protection of that prudent devil
> Of yours, to tell him not to go too far.[1]

And, as if to rub the parallel in, Mrs. Carghill finds Michael 'the image' of what his father was when she knew him (pp. 72–3). The great difference is that, as Gomez indicates, Michael is weaker than his father. He lacks the restraining influence of the 'prudent devil' which prevented his father from sinning unreservedly and becoming aware of his sin as sin. The greater sinner is more liable to have a sudden revulsion from sin than the mild sinner and in this revulsion to find contrition. Michael's weakness might be his salvation, if he did not have in Gomez 'a custodian of [his] morals' who will have the same influence on him that his father had on Fred Culverwell (p. 94). It is not surprising that Michael has found his inheritance a burden:

> I was just your son—that is to say,
> A kind of prolongation of your existence,
> A representative carrying on business in your absence (p. 68).

His solution to the frustration of life in his father's shadow is to go abroad where he can 'be somebody on [his] own account' (p. 67). He might even, he says, take a different name. For him, as for his father and Gomez, this would symbolize an attempt to cut adrift from the earlier self, to escape, in effect, from one's essential identity. He will become 'a fugitive from reality', his father warns him:

> Those who flee from their past will always lose the race.
> I know this from experience. When you reach your goal,
> Your imagined paradise of success and grandeur,
> You will find your past failures waiting there to greet you (p. 70).

But experience cannot be passed on, and there is between Michael and his father none of the love or respect which might make him take his father's word for it. In his passion for domination, Lord

[1] p. 34. The 'prudent devil' is previously referred to on p. 32.

Claverton has rejected his son's love; love cannot develop unless there is acceptance of the other person in his own right and not as an image of one's own creation or a projection of oneself. Just as he has thwarted the 'gift of friendship' in Gomez and abused the 'capacity for loving'—slight though it may have been—in Mrs. Carghill, so he has denied his own son's capacity for family affection (p. 72).

Coming on top of the reminders of his earlier failures, the bitter realization of what he has done to his son shocks Lord Claverton into a re-evaluation of himself:

> Do I understand the meaning
> Of the lesson I would teach? Come, I'll start to learn again.
> Michael and I shall go to school together.
> We'll sit side by side at little desks
> And suffer the same humiliations
> At the hands of the same master (p. 79).

He has begun to acquire what Eliot calls in *East Coker* 'The only wisdom we can hope to acquire', 'the wisdom of humility'.[1]

Conscience has never quite died in him, but it has been distorted into a passion for self-justification:

> Some dissatisfaction
> With myself, I suspect, very deep within myself
> Has impelled me all my life to find justification
> Not so much to the world—first of all to myself (p. 44).

In the case of Gomez and Mrs. Carghill, he might still find reason for placating his conscience, for justifying himself to himself. They have both achieved more worldly success as a result of their relations with him than they would otherwise have done (p. 86). But this, ironically, is a symptom of their deterioration as human beings. Lord Claverton comes to admit his responsibility for both eventualities, and in accepting responsibility he at last faces his ghosts of the three people who 'died' as a result of his misdeeds—Freddy Culverwell, Maisie Batterson, and Dick Ferry, his earlier self, 'people with good in them' (p. 87) which he helped to stifle. He recognizes that he has been ignoring the implications of

---

[1] *Four Quartets*, p. 18.

his behaviour. What, he now asks himself, did he make of Freddy's admiration for himself?

> How easily we ignore the fact that those who admire us
> Will imitate our vices as well as our virtues—
> Or whatever the qualities for which they did admire us!
> And that again may nourish the faults that they were born with.
> And Maisie loved me, with whatever capacity
> For loving she had—self-centred and foolish—
> But we should respect love always when we meet it;
> Even when it's vain and selfish, we must not abuse it (p. 87).

By acknowledging his failure and facing up to the reality of his guilt, he makes contact with reality again, and the real self, the self which sinned, can revive:

> I see myself emerging
> From my spectral existence into something like reality.[1]

And not only can the real self revive; it can find absolution.

The decisive step 'towards [his] freedom' (p. 89) consists in his confession to the one person he really loves, Monica. Preparing the way for this confession and pointing its significance, he says:

> If a man has one person, just one in his life,
> To whom he is willing to confess everything . . .
> Then he loves that person, and his love will save him (p. 83).

Absolution will come through love as the manifestation and operation of the Divine in ordinary life. However, as he goes on to explain, Lord Claverton's particular difficulty is that he has so long played a part that he finds it hard to drop the pretence, especially before Monica, who has, he fears, so idolized him in the part he has played that disillusionment will kill her love. But this is a risk which he must and which, with her reassurance, he does take. And thus he achieves his freedom:

> I've been freed from the self that pretends to be someone;
> And in becoming no one, I begin to live.
> It is worth while dying, to find out what life is (p. 106).

---

[1] p. 85. Cf. p. 89.

He has become an explorer such as Eliot says old men should be:

> Old men ought to be explorers
> Here and there does not matter
> We must be still and still moving
> Into another intensity
> For a further union, a deeper communion. . . .[1]

Having found this spirit of acceptance and peace, Lord Claverton can impart it to others, and not by words alone, for

> "on whatever sphere of being
> The mind of a man may be intent
> At the time of death"—that is the one action
> (And the time of death is every moment)
> Which shall fructify in the lives of others.[2]

His serenity and sense of spiritual reality will strengthen the spiritual life of Monica and Charles. But it is not only by his attitude at the moment before death that Lord Claverton can influence his daughter:

> what the dead had no speech for, when living,
> They can tell you, being dead: the communication
> Of the dead is tongued with fire beyond the language of the
> living.[3]

So, at the end of the play, Monica knows of his death intuitively:

> In becoming no one, he has become himself.
> He is only my father now, and Michael's.

[1] *Four Quartets*, pp. 22–3.

[2] *Ibid.*, p. 31. The quotation is from the *Bhagavad-Gita*, viii. 6. The previous section is also relevant to *The Elder Statesman*. The whole passage, in which Krishna, an incarnation of the Divine, is giving instruction in the manner of achieving ultimate reality, runs thus:

'At the hour of death, when a man leaves his body, he must depart with his consciousness absorbed in me. Then he will be united with me. Be certain of that. Whatever a man remembers at the last, when he is leaving the body, will be realized by him in the hereafter. . . .'

—*Bhagavad-Gita*, translated by Swami Prabhavananda and Christopher Isherwood, Phoenix House, London, 1947, p. 95. This would seem to be the explanation of the apotheosis of Lord Claverton.

[3] *Four Quartets*, p. 36.

And I am happy. Isn't it strange, Charles,
To be happy at this moment?
                    CHARLES
         It is not at all strange.
The dead has poured out a blessing on the living (p. 108).

Perhaps the most striking difference between *The Elder States-man* and the earlier plays is that, apart possibly from this ending, there is no suggestion that the hero has an exceptional spiritual destiny. The tendency in the course of the plays for the exceptional person to be pushed further and further from the centre of the picture here reaches its logical conclusion. There is in fact for the first time no discovery of a special election and, as in *The Confidential Clerk*, no one expiates the sins of others. Each man expiates his own sins. The son will have to work out his own salvation, just like his father. The sins, moreover, in this play are misdemeanours of youth such as are not uncommon in ordinary life. Many people, perhaps most people, would dismiss them. Lord Claverton himself recognizes that they may seem trivial:

> You think that I suffer from a morbid conscience,
> From brooding over faults I might well have forgotten.
> You think that I'm sickening when I'm just recovering!
> It's hard to make other people realise
> The magnitude of things that appear to them petty;
> It's harder to confess the sin that no one believes in
> Than the crime that everyone can appreciate.
> For the crime is in relation to the law
> And the sin is in relation to the sinner.[1]

Eliot seems to be indicating that the stirring of the spirit can come from quite ordinary incidents. What is more, the hero finds his salvation not by rejection of ordinary, family life, but by puri-

---

[1] pp. 89–90. Cf. *Four Quartets*, pp. 20–1:
> Our only health is the disease
> If we obey the dying nurse
> Whose constant care is not to please
> But to remind of our, and Adam's curse,
> And that, to be restored, our sickness must grow worse.

fication of his life within the family. There is, in fact, a new emphasis upon the efficacy of love, especially of

> love within a family, love that's lived in
> But not looked at, love within the light of which
> All else is seen, the love within which
> All other love finds speech (p. 72).

This new emphasis is the culmination of a long development, the beginnings of which we can see in the *Four Quartets*. In *Burnt Norton* (1935), which originated, I understand, in fragments left over from the writing of *Murder in the Cathedral*, the chief value of life inheres in the moment of illumination, the moment in the rose-garden. For those who have experienced it,

> Ridiculous the waste sad time
> Stretching before and after.[1]

This is the experience dramatized in *The Family Reunion* (1939). The insight Harry gains in the moment of communion with Agatha leads him away from the family, away from normal love. In *East Coker* (1940) the poet records a change in his outlook:

> As we grow older
> The world becomes stranger, the pattern more complicated
> Of dead and living. Not the intense moment
> Isolated, with no before and after,
> But a lifetime burning in every moment
> And not the lifetime of one man only
> But of old stones that cannot be deciphered.
> There is a time for the evening under starlight,
> A time for the evening under lamplight
> (The evening with the photograph album).[2]

The continuum between 'the intense moment / Isolated' and the rest of life is emphasized, and a value is found in cultural tradition and family life. The *Quartets* move through rejection of sensuous images—'Desiccation of the world of sense'[3]—to a re-acceptance of the world in a new spirit:

[1] *Four Quartets*, p. 13.   [2] *Ibid.*, p. 22.
[3] *Ibid.*, p. 11. Cf. p. 20.

There are three conditions which often look alike
Yet differ completely, flourish in the same hedgerow:
Attachment to self and to things and to persons, detachment
From self and from things and from persons; and, growing
    between them, indifference
Which resembles the others as death resembles life,
Being between two lives—unflowering, between
The live and the dead nettle. . . .
             See, now they vanish,
The faces and places, with the self which, as it could, loved
    them,
To become renewed, transfigured in another pattern. . . .[1]

In keeping with this movement from attachment to detachment, which, as these lines point out, is not at all like indifference, the later *Quartets* move away from the emphasis on the experiences symbolized by 'the still point' and the 'rose-garden' (the moments 'out of time' experienced by the saint and the spiritually elect) towards a greater tolerance of the life of man in time.[2]

    This change bears its greatest fruit in the plays, as one would expect, since plays must deal primarily with life *in* time. Without it, we might not have these plays at all, and, even if we did, they would probably be very different. In the earlier plays, the moment of transcendence of time is all-important. In the later plays, this isolated moment becomes progressively remote—it is never again fully experienced on-stage, though there are vestiges of it— just as the exceptional person who is capable of experiencing it is moved further and further from the centre of the canvas. *The Cocktail Party*, with its double plot, dramatizes the transition, but already ordinary life occupies most of the canvas. The saint's sacrifice is seen to affect the Chamberlaynes, but they have to make the best they can of life without direct illumination. In *The Confidential Clerk* a less exceptional person has more obvious and precise influence on the lives of those with whom he comes into contact. In *The Elder Statesman* Everyman has taken the centre

---

[1] *Four Quartets*, pp. 40-1.

[2] For several observations in this section, I am indebted to the lectures of Mr. Leonard Unger and to his book, *The Man in the Name* (The University of Minnesota Press, Minneapolis, 1956), pp. 188, 220-8.

of the stage and his influence is limited to his relatives and friends, but is clearly defined; it is an influence for evil transmuted in the course of the play into an influence for good.

This gradual disappearance of the exceptional person is accompanied by a transformation of the problem of communication, which is in part explained by the lessening of the discrepancy between the experience of the hero and that of other people, but not entirely. In *The Family Reunion* the failure in communication is due to the obtuseness of the spiritually blind and seems irreparable. In *The Cocktail Party* the failure is seen to be inherent in the nature of things—people change so rapidly that we cannot keep pace with the change—and the emphasis is upon the need to accept the limits of understanding. In *The Confidential Clerk* the emphasis seems to have shifted slightly and to be now upon the need to try to keep up with the change and thus to surmount the limits of understanding. In *The Elder Statesman*, however, although we have a demonstration of the failure to communicate the wisdom of experience and a momentary emphasis upon the limitations of language itself (p. 107), a much more optimistic view is taken of the whole problem. The limits of expression and understanding are seen to be transcended by love. Where love does not exist, as between Michael and his father in the earlier part of the play, expression is hampered and understanding is impossible; where it does exist, as it does increasingly between Monica and her father, expression is made easier and the shortcomings of expression are remedied by understanding at a deeper level.

We are encouraged to believe that the last step in this development is the fruit of Eliot's own experience by the dedication of the play, in which he speaks of his wife and himself as lovers

Who think the same thoughts without need of speech
And babble the same speech without need of meaning:

    .   .   .   .

The words [of the play] mean what they say, but some have a
    further meaning
            For you and me only.[1]

[1] See also the interview by Henry Hewes, 'T. S. Eliot at Seventy', *The Saturday Review of Literature*, September 13, 1958, p. 32.

The last lines are an exact parallel to the experience of Monica and Charles in a passage which begins with an echo of Harry's experience with Mary in *The Family Reunion* (p. 59), goes on to throw new light upon one of the main themes of *The Cocktail Party*—the change which makes people strangers is here countered by the change which lovers induce in each other as they grow into a new unity—and ends with the fulfilment of an aspiration that was thwarted in Colby's case. It will be recalled that he hoped to find a loved one as companion in his 'garden', or private world, and in this way to achieve continuity between it and the public or everyday world through the fact that the loved one would share *both* worlds. Charles and Monica achieve such communion; the moment in the rose-garden has become the common experience of lovers:

MONICA

How did this come, Charles? It crept so softly
On silent feet, and stood behind my back
Quietly, a long time, a long long time
Before I felt its presence.

CHARLES

        Your words seem to come
From very far away. Yet very near. You are changing me
And I am changing you.

MONICA

        Already
How much of me is you?

CHARLES

        And how much of me is you?
I'm not the same person as a moment ago.
What do the words mean now—*I* and *you*?

MONICA

In our private world—now we have our private world—
The meanings are different.[1]

It seems to me that Eliot escapes the charge of writing a kind of private shorthand intelligible only to students of his work—

[1] p. 13. Cf. *The Confidential Clerk*, pp. 52-4, and, on the matter of change, pp. 55-6, which mark a half-way stage between *The Cocktail Party* and *The Elder Statesman*.

nothing in the passage is unintelligible in its own right, even though most of it is greatly enriched by knowledge of the earlier works—but the passage is so packed with ideas and so thin in its *imagery* that its effect is liable to be somewhat inappositely cerebral unless the acting can make the necessary compensation.

Here and elsewhere in the play the experience of the lovers is sketched in rather than fully drawn. They are somewhat idealized, as are the young lovers in Shakespeare's last plays, and in view of the mellowing of Eliot's attitude to human love it is not surprising, but, whereas in Shakespeare the idealization is not effected at the expense of human warmth—the poetry remains sensuous and concrete—in Eliot there is a certain coldness and aloofness. The lovers do not share the richness of their experience with us; the secret meanings elude us and what remains is inclined to be banal. As *The Times* critic remarked in his notice of the play's first performance, 'Coming from the author of the "Four Quartets," the language of the love scene is curiously conventional.'[1] Eliot occasionally illuminates the cliché, as in Monica's lines:

> I've loved you from the beginning of the world.
> Before you and I were born, the love was always there
> That brought us together (p. 107),

where the feeling common among lovers that they have always loved each other is made intelligible in the light of the Creative Love. But for the most part Eliot tends to leave it to the actor to inform the love scenes with an emotion that will lift them above the trite, and this is part of a significant development in the direction of naturalism which is one of the most striking factors in the play's technique. The poet tends to leave more unsaid, to let it be inferred, and this intensifies a problem which is basic to the writing of religious plays.

Eliot's concern with the spiritual life has been his great strength and his great weakness as a dramatist. It has been his strength in that it has led him to write passages of spiritual exploration and communion such as we have hardly known in English drama outside a few moments in Shakespeare. It has been his weakness in that such passages tend to be static and do not in themselves fulfil our expectations of a play. The spiritual life does not lend

[1] *The Times*, 26 August, 1958, p. 11.

itself to drama, which requires a certain amount of physical action, and the groping *towards* spiritual understanding, which is what we mostly have in the plays in contemporary settings, as in the life they represent, is hardly more dramatic. In fact, the tension of drama seems to arise more naturally if one *starts* from a religious basis. Damnation or the threat of damnation is more dramatic, for instance, than salvation or the hope of salvation, perhaps since it is more liable to involve physical action, being essentially a turning away from the Creator to the creature.[1] Nothing is more intense than the conflict between good and evil, nothing more compelling than the attack evil makes upon good. Temptation is one of the most absorbing and suspenseful forms of drama. The difficulty is to objectify it for dramatic representation.

In *Murder in the Cathedral* Eliot was able to start from a common religious basis, to objectify temptation by conventional means, and to go on to an exciting historical action. In the later plays, he has not been able to assume common belief; he has had to adapt his source-material much more; and he has not thought it desirable to employ conventions but has conformed more and more to the tenets of naturalism. Having failed in his attempt to objectify Harry's conflict by means of the Erinyes-Eumenides, he has not since had recourse to such a device, and in *The Elder Statesman* solves a similar problem by making the Furies real people. In between, he has had to express spiritual conflict and development by letting his characters tell one another about it, which is perhaps the method of the confessional box rather than the theatre. The great scenes in *The Cocktail Party* and *The Confidential Clerk* are those in which the characters lay bare their spiritual difficulties and aspirations. In *The Elder Statesman* too the stages of inner development are defined in this way; Lord Claverton voices his inmost thoughts and feelings to his daughter and her fiancé. This is more poignantly done than in *The Cocktail Party*, where the fact that the disclosures are made to a psychiatrist introduces a clinical note, but less poignantly than in *The Confidential Clerk*, where the revelations have intense relevance to the

[1] It is noticeable that in his plays of salvation, *Hamlet* and *King Lear*, Shakespeare introduces a great deal of extraneous excitement, whereas in the plays of damnation, *Othello* and *Macbeth*, he is able to extract much more excitement from the spiritual action itself.

predicament of the listener as well as the speaker. This relevance is not so intense in *The Elder Statesman*, but the later play has a better balance between introspection and outward action than any of the earlier plays in a contemporary setting. The inner action of the play is largely identified with the outer action in the scenes with Gomez and Mrs. Carghill. What remains to be told is given in their shrewd guesses about the motives and feelings of Lord Claverton and in the passages of introspection and confession which are interspersed with the phases of outward action and are closely linked with them.

As a piece of construction, in fact, the play marks a considerable advance upon its predecessors. In *The Cocktail Party* the last Act is something of an anti-climax; in *The Confidential Clerk* the First Act is somewhat flat. *The Elder Statesman* has a more satisfactory shape; the climactic phase of inner development arises directly out of the climactic scene of the outward action, the scene with Michael at the end of the Second Act, but is quite naturally delayed—the shock needs time to do its work—until the Third Act.

The play begins brightly with the return of the young lovers from a shopping expedition. Charles engages our sympathy immediately because he is obviously being led a dance. Then suddenly the feeling deepens and we have the short love-passage already discussed. This effects a transition to an expository passage in which we see a more serious Monica, a figure capable of playing Antigone to her father's Oedipus. The happiness of the lovers is seen to be closely involved with the predicament of Lord Claverton, for Monica will not agree to become engaged while her father is so dependent upon her. Our interest in him thus aroused, Lord Claverton enters, and by means of the engagement book on which he has been brooding we are led immediately to an exploration of his dismay at the prospect before him. Attention shifts to a silver salver—we note how skilfully Eliot is crystallizing his exposition about appropriate concrete objects—and this leads Lord Claverton to express his disillusionment about his success as a public figure. He recognizes himself as a ghost, and, on this cue, Gomez, the first of the companion ghosts, is announced. After a momentary suspense—if Lord Claverton sees him in the library, *we* won't see him—the revelation of the dark places in Lord Claverton's past begins. Eliot here returns to the Ibsenian technique he employed in *The Family Reunion*, by which the drama develops through the revelation of the past embedded in the present. The long dialogue is broken by the entrances of Lambert, the first to satisfy Gomez' request for whisky—this provides business for Gomez, some of it comic—and the second in accordance with the pre-arranged plan to get rid of Gomez— an interruption which injects humour into the situation *and* serves to hasten his departure. The effect of the visit on Lord Claverton is pointed in a short scene which leads to an ominous 'curtain'.

Act Two begins gently with an atmosphere somewhat lightened but slightly overcast: 'I only hope that it will last . . .' [1] Then Mrs. Piggott bustles in to get the Act moving. Her comic re-entry recalls Julia's in *The Cocktail Party*, but is more boisterously amusing, because the timing is speeded up. It is purely functional, moreover, having none of the symbolic overtones of Julia's fussiness.[2] Eliot squeezes every bit of humour out of the situation ('She'll come back to tell us more about the peace and quiet') and makes it serve as preparation for the entry of Mrs. Carghill. Put on his guard, Lord Claverton tries evasive tactics, which she characteristically circumvents. The humour carries over into the scene with her but becomes sardonic. Afterwards, the game of shielding him begins again, but it is now ironic; the real intrusion has been made, and the intruder is one of the players. She leaves as a hint to Mrs. Piggott, who has flown to rescue him from her, and Monica flies to rescue him from Mrs. Piggott. Monica's entry also serves to introduce her brother, and through this episode of near-farce we move to the tragic climax of the Act. After this scene with Michael the past presses in upon Lord Claverton; the ghosts congregate and threaten to join forces. The Act ends with the anxious question, 'Is it too late for me?' [3]

[1] p. 43. The weather is used to reinforce this unease (pp. 43-4, 47) just as it is later used to underline Lord Claverton's release from the bondage of circumstance (p. 106). From the famous opening of *Prufrock* onwards, Eliot has used the weather as an extension of the mood of his characters.

[2] Cf. *The Cocktail Party*, pp. 21, 29, 48, 59. Julia's fussiness might be said to be the comic aspect of her guardianship. Cf. Alex's fussiness, pp. 35, 47.

[3] p. 79. Ironically, the other 'ghosts' have answers to the question. Cf. the title of Mrs. Carghill's song, *It's Not Too Late For You to Love Me* (p. 55) and Gomez' comment, 'Better late than never' (p. 97).

Act Three begins with the reunion of the lovers, who now become engaged, but in an atmosphere subdued by Monica's anxiety about her father. He enters while she is affirming that she cannot imagine his having 'a guilty secret in his past' (p. 82) and this challenges him to confess. The significance of the confession is prepared in a long speech, as we have noted, and Lord Claverton allays the suspicions the lovers have been nursing. He rises clear of the melodramatic situation and frees himself absolutely from the threats of blackmail through the contrition which 'frees all faults'. Unlike the abrupt dismissal of the thriller interest in *The Family Reunion*, this sudden resolution of the suspense has been carefully prepared. In that the blackmail is emotional and not financial, we have been led to expect that Lord Claverton is going to find the solution inside himself, if anywhere, and not in any mechanistic device. Even so, the critic of *The Times* suggested that some disappointment is felt at the easy resolution and that when Lord Claverton

'decides to submit himself to his daughter's judgment we are conscious of some surprise that already his battle should have been won. Our sense of the inner conflict has been stirred, but evidently not stirred deeply enough. And we are mistaken if we suppose that Claverton will have to fight his battle over again with his daughter. It is part of Mr. Eliot's design that Monica should make things very easy for him. . . . The intention is that the shriving of Claverton should attest the charity of the shrivers and that the young people should be helped by the old man's purified moral vision to see into their own hearts. They must be fit to receive the illumination of love stretching out to them from the resting place which the elder statesman, like Oedipus at the end of his wanderings, is to find without help from human hands.' [1]

I believe that we recognize instinctively that the conflict within Lord Claverton must be resolved largely in silence, so that we are not particularly disturbed by the fact that it has been resolved off-stage. Certainly Eliot has skilfully suggested the last pangs of the conflict in the hesitation which underlies and, from a naturalistic point of view, justifies Lord Claverton's preliminary explanation

[1] *The Times*, 26 August, 1958, p. 11.

of the significance of his confession (pp. 82–6). On the other hand, the analysis of the poet's design seems sound. Moreover, the fact that the lovers have already achieved their own clarity of moral vision diminishes the illumination they receive from, and minimizes the effect of, Lord Claverton's death. But this is in keeping with the implication of other parts of the play, that, essentially, every man must achieve his own salvation.

This is most clearly shown in the case of Michael and it determines the action of the last part of the play. Lord Claverton himself is saved by his confession and is freed from his ghosts, but the consequences of his misdeeds remain and the ghosts return to batten on his son, who, against all warnings, is repeating his mistakes. As Mrs. Carghill has effected the meeting between Gomez and Michael which has led to the arrangement between them, so it is she who brings the news of these developments. She seems to be taking a malicious delight in separating father and son. Michael's departure comes after a scene in which the ironies of the situation are underlined; in helping Michael, Gomez is repaying his father for the 'help' he received from him (pp. 94, 97). The sensations of melodrama are present here to some extent. Will the three good people rescue the young man from the bad people in the nick of time? But although, as we shall see, Eliot is using some of the elements of melodrama, he transforms them, just he as transforms the farcical elements in *The Confidential Clerk*, so that we get spiritual farce in the one case and spiritual melodrama in the other. And of course there is no simple way out for Michael; the victory of good is not as easy as that. But a concrete hope is implied in Monica's promise that when he returns:

> Whoever you are then
> I shall always pretend that it is the same Michael (p. 100).

He will not be able to deny his old self entirely.

With some consolation in the knowledge of Monica's love for Michael, great comfort in Monica's and Charles' love for each other, and a new understanding of the meaning of love, Lord Claverton goes serenely to his death. This is the only point at which the naturalistic surface of the play is definitely broken. He senses that death is upon him and Monica knows intuitively when it has come. Naturalism might go even this far, but supernaturalism alone will account for the ending. Here the Sophoclean apotheosis is translated into spiritual illumination, and the play ends in 'a dry and clear beatific serenity'. [1]

This serenity is the last touch in the most skilful variation of mood and atmosphere that Eliot has achieved since *Murder in the Cathedral*. One of the weaknesses of *The Family Reunion* is the lack of variety in the central role. Powerfully rendered though the sense of horror is, it becomes somewhat oppressive through repetition, and even after Harry comes to see the meaning of the horror there is little relief from grimness. All of this is in the nature of the experience, of course, but an audience is apt to emerge depressed and feeling little or none of the elation that accompanies the genuine tragic feeling. In *The Elder Statesman*, we move from the tremendous brooding of Lord Claverton's early speeches [2] by a gradation of moods to the peace of the ending; we move from the terror of loneliness and hopelessness through the anguish involved in recovery of contact with other human beings to the release from the prison of self at the point where the human is taken up into the divine.

The play reveals a healthy sense of proportion. Lord Claverton's experience is seen in perspective. In *The Family Reunion* we see with the eyes of Harry, Agatha and Mary, or not at all. Here, while we are admitted to Lord Claverton's mind, we can also

---

[1] *Ibid.* The consonance between the end of life and the end of the day allows the stage electrician to contribute something to the atmosphere.

[2] The finest example of this is the extended image of the deserted railway station (p. 20), which may be an elaboration of the similar image in *The Ambassadors*. This occurs in the magnificent scene where Strether suddenly realizes that he has missed a great deal in life, that he hasn't relished life to the full, and advises young Bilham:

'Live all you can; it's a mistake not to. . . . This place and these impressions . . . have had their abundant message for me, have just dropped *that* into my mind. I see it now. I haven't done so before—and now I'm too old; too old at any rate for what I see. Oh I *do* see at least; and more than you'd believe or I can express. It's too late. And it's as if the train had fairly waited at the station for me without my having had the gumption to know it was there. Now I hear its faint receding whistle miles and miles down the line.'

—Henry James, *The Ambassadors*, Charles Scribner's Sons, New York, 1909, Vol. I, Book V, chap. 2, p. 217.

The naturalness with which Eliot works into the image is particularly impressive.

see the situation more objectively. This is largely because Eliot has successfully objectified his symbols. Ezra Pound, one of Eliot's poetic masters, pointed out as far back as 1912 the ground on which symbolism and naturalism may be reconciled, when he suggested

'that the proper and perfect symbol is the natural object, that if a man use "symbols" he must so use them that their symbolic function does not obtrude; so that *a* sense, and the poetic quality of a passage, is not lost to those who do not understand the symbol as such, to whom, for instance, a hawk is a hawk.' [1]

So here: the ghosts of the past are real people, not just objectifications of elements in Lord Claverton's conscience. They exist in their own right, but they are also reminders for him of the wrongs he has committed. The naturalistic surface is not broken; it merely takes on more-than-natural significance. And this is much truer to general experience than the discontinuity between the natural and the supernatural that we find in *The Family Reunion*.

In one respect, the play goes back to the kind of drama that naturalism ousted. As I have already suggested, it is to some extent a melodrama. The melodramatic plot, however, functions alongside the spiritual plot, if I may for convenience call it that, and is not integrated with it. The blackmail is the occasion of the spiritual awakening rather than its cause. The running over the old man which Gomez threatens to disclose is irrelevant to Lord Claverton's corruption of Gomez, which is the really important issue. It pinpoints Gomez' claim upon him and helps to put the dramatic machinery into motion, but what sets the spirit in motion is the fact that, through his influence, Gomez has become, the sort of man who will descend to blackmail, even if it is emotional, not financial, blackmail. The letters which Mrs. Carghill hints she might auction are more germane to his desertion of her, but this more subtle threat doesn't touch him any more nearly, disillusioned as he now is about his public stature. The really disturbing fact is that both of these people have become, through his influence on them, the stunted creatures of melo-

[1] 'Prolegomena', *The Poetry Review*, Vol. I, No. 2 (February, 1912), p. 73, reprinted in *Literary Essays of Ezra Pound*, edited with an introduction by T. S. Eliot (Faber and Faber, London; and New Directions, New York, 1954), p. 9.

drama. He is able, once he has realized this, to ignore their claims —he cannot now honestly respond in the way they require, any-way—and to rise above the melodramatic situation and achieve full humanity. Meanwhile his tormentors turn their attention to his son and try to exact their revenge through him. Gomez, who is the more obviously villainous, seems wholly content with this form of revenge. Mrs. Carghill, who is throughout more subtle and is at times quite terrifying, continues to make her claim upon him, and, in the light of her earlier comment about the possibility of their always being together (p. 57), her parting remark, 'We must always keep in touch' (p. 103), has a terrible sense of menace.

But if Gomez and Mrs. Carghill are recognizable melo-dramatic types—the young innocent corrupted by his worldly elder and lacking his elder's restraint, and the 'old flame' (so often an actress) who suddenly and inconveniently lets it be known that she has sentimentally preserved the love-letters of a now respectable man's wayward youth—Eliot has contrived to suggest the potentialities for good they once had by which they might have achieved human stature, and thus has made them something more than stereotypes. With this play, in fact, he moves a step nearer the Theatre of Character he desiderated in an interview of 1949:

'It seems to me that we should turn away from the Theatre of Ideas to the Theatre of Character. The essential poetic play should be made with human beings rather than with ideas. It is not for the dramatist to produce an analysed character, but for the audience to analyse the character.' [1]

Obviously, Eliot does not carry out this theory rigorously. To do so would be to end in pure naturalism. He continues to let his characters analyse themselves to some extent. But he tends to let motives be inferred more and more and to distinguish the characters by naturalistic means, notably by style of speech.

He has always tended to characterize by poetic rhythm and, to a lesser extent, by diction, but this tendency has become in-creasingly noticeable and it is very marked in this play, where

[1] *World Review*, November, 1949, p. 22.

diction begins to assume an importance comparable to that of rhythm. Lord Claverton's slightly stilted manner of speech, with its steady rhythm and careful choice of word—the result of years of 'responsible' public speaking—is contrasted, for instance, with the manner of Gomez, whose flexible, wily, insinuating rhythm is balanced by raciness of idiom, and with that of Mrs. Carghill, who flits or gushes, but almost never rises above the kind of commonplace phrase that such a person would subsist on. She probably has the most 'characteristic' style of any character in the plays, and her loquacity has a very amusing extension in Effie, whose comments are always so much to the purpose that one begins to wonder whether she is not, like Mrs. Gamp's friend, a convenient second self, even though there is evidence for her existence. Successful though Mrs. Carghill and Effie are as comic creations, however, they do not entirely hide the risk the poetic dramatist takes in emulating the banality of ordinary speech. We recall that Shakespeare was able to use prose for such characters and that, in any case, he tended to exploit the picturesque potentialities of vulgar speech.[1]

The danger in verisimilitude for the poetic dramatist is that he will sacrifice too much of his own power of speech, the thing that gives poetic drama its distinctive quality in the first place. Our everyday speech, which is what verisimilitude emulates, is usually 'stale, flat, and unprofitable'. Eliot avoids the danger most of the time. Most of his dialogue remains distinguished, and he bolsters it with his customary wry humour,[2] with an occasional sententiousness which he began to exploit for its humorous pos-

---

[1] In our own day, Christopher Fry has done the same, arguing that

'Almost anyone is *capable* of a vivid use of language without even noticing it, not only in the metaphors and similes they have accepted on trust from their parents and grand-parents, but in expressions of their own coining. . . . During the war there was a report in the papers of two miners who went poaching. They were leaving a wood in darkness when John decided to unload, and accidentally the gun was discharged. This is how John told the story at the inquest on Arthur. "I looked at Arthur and saw that he stood withering on his feet." . . .

'What poet could do better than "he stood withering on his feet"? . . . This is where poetry and common speech need no adjustment to become one.'
—'Poetry and the Theatre', *Adam* International Review, Nos. 214–15 (1951), p. 9.

[2] e.g. pp. 20–1 and 48–9.

sibilities in *The Confidential Clerk*,[1] and with a new application of his sense of the paradoxical—at least, I do not recall that he has before applied it to social behaviour—that is almost Shavian.[2] But there are passages which come perilously close to the banal at moments when the dramatic situation requires something more.

On the other hand, there is once or twice in the play a tendency to inflation. For example, Lord Claverton's anguish tends to become sheer rhetoric in his cry:

> Oh Michael! If you had some aim of high achievement,
> Some dream of excellence, how gladly would I help you!
> Even though it carried you away from me forever
> To suffer the monotonous sun of the tropics
> Or shiver in the northern night (p. 70).

The echo of the Third Priest's magnificently scornful dismissal of the Knights, 'Go to the northern seas . . .',[3] muted though it is, sounds grandiloquent in this context. I remind myself that Lord Claverton is prone to pompous utterance and that he has not yet been moved to genuine sympathy with his son, but my reaction remains unmodified. And Monica's protestation, 'Father! You know that I would give my life for you' (p. 71), seems to me to display a similar miscalculation. She immediately apologizes for it ('Oh, how silly that phrase sounds!') and then explains why 'love within a family . . . is silent' (pp. 71–2). The explanation is one of the finest passages in all Eliot, but it emphasizes why she should not have tried to voice her love directly. 'What [then] shall [Monica] speak? Love, and be silent.' [4] Well, not exactly, for obviously she must say something at this point, and no one would want to lose the superb explanation. But one wishes that

[1] e.g. pp. 53, 56. This is another habit of speech in which Mrs. Carghill resembles Lady Elizabeth.

[2] e.g. pp. 26, 33. It may be a quirk of Eliot's humour to put these Shavianisms into the mouth of Gomez, who is a sort of devil's advocate.

[3] *Murder in the Cathedral*, p. 84.

[4] *King Lear*, I. i. 61. I could not resist this quotation, and it gives me an opportunity to point out the resemblance of Eliot's play to Shakespeare's, which also deals with a retired statesman who achieves purgation with the help of a daughter. I have noticed no specific allusion, however, unless the speech of Monica's under discussion is an echo of Cordelia's.

there had been a less obtrusive way of introducing this passage. Of course, the original Antigone did die out of loyalty to some-one she loved, but heroics ring false in a modern family situation.

These examples seem to betray an uncertainty of tone, a dis-turbance of the poise which is usually so assured in Eliot's work, and this may indicate that he has reached a turning point. In *Poetry and Drama* he said:

'I . . . believe that while the self-education of a poet trying to write for the theatre seems to require a long period of disciplining his poetry, and putting it, so to speak, on a very thin diet in order to adapt it to the needs of the stage, he may find that later, when (and if) the understanding of theatrical technique has become second nature, he can dare to make more liberal use of poetry and take greater liberties with ordinary colloquial speech.' [1]

There are some signs in the play that Eliot is beginning to allow himself a 'more liberal use of poetry'. The rendering of the apotheosis as obvious poetry is the most striking, but not perhaps the most significant. If one is going to reintroduce poetry, then the ending is the obvious place to start, since the whole play will be a preparation for it. And just before this, stepping up the poetic voltage, so to speak, is a vestigial lyric duet (p. 107). More signi-ficant, therefore, is the vestige of the moment in the rose-garden which comes within five pages of the opening of the play. It is, of course, partly justified as a love-scene, but it is essentially unnaturalistic and markedly unlike anything Eliot allows himself in the first act of either *The Cocktail Party* or *The Confidential Clerk*.

For the most part, however, the play has a naturalistic surface, and the question once again poses itself: What distinguishes such a play from a prose play? Well, the verse form gives greater control in the rendering of character and greater precision in the delineation of emotion; the rhythms are more clearly defined than they would be in prose, even if the vocabulary is frequently commonplace. And though the imagery is pared down to a minimum, there is still sufficient to convey the basic concepts of character and character change. A distinctive quality of the poet is that he thinks in the concrete terms of imagery rather than the

[1] *Poetry and Drama*, pp. 32–3 (*On Poetry and Poets*, pp. 85–6).

abstract terms of science, in terms of masks and ghosts, for example, instead of repression and complexes. His language is intuitive and therefore intelligible to people who have no scientific knowledge or even no capacity for abstract thought. It creates an immediate link with their own experience, so that the experience of the protagonist of a poetic play is universalized and can draw upon the depths of common and communal experience. As Mr. Leslie Paul has very neatly put it, the characters in *The Elder Statesman*

'are types which represent human dilemmas rather than actual people the playwright has enjoyed observing. But this typological use of his characters tells us something important about the dramatist's intentions. One feels that it is almost an accident that Mr. Eliot chose stock situations and characters out of Edwardian drama. He knows that we can be counted on to fill in all about them which he thinks inessential, for his purpose seems to be not to exploit them humanly and realistically, as Arthur Miller or John Osborne might have done, . . . but to use them as mouth-pieces, as Greek drama does, to speak to the ultimates of the human situation—sin, loneliness, failure, despair, death. . . .

' "The Elder Statesman" . . . is a play not so much about Lord Claverton as about Everyman. . . . [For] the structure as well as the versification of the morality plays is to be found in his dramas. He is writing moralities in the idiom of our times and in his own highly idiosyncratic way about eternal values. Like an ancient morality play, "The Elder Statesman" uses a simple and quickly grasped situation presented by uncomplicated characters to speak profound and difficult things about the human spirit. It is the effort to do this which gives to all T. S. Eliot's dramas a timeless and placeless quality.' [1]

[1] From a talk in the B.B.C.'s European Service reprinted in *The Listener*, 4 September, 1958, p. 341.

Chapter Eight

Conclusion

THE unity of Shakespeare's work is such that none of his plays can be fully understood in isolation; some of the implications of each play will emerge only when it is seen in the context of the whole canon. After commenting on this in his essay on John Ford, Eliot goes on to suggest that 'the measure in which dramatists and poets approximate to this unity in a lifetime's work, is one of the measures of major poetry and drama.' [1] Even though Eliot's own creative work is not yet complete, it is already clear that it will go a long way towards achieving such a unity. The poetry has a pattern of its own. Starting with a series of portraits from and snapshots of the modern scene, it moves on in *The Waste Land* to a panoramic survey which makes a diagnosis of the disease of modern life and adumbrates a remedy. The later poetry is a working out of the personal implications of that remedy. It is to the plays that we must turn for a demonstration of the social implications.

In a sense, therefore, the plays arise out of the poetry, and are illuminated by it.[2] Starting with a full-scale study of martyrdom, Eliot moves on to illustrate the way in which the self-sacrifice of the spiritually elect fertilizes the lives of ordinary people and makes possible a fruitful communal life. The emphasis now shifts to the

---

[1] *Selected Essays*, p. 194.

[2] The numerous references to the poems throughout this book will have indicated the extent to which they illuminate the plays, and a further demonstration is given in Appendix II.

group and the saint's sacrifice seems to become more and more remote, just as it seems to be remote from contemporary life. But the saint's standards, the Christian standards, of moral honesty and spiritual integrity still apply. The financier discovers the need for integrating the public and private worlds; 'the elder statesman' finally drops the mask and allows the real self to emerge. Throughout these plays in contemporary settings run a number of themes: the need to lay one's ghosts and to build the future upon the real past, the danger of hiding the real self and letting it atrophy beneath a social mask, the problem of psychological change and the difficulty of communication with others—these and related themes interweave from play to play, now one strand and now another becoming most prominent in the design. Consequently, each play is illuminated by the others and, in turn, illuminates them.

But while the plays are closely interlinked in this way, each one is quite distinct and has its own atmosphere. Each play is to some extent a separate experiment. Eliot has said:

'Everything should be an experiment to the extent that it should not be a repetition of what one has done before, and that it should give one hints on what to attempt and what to avoid in the future.' [1]

And modern poetic drama

'is still very experimental. I do not believe that there is one poet in the theatre today, who can feel assured that he has found the right form, the right idiom, the right range of human emotions and experience to manipulate. In consequence, one is, in every play, trying something a little different.' [2]

Each experiment, however, is part of a larger experiment. As the ultimate goal, there is the

'ideal towards which poetic drama should strive. It is an unattainable ideal: and that is why it interests me, for it provides an incentive towards further experiment and exploration, beyond any goal which there is prospect of attaining.' [3]

[1] *World Review*, November, 1949, p. 21.   [2] *The Aims of Drama*, p. 3.
[3] *Poetry and Drama*, p. 33 (*On Poetry and Poets*, p. 86).

As a more immediate goal, there is the re-establishment of poetry in the theatre.

Eliot thinks of his work as a preparatory stage in the creation of a modern poetic drama. 'The creation of any form', he has said,

'cannot be the work of one man or of one generation of men working together, but has to evolve by the small contributions of a number of people in succession, each contributing a little. Shakespeare himself did not invent suddenly. . . .' [1]

So he thinks of poetic drama 'as a social creation':

'I regard our work today as that of the first generation only: my greatest hope is that we shall lay some foundations upon which others will come to build.' [2]

In order to help lay these foundations, Eliot has made himself into a popular dramatist by self-discipline. He said of Yeats that

'He cared . . . more for the theatre as an organ for the expression of the consciousness of a people, than as a means to his own fame or achievement; and I am convinced that it is only if you serve it in this spirit that you can hope to accomplish anything worth doing with it.' [3]

He himself has served it in this spirit. No great man of our time is less prone to seek the limelight; but he has endured it in the cause of poetry. No writer of our time, one would have thought, was less likely to accept the limitations of the contemporary stage; he began in revolt against them. But he has taught himself to work inside the limitations of naturalism in order to establish poetry at the centre of our theatre, presumably because he feels that poetic drama can be revived only by gradual transformation of what people are accustomed to. The violence of revolution is abhorrent to him. It tends only to swing the pendulum to an extreme, from which it is likely to return to the opposite extreme. It is hardly likely to gain a permanent place for poetry in the theatre. To equip himself for this strategy, he has put himself to school to men of the theatre, notably to Mr. E. Martin Browne. If ever the

[1] 'The Need for Poetic Drama', *The Listener*, 25 November, 1936, p. 994.
[2] *The Aims of Drama*, p. 7.   [3] *On Poetry and Poets*, p. 261.

full story of their collaboration is told, it will reveal a tremendous humility on the part of Eliot.[1]

To the same end, he has abrogated much of the power of his own style, has put his poetry 'on a very thin diet', as he says.[2] And with the support of Christopher Fry, whose tactics have been somewhat different, he has made theatrical poetry into a 'commercial proposition'. Some part of his success in the West End and on Broadway has unfortunately been due to cultural snobbery. With *The Cocktail Party*, he became 'fashionable'. In an article written in 1950, James Thurber describes how

'Ever since the distinguished Mr. T. S. Eliot's widely discussed play came to town, I have been cornered at parties by women, and men, who seem intent on making me say what I think *The Cocktail Party* means, so they can cry, "Great God, how naive!" '[3]

The unravelling of his meaning became in some circles a kind of parlour game, which one might call 'hunt the symbol.' Moreover, it is bitterly ironic that in *Murder in the Cathedral*, where he wrote at full stature, or something very like it, he succeeded magnificently in speaking to all sorts and conditions of men, whereas in the later plays, while deliberately simplifying his style for the benefit of the ordinary theatregoer, he has gained a reputation for 'obscurity'. This so-called obscurity is of course largely fictitious. Unable to reach an audience of the uneducated as he wished,[4] Eliot has reached the half-educated and the ill-educated, whose sophistication will not allow them to rest content in simplicity of statement; they must always be searching frantically for hidden meanings. If this were the whole story, it would be a sad one, indeed. Fortunately, the audiences in the West End and on Broadway, although by no means cross-sections of the community, do contain some wholly and well-educated people and

---

[1] Part of the story can be gathered from an interview with Mr. Martin Browne by Burke Wilkinson in *The New York Times*, 7 February, 1954, Section 2, p. 1, col. 5, and from Mr. Browne's article 'From *The Rock* to *The Confidential Clerk*', in Braybrooke's *Symposium*, pp. 57–69. Another part can be gleaned from the series of prefatory notes to the plays.

[2] *Poetry and Drama*, p. 32 (*On Poetry and Poets*, p. 85).

[3] James Thurber, '*What* Cocktail Party?', *The New Yorker*, 1 April, 1950, p. 26.

[4] See *The Use of Poetry and the Use of Criticism* (1933), p. 152.

others who know they are not. And even the middle sort cannot remain untouched. An audience for poetry is in the making.

Even so, the question arises: Can poetic drama be recreated 'by willing and contriving'? One might admit the great virtues of poetic drama, but doubt whether they can be secured by an effort of will. Eliot faced the question and the doubt before starting his career as dramatist. In the 'Dialogue on Dramatic Poetry' of 1928, one of the interlocutors argued that a revival of the greatness of Elizabethan drama was unlikely because no nation had ever had two great periods of drama. True, answered one of the other speakers, but

'we are not going to be deterred by a fatalistic philosophy of history from wanting a poetic drama, and from believing that there must be some way of getting it. Besides, the craving for poetic drama is permanent in human nature.' [1]

We may applaud the resolution and approve the final comment, but still wonder whether it is possible to recover the wholeness of outlook which seems to be a prerequisite of poetic drama.

Considered as a literary problem, the revival of poetic drama is feasible, for as Eliot has said: 'A literature is different from a human life, in that it can return upon its own past, and develop some capacity which has been abandoned.' [2] But the problem is not a purely literary problem. Eliot has perceived this more clearly than anyone, and has perceived also that the requisite wholeness of outlook can only come from religion, for nothing else comprehends all aspects of human life. And, from one point of view, his plays have been a subtle demonstration of the relevance of religion to all spheres of human activity. They throw light on aspects of modern life normally thought of as removed from the 'sphere' of religion as well as on areas of experience that modern psychology and sociology fail to take account of. Because they are implicitly and not explicitly Christian, they surprise people into an awareness of the meaning and implications of Christianity. In *The Idea of a Christian Society*, Eliot says: 'A Christian education would primarily train people to be able to think in Christian categories.' [3] This is, in a sense, what his later plays have been unobtrusively

[1] *Selected Essays*, p. 56.   [2] *On Poetry and Poets*, p. 168.
[3] *The Idea of a Christian Society* (Faber and Faber, 1939), p. 28.

doing. Eliot has therefore been contributing to the creation of the kind of wholeness of outlook without which poetic drama cannot be accepted as the normal mode of drama.

Whether or not, however, a new tradition of poetic drama is created, Eliot's work is assured of a permanent place in dramatic literature. Of the greatness of *Murder in the Cathedral*, there can be no doubt—it may even be the greatest religious play ever written —and the other plays will survive if only as parts of the unity of which it is the finest element. It is difficult, however, to be sure of their individual stature. One cannot yet distinguish between their intrinsic merit and their importance as steps towards the re-estab-lishment of poetic drama. It is a distinction we must leave for posterity to make. Meanwhile, fortunately, Eliot is still pursuing his ideal:

'I have before my eyes a kind of mirage of the perfection of verse drama, which would be a design of human actions and of words, such as to present at once the two aspects of dramatic and of musical order. . . . To go as far in this direction as it is possible to go, without losing that contact with the ordinary everyday world with which drama must come to terms, seems to me the proper aim of dramatic poetry. For it is ultimately the function of art, in imposing a credible order upon ordinary reality, and thereby eliciting some perception of an order *in* reality, to bring us to a condition of serenity, stillness and reconciliation; and then leave us, as Virgil left Dante, to proceed toward a region where that guide can avail us no farther.' [1]

[1] *Poetry and Drama*, pp. 34–5 (*On Poetry and Poets*, p. 87).

Appendix I

Criticism of 'Murder in the Cathedral'

FOR the critic reading the play in the isolation of his study or applying naturalistic standards of characterization, the portrayal of Becket seems to exhibit flaws which are not apparent to the ordinary member of an audience sharing a group experience and unhampered by critical preconceptions. Even such a sensitive and intelligent critic as Miss Helen Gardner succumbs to the hazards of her profession on several points:

(a) 'Thomas can hardly be said to be tempted, for the play opens so near its climax that any inner development is impossible. Except for the last, the temptations are hardly more than recapitulations of what has now ceased to tempt, an exposition of what has happened rather than a present trial; and the last temptation is so subtle and interior that no audience can judge whether it is truly overcome or not' (*The Art of T. S. Eliot*, p. 134).

It is true that the first three temptations are largely retrospective (cf. pp. 44–5) and that they therefore present something of a challenge to the director and the actors. But it may be assumed that they have not entirely lost their power, that, as Thomas says of the first temptation:

> The impossible is still temptation.
> The impossible, the undesirable,

216

Voices under sleep, waking a dead world,
So that the mind may not be whole in the present (p. 26).

Perhaps the layman is apt to underestimate the appeal of the world to the churchman. Certainly, I was surprised when a bishop told me that we had not, in my production, made enough of the continuing struggle with the world. The problem is to create a mounting tension and yet to preserve the distinction between the first three, expected temptations and the unexpected fourth. The clues are there, however, for the skilful director and actors to follow out. The first temptation barely touches Thomas, just preventing the mind from being whole in the present; the second rouses him to a considerable effort ('No! shall I, who keep the keys . . .', p. 30); the third moves him to a more subdued emotion ('O Henry, O my King!', 'If the Archbishop cannot trust the Throne . . .', pp. 32, 34), providing a relaxation before the final, relentless turn of the screw.

As for the difficulty of judging whether the last temptation has been overcome, Miss Gardner accounts for it herself, though somewhat grudgingly:

'a question has been raised that cannot be answered dramatically and that has simply to be set aside. We have to take it for granted that Thomas dies with a pure will, or else, more properly, ignore the whole problem of motives as beyond our competence and accept the fact of his death '(*loc. cit.*).

It is true that we are here at the frontiers of drama, and if Eliot drew back he is in good company: *Hamlet* and *King Lear* show that Shakespeare in not dissimilar circumstances could do little more. But I suggest that both Eliot and Shakespeare knew the limitations of their art and bypassed them with the aid of the conventions at their disposal. For my part, I have no difficulty in taking Thomas at his word when he tells me that 'Temptation shall not come in this kind again' (p. 44) and nothing in his action from then on contravenes this. To expect more than this is to misunderstand the nature of Eliot's art.

(*b*) 'If in the first act the strife is with shadows, in the second there is no strife at all' (Gardner, *loc. cit*).

I should prefer to say that whereas in the first part the conflict is inward, in the second part it is mainly external. Perhaps Miss Gardner means that the outcome of the conflict is foreknown. But that merely means that suspense is lacking, not that the conflict is undramatic. We should have to dismiss large areas of ancient and modern drama if we thought otherwise. It seems to me that there is adequate dramatic interest in the way Becket receives the Knights and that the audience's sympathy with Becket is skilfully engineered by Eliot's treatment of them.

(c) 'There is more than a trace in the Archbishop of the "classic prig" who disconcerts us so deeply in Milton's presentation of the tempted Christ in *Paradise Regained*. There is a taint of professionalism about his sanctity; the note of complacency is always creeping into his self-conscious presentation of himself' (Gardner, p. 135).

I suggest that Miss Gardner mistakes the explicitness of Eliot's art for self-consciousness in Thomas. There are times when, within the limitations of dramatic form—Milton's poem is another matter—it is only out of Thomas's own mouth that Eliot can make clear the significance of his actions. To put expressions of humility into a man's mouth is, in our naturalistic theatre, to risk making him appear the opposite of humble. It might be argued that Eliot is wrong to trust the convention of depersonalization in an age dominated by naturalism, but, as I have already said, I do not think that a popular, unsophisticated audience has normally any difficulty in making the necessary adjustments and does it quite unconsciously. Difficulty may arise if the performance is unsympathetic, but there is nothing in the part which will be objectionable in a truly sympathetic performance.

Appendix II

'Fare Forward'

THE kind of light that Eliot's poems can throw upon his plays is well illustrated in his use of the phrase 'fare forward'. In *Animula*, the short poem of 1929 which depicts the progress of the ordinary soul from birth to death, the soul is 'Unable to fare forward or retreat'.[1] In *Murder in the Cathedral*, Thomas seems to be caught in the same impasse when the Fourth Tempter counsels him to 'Fare forward to the end' (p. 36), but he finds that, by losing his will in the will of God and no longer desiring anything for himself, 'not even the glory of being a martyr' (p. 49), he is able to resolve the dilemma under which ordinary men stagger. Turning to the *Four Quartets* for further clarification, we find that Thomas has been able to put into practice Krishna's advice:

> And do not think of the fruit of action.
> Fare forward (p. 31),

or, in Krishna's own words:

'Desire for the fruits of work must never be your motive in working. . . . Perform every action with your heart fixed on the Supreme Lord. Renounce attachment to the fruits . . . .

'In the calm of self-surrender you can free yourself from the bondage of virtue and vice during this very life. Devote yourself, therefore, to reaching union with Brahman. To unite the heart

---

[1] *Collected Poems*, p. 111.

with Brahman and then to act: that is the secret of non-attached work. In the calm of self-surrender, the seers renounce the fruits of their actions, and so reach enlightenment.'[1]

Thomas finds that, as it is put in the third of the Quartets:

> right action is freedom
> From past and future also (p. 33),

or, as Krishna puts it: 'Action rightly performed brings freedom.'[2] By apprehension of 'the still point of the turning world . . . Where past and future are gathered',[3] he transcends the limits of time and rises clear of the impasse.

The contrast between the ordinary man and the saint is at the heart of *The Cocktail Party* and, while Celia is able to 'fare forward', Edward and Lavinia discover that they 'can go neither back nor forward', but must accept their predicament and 'make the best of a bad job'.[4]

Another detail of *Animula* throws light on *Murder in the Cathedral*. We note that the ordinary man dies 'Leaving disordered papers in a dusty room'.[5] And from this a tiny detail of the saint's behaviour takes on significance. When Thomas returns from France, the Second Priest says: 'Your Lordship will find your rooms in order as you left them,' and he replies: 'And will try to leave them in order as I find them' (p. 22). And then at the moment when he recognizes that death is at hand he says:

> On my table you will find
> The papers in order, and the documents signed (p. 59).

The tidiness of the saint's life, his conformance to the divine plan, is quietly underlined in a petty, everyday detail. Such is the economy of Eliot's art.

[1] *Bhagavad-Gita*, ii. 47–51, translated by Swami Prabhavananda and Christopher Isherwood (Phoenix House, London, 1947), p. 46.

[2] *Ibid.*, v. 2, trans. cit., p. 69.

[3] *Four Quartets*, p. 9.

[4] *The Cocktail Party*, p. 111. Cf. the passage from *Four Quartets* quoted on p. 132 above.   [5] *Collected Poems*, p. 112.

Bibliography

THOMAS STEARNS ELIOT (b. 1888)

PLAYS

1926-7   *Sweeney Agonistes*. Fragments of an Aristophanic Melodrama (reprinted in *Collected Poems, 1909-35*, pp. 117-32).

1934   *The Rock*. A Pageant Play written for performance at Sadler's Wells Theatre, 28 May-9 June, 1934, on behalf of the Forty-Five Churches Fund of the Diocese of London (Faber and Faber, 1934).
       (The Choruses are reprinted in *Collected Poems*, pp. 157-81.)

1935   *Murder in the Cathedral*. Canterbury Festival, 1935 (Faber and Faber, 1935; fourth edition, 1938).

1939   *The Family Reunion* (Faber and Faber, 1939).

1949   *The Cocktail Party*. Edinburgh Festival, 1949 (Faber and Faber, 1950; revised for fourth impression, September, 1950).

1953   *The Confidential Clerk*. Edinburgh Festival, 1953 (Faber and Faber, 1954).

1958   *The Elder Statesman*. Edinburgh Festival, 1958 (Faber and Faber, 1959).

RELEVANT PROSE

'The Duchess of Malfi at the Lyric: and Poetic Drama', *Art and Letters* (N.S.), Vol. III, No. 1 (Winter, 1920), pp. 36-9.

'The Poetic Drama' (A review of *Cinnamon and Angelica* by John Middleton Murry), *Athenaeum*, No. 4698, 14 May, 1920, pp. 635-6.

'The Possibility of a Poetic Drama', *The Sacred Wood* (Methuen, London, 1920).

Introduction to *Savonarola: A Dramatic Poem* by Charlotte Eliot (R. Cobden-Sanderson, London, 1926).

Introduction to *The Wheel of Fire* by G. Wilson Knight (Oxford University Press, 1930).

Selected Essays (Faber and Faber, 1932; revised, 1951). Sections II and III.

The Use of Poetry and the Use of Criticism (Faber and Faber, 1933), pp. 152-5.

Letter on *The Rock*, *The Spectator*, 8 June, 1934, p. 887.

'Audiences, Producers, Plays, Poets', *New Verse*, No. 18 (December, 1935), pp. 3-4.

'The Need for Poetic Drama', *The Listener*, XVI, 411 (25 November, 1936), pp. 994-5.

'Religious Drama: Mediaeval and Modern', *The University of Edinburgh Journal*, Vol. IX, No. 1 (Autumn, 1937), pp. 8-17.
(An address delivered to the Friends of Rochester Cathedral in 1937. Reprinted in book form by House of Books Ltd., New York, 1954, with a prefatory note by Eliot.)

'Five Points on Dramatic Writing' (A Letter to Ezra Pound), *Townsman*, I, 3 (July, 1938), 10. Reprinted in J. Isaacs, *An Assessment of Twentieth-Century Literature* (Secker and Warburg, 1951), pp. 159-60.

'The Music of Poetry', the third W.P. Ker Memorial Lecture delivered at Glasgow University in 1942, and published by Glasgow University Press in the same year (reprinted in *On Poetry and Poets*, 1957, pp. 26-38).

Introduction to *Shakespeare and the Popular Dramatic Tradition* by S. L. Bethell (King and Staples, London, 1944).

'The Social Function of Poetry', *The Adelphi*, Vol. 21, No. 4 (July-September, 1945), pp. 152-61.
(Described as the original text of an address, 'Le rôle social des poètes', delivered to an audience in Paris in May, 1945. This is possibly the text delivered at the British-Norwegian Institute in London in 1943. It differs somewhat from the text printed in *On Poetry and Poets*, pp. 15-25, particularly in the short section on drama. Cf. *Adelphi*, p. 153, with *On Poetry and Poets*, p. 17.)

The Aims of Poetic Drama: The Presidential Address to the Poets' Theatre Guild (London, The Poets' Theatre Guild, 1949).

'The Aims of Poetic Drama', *Adam* International Review, ed. Miron Grindea, No. 200 (November, 1949), pp. 10-16.
(The last two differ completely.)

Poetry and Drama. The Theodore Spencer Memorial Lecture, Harvard University, 21 November, 1950 (Faber and Faber, 1951). Reprinted, with an additional note, in *On Poetry and Poets* (Faber and Faber, 1957), pp. 72-88.

The Three Voices of Poetry—The eleventh Annual Lecture of the National Book League, delivered in 1953 and published for the

N.B.L. by the Cambridge University Press. Reprinted in *On Poetry and Poets*, pp. 89–102.

'Gordon Craig's Socratic Dialogues', *Drama*, Spring, 1953 (New Series, No. 36).

INTERVIEWS

Shahani, Ranjee, 'T. S. Eliot Answers Questions', *John O'London's Weekly*, Vol. LVIII, No. 1369 (Friday, 19 August, 1949), pp. 497–8.

Hailey, Foster, 'An Interview with T. S. Eliot', *The New York Times*, 16 April, 1950, section 2, p. 1, col. 5.

Hamilton, Iain (see bibliography for *The Cocktail Party*).

'Eliot says Play is to Entertain', *The New York Herald Tribune*, 14 May, 1950, sec. 5, p. 2.

(The occasion was the New York production of *The Cocktail Party*, but most of Eliot's remarks apply to the other plays.)

Hewes, Henry, 'Eliot on Eliot: "I feel younger than I did at 60"', *The Saturday Review of Literature*, 13 September, 1958, p. 32.

CRITICAL STUDIES, REVIEWS, ETC.

Note: I have excluded items in newspapers and weekly publications, except for a few of outstanding interest. This is an arbitrary limitation, but without it the list would have been swollen with items of little or no value to the student. As it is, a number of items of very slight value have found their way in. But, in general, writers preparing items for periodicals published not more often than once a fortnight have the opportunity for more careful consideration.

Within these limits, I have tried to make the list a complete record of items written in the main languages of Western Europe. I know, however, of the existence of a number of items that I have not been able to track down, and no doubt there are others that I do not know about. I should be grateful, therefore, for details of any omissions.

Even though limited and incomplete, the list is formidable, and to assist readers who have no previous acquaintance with this body of criticism but wish to pursue the study of Eliot's plays, I have indicated by asterisks the items which I have found most helpful.

CRITICAL STUDIES OF MORE THAN ONE PLAY

Note: Unless otherwise indicated, these studies deal with all the plays written before the date of publication.

*Arrowsmith, William, 'Transfiguration in Eliot and Euripides', *The Sewanee Review*, LXIII (1955), 421–42. Reprinted in *English Stage*

Comedy, ed. W. K. Wimsatt, Jr. *English Institute Essays 1954* (New York, Columbia U.P.; London, Cumberlege, 1955), pp. 148–72.
(*The Cocktail Party* and *The Confidential Clerk*.)

Battenhouse, Henry M. *Poets of Christian Thought*. Evaluations from Dante to T. S. Eliot (The Ronald Press Co., New York, 1947), pp. 167–70.
(*Murder in the Cathedral* and *The Rock*.)

Blackmur, R. P. 'T. S. Eliot: From *Ash Wednesday* to *Murder in the Cathedral*', *The Double Agent* (Arrow Editions, New York, 1935), pp. 184–218. Reprinted in Unger's *Critique*, pp. 236–62.
(*The Rock* and *Murder in the Cathedral*.)

Bland, D. S. 'The Tragic Hero in Modern Literature', *The Cambridge Journal*, Vol. III, No. 4 (January, 1950), pp. 214–23.
(*Murder in the Cathedral* and *The Family Reunion*.)

Bradbrook, M. C. *T. S. Eliot* (Writers and Their Work No. 8, Published for the British Council by Longmans, Green and Company, 1950. Revised, 1955).

Braybrooke, Neville (Ed.) *T. S. Eliot. A symposium for his seventieth birthday* (Farrar, Straus and Cudahy, New York, 1958).
(Relevant items are listed under their authors in the appropriate sections of this bibliography. This collection is referred to throughout as Braybrooke's *Symposium*.)

Brenner, Rica. *Poets of Our Times* (Harcourt, Brace and Co., New York, 1941), pp. 193–7.
(Does little more than refer to *The Rock* and *Murder in the Cathedral* and is perfunctory on *The Family Reunion*.)

Browne, E. Martin. 'The Poet and the Stage', *The Penguin New Writing*, ed. John Lehmann, No. 31 (1947), pp. 81–92.

*——— 'The Dramatic Verse of T. S. Eliot', in March's *Symposium*, pp. 196–207.

——— 'Theatre Aims of T. S. Eliot', *The New York Times*, 15 January, 1950, sec. 2, p. 3.
(*Murder in the Cathedral*, *The Family Reunion*, and *The Cocktail Party*.)

*——— 'From *The Rock* to *The Confidential Clerk*' in Braybrooke's *Symposium*, pp. 57–69.

Cookman, A. V. 'The Verse Play', *The Year's Work in the Theatre 1949–50* (published for the British Council by Longmans, Green & Co., London, 1950).

Daniells, Roy. 'The Christian Drama of T. S. Eliot', *The Canadian Forum*, Vol. 16, No. 187 (1936), pp. 20–1.
(*The Rock* and *Murder in the Cathedral*.)

Downey, Harris. 'T. S. Eliot—Poet as Playwright', *The Virginia Quarterly Review*, Vol. 12, No. 1 (January, 1936), pp. 142–5.
(Review of *The Rock* and *Murder in the Cathedral*.)

Dukes, Ashley. 'Re-enter the Chorus', *Theatre Arts Monthly*, XXII (May, 1938), pp. 337, 340.
(Brief references.)

—— 'T. S. Eliot in the Theatre', in March's *Symposium*, pp. 112–19.

Engel, Claire-Éliane. *Esquisses Anglaises* (Collection: Les Essayistes. Éditions 'Je Sers', Paris, 1949).
(*Murder in the Cathedral*, pp. 106, 113–15, 126, 156–61: *Family Reunion*, 161–70.)

Evans, B. Ifor. *A Short History of English Drama* (Penguin Books, 1948), p. 168.

*Findlater, Richard. *The Unholy Trade* (Gollancz, London, 1952), pp. 130–146.

Frankenberg, Lloyd. *Pleasure Dome:* On reading modern poetry (Houghton Mifflin Co., Boston, Mass., 1949), pp. 78–96.

Fry, Edith M. 'The Poetic Work of T. S. Eliot', *The British Annual of Literature*, Vol. V (1948), pp. 11–12.
(Brief references to *Murder in the Cathedral* and *The Family Reunion*.)

Gamberini, Spartaco. *La Poesia di T. S. Eliot* (Pubblicazioni dell' Istituto Universitario di Magistero, Genova, 1954).

*Gardner, Helen. *The Art of T. S. Eliot* (The Cresset Press, London, 1949).

Gassner, John. *Masters of the Drama.* Third revised and enlarged edition (Dover Publications Inc., New York, 1954), pp. 729–31.

—— 'T. S. Eliot: The Poet as Anti-Modernist', in *The Theatre in Our Times* (Crown Publishers Inc., New York, 1954), pp. 267–81.
(Deals chiefly with *The Cocktail Party* but also touches on the earlier plays.)

Graves, Robert. *The Common Asphodel.* Collected Essays on Poetry, 1922–49 (Hamish Hamilton, London, 1949), pp. 286–9.
(*The Rock* and *Murder in the Cathedral*. This portion of the book written in collaboration with Laura Riding.)

*Harding, D. W. 'Progression of Theme in Eliot's Modern Plays', *The Kenyon Review*, Vol. XVIII, No. 3 (Summer, 1956), pp. 337–60.

Hassall, Christopher. *Notes on the Verse Drama* (*The Masque* No. 6, London, The Curtain Press, 1948).
(Refers briefly to *Murder in the Cathedral*, pp. 20–21, and *The Family Reunion*, pp. 9, 13, 21.)

Henn, T. R. *The Harvest of Tragedy* (Methuen, London, 1956).

Isaacs, J. *An Assessment of Twentieth-Century Literature.* (Secker and Warburg, London, 1951), pp. 135–60.

Kerr, Walter. *How Not to Write a Play* (Max Reinhardt, London, 1956), pp. 230–1.

Lambert, J. W. 'The Verse Drama' in *Theatre Programme*, ed. J. C. Trewin (Frederick Muller Ltd., London, 1954), pp. 63–6. (See also pp. 125–6, 190–1.)

Leggatt, Alison. 'A Postscript from Mrs. Chamberlayne and Mrs. Guzzard', Braybrooke's *Symposium*, pp. 79–80.
   (*The Cocktail Party* and *The Confidential Clerk.*)

Lobb, Kenneth Martyn. *The Drama in School and Church.* A short survey (George G. Harrap, London, 1955), pp. 115, 117–19.

Lumley, Frederick. *Trends in Twentieth-Century Drama.* A survey since Ibsen and Shaw (Rockliff, 1956), pp. 80–90.

March, Richard and Tambimuttu (compilers). *T. S. Eliot: a symposium* (Editions Poetry London, 1948).
   (Relevant items listed under individual authors in appropriate sections. This collection is throughout referred to as March's *Symposium.*)

*Matthiessen, F. O. *The Achievement of T. S. Eliot* (Oxford University Press, 1935. Second edition, 1947. Third edition, with a chapter on Eliot's later work by C. L. Barber, 1958).

*Maxwell, D. E. S. *The Poetry of T. S. Eliot* (Routledge and Kegan Paul, London, 1952).

*Melchiori, Giorgio. *The Tightrope Walkers.* Studies of mannerism in modern English literature (Routledge and Kegan Paul, London, 1956).
   (N.B. *The Confidential Clerk* is discussed on pp. 248–54.)

*Murry, John Middleton. *Unprofessional Essays* (Cape, London, 1956), pp. 151–91.

Nicholson, Norman. *Man and Literature* (S.C.M. Press, London, 1943), pp. 197–201.

Nicoll, Allardyce. *British Drama.* An historical survey from the beginnings to the present time (George G. Harrap & Co., Ltd., 1925. Fourth edition, 1947), p. 481.

—— *World Drama* from Aeschylus to Anouilh (George G. Harrap, London, 1949), pp. 871–3.

Orsini, Napoleone. 'T. S. Eliot e la teoria delle convenzioni drammatiche', *Letterature Moderne*, IV, n. 6 (novembre–dicembre, 1953), pp. 621–35.

*Peacock, Ronald. *The Poet in the Theatre* (Routledge and Kegan Paul, London, 1946), pp. 1–20.

Bibliography

Peacock Ronald, 'Public and Private Problems in Modern Drama', *Bulletin of the John Rylands Library* (Manchester), Vol. 36 (1953–4), pp. 38–55. Reprinted in *The Tulane Drama Review*, Vol. 3, No. 3 (March, 1959), pp. 58–72.
> (Refers only to *The Family Reunion* and *The Cocktail Party*, but is relevant to all the plays in contemporary setting.)

Policardi, Silvio. *La Poesia di T. S. Eliot* (Edizioni Universitarie, Milano–Venezia, 1948–9), pp. 129–87.

Pottle, Frederick A. 'Drama of Action', *The Yale Review*, N.S., Vol. XXV, No. 2 (December, 1935), pp. 426–30.
> (Review of *The Rock* and *Murder in the Cathedral*.)

Powell, Dilys. *Descent from Parnassus* (The Cresset Press, London, 1934).
> (Pp. 74–5, *Sweeney Agonistes*; pp. 78–80, *The Rock*.)

Read, Herbert. *The True Voice of Feeling*, Studies in English Romantic Poetry (Faber and Faber, London, 1953), pp. 139–50.

Reed, Henry. 'Towards "The Cocktail Party".' Two radio talks printed in *The Listener*, 10 and 17 May, 1951, Vol. XLV, pp. 763–4 and 803–4.

Robbins, Rossell Hope. *The T. S. Eliot Myth* (Henry Schuman, New York, 1951), pp. 17–18, 21–4, 39–46, 61–5, 86–7, 92–112, 131–2, 143–5, 147–53, 160, 165, 174, 176, 177–8, 181, 183, 184.
> (Attacks all the plays, but most frequently *The Cocktail Party*.)

Rosati, Salvatore. 'Verso e linguaggio poetico nelle opere drammatiche di T. S. Eliot', *Galleria* I (gennaio-febbraio, 1953), pp. 21–4.

Sampson, George. *The Concise Cambridge History of English Literature* (Cambridge University Press, 1941), p. 1023.

Schaeder, Grete. 'T. S. Eliots dramatische Dichtungen, "Sweeney Agonistes", "The Family Reunion", "Murder in the Cathedral" ', *Neue Schweizer Rundschau*, April, 1948. Heft Nr. 12 (pp. 728–42).

★Schaeder, Grete und Hans Heinrich. *Ein Weg zu T. S. Eliot* (Verlag der Büchsterstube Fritz-Seifert, Hameln, 1948).
> (Deals with *Murder in the Cathedral* and *The Family Reunion*.)

Smidt, Kristian. *Poetry and Belief in the Work of T. S. Eliot*. Skrifter utgitt av Det Norske Videnskaps-Akademi i Oslo II Hist.—Filos. Klasse 1949, No. 1 (Oslo, I Kommisjon Hos Jacob Dybwad, 1949).
> (Incidental references throughout, notably p. 198 on *The Family Reunion*.)

★Smith, Grover, Jr. *T. S. Eliot's Poetry and Plays*. A study in sources and meaning (University of Chicago Press, 1956).

Speaight, Robert. *Drama Since 1939* (Longmans, Green & Co. for the British Council, London, 1947), pp. 43–5.

Speaight, Robert. 'Interpreting Becket and Other Parts', in Braybrooke's *Symposium*, pp. 70–8.
(*Murder in the Cathedral, The Family Reunion, The Cocktail Party*
and *The Confidential Clerk.*)

Tordeur, J. *A la Rencontre de T. S. Eliot.* Un Classique vivant (La
Sixaine, Bruxelles, 1946), pp. 36–41, 44–5.

Trewin, J. C. *Dramatists of Today* (Staples Press, 1953).

Tynan, Kenneth. 'Prose and the Playwright', *The Atlantic Monthly*,
December, 1954, pp. 72–6.

*Unger, Leonard (ed.). *T. S. Eliot: a selected critique* (Rinehart & Co.,
Inc., New York, 1948).
(Relevant articles listed under individual authors in appropriate
sections. This very useful compilation is referred to throughout
as Unger's *Critique.*)

* ——*The Man in the Name.* Essays on the experience of poetry
(University of Minnesota Press, Minneapolis, 1956), pp. 181–5
(*The Family Reunion*), 211–15, 219–26. (*The Cocktail Party* and
The Confidential Clerk.)

Vallette, Jacques. 'Remarques sur le théâtre de T. S. Eliot', *La Nef*,
2ᵉ année, numéro 7 (juin, 1945), pp. 119–24.

Vigée, Claude. 'Les Artistes de la faim', *Comparative Literature*, Vol.
IX, No. 2 (Spring, 1957), pp. 97–117.
(Touches briefl y on plays in contemporary setting as showing
symptoms of a new asceticism: pp. 98, 99, 110–11, 116, 117.)

Wells, Henry W. *New Poets from Old.* A Study in Literary Genetics
(Columbia University Press, New York, 1940).
(Brief references to *The Family Reunion* on p. 71 and *Sweeney
Agonistes* on p. 75.)

Whicher, George F. 'Loopholes of Retreat', *The Literature of the
American People.* An historical and critical survey. Ed. Arthur
Hobson Quinn (Appleton-Century-Crofts Inc., New York,
1951), pp. 897–8.

*Wildi, Max. *Die Dramen von T. S. Eliot* (Kultur- und Staatswissen-
schaftliche-Schriften. Heft 97: Polygraphischer Verlag A-G.,
Zurich, 1957).

*Williams, Raymond. *Drama from Ibsen to Eliot* (Chatto and Windus,
London, 1952), pp. 223–46, 273–7.
(The chapter entitled 'Criticism into Drama' was published in
Essays in Criticism, Vol. I, No. 2, April, 1951, pp. 120–38.)

—— *Drama in Performance* (Frederick Muller, London, 1954), pp.
109–16.

Williamson, Audrey. 'Poetry in the Theatre: Eliot and Fry', *Chrysalis*,
IV, Nos. 5-6 (1951), pp. 3–12. (Reprinted with additions in her

Theatre of Two Decades, Rockliff, London, 1951, pp. 127–30, 134–44).
(*Murder in the Cathedral*, *The Family Reunion*, and *The Cocktail Party*.)

Wilson, Frank. *Six Essays on the Development of T. S. Eliot* (The Fortune Press, London, 1948), pp. 41–53.
(Does not deal with *The Rock*.)

Wynn, Dudley. 'The Integrity of T. S. Eliot', *University of Denver Publications, Studies in Humanities*, No. 1: 'Writers of Our Years', ed. A. M. I. Fiskin (The University of Denver Press, 1950), pp. 59–78.
(*The Rock, Murder in the Cathedral*, and *The Family Reunion*.)

CRITICAL STUDIES OF SINGLE PLAYS

Sweeney Agonistes

Barker, George. (Review) *The Adelphi*, Vol. 5, No. 4 (January, 1933), pp. 310–11.

Coghill, Nevill. 'Sweeney Agonistes', in March's *Symposium*, pp. 82–7.

*Jayne, Sears. 'Mr. Eliot's Agon', *Philological Quarterly*, XXXIV (1955), pp. 395–414.

Moore, Marianne. 'Sweeney Agonistes' (Review) *Poetry: A magazine of verse*, Vol. XLII, No. 11 (May, 1933), pp. 106–9.

Sitwell, Edith. *The American Genius*. An Anthology . . . with a Preface (John Lehmann, London, 1951), pp. xvii–xix.

Spender, Stephen. 'T. S. Eliot in his Poetry', *The Destructive Element* (Cape, London, 1936). Reprinted in Unger's *Critique* (pp. 274–5 on *Sweeney Agonistes*).

Thompson, T. T. 'The Bloody Wood', *London Mercury*, XXIX (1934), pp. 233–9. Reprinted in Unger's *Critique*, pp. 161–9.

Williamson, George. *Reader's Guide to T. S. Eliot* (The Noonday Press, New York, 1953), pp. 191–5.

The Rock

A. M. (Review of the book) *Blackfriars*, Vol. XV, No. 174 (September, 1934), pp. 642–3.

Harding, D. W. 'The Rock', *Scrutiny*, Vol. III, No. 2 (September, 1934), pp. 180–3.

Moore, Harry Thornton. (Review) *The Adelphi*, Vol. 9, No. 3 (December, 1934), pp. 188–9.

Theatre Arts Monthly, Vol. XVIII, No. 12 (December, 1934), pp. 927–8. '*The Rock*: Ecclesiastical Revue'. (Accompanied by photographs of the production.)

Zabel, M. D. 'Poetry for the Theatre', *Poetry: A magazine of verse*, Vol. 45 (1934), 152–8.

Murder in the Cathedral

★Adair, Patricia. 'Mr. Eliot's "Murder in the Cathedral"', *The Cambridge Journal*, Vol. IV, No. 2 (November, 1950), pp. 83–95.

Barnes, T. R. 'Poets and the Drama', *Scrutiny*, Vol. IV, No. 2 (September, 1935), pp. 189–91.

★Boulton, J. T. 'The Use of Original Sources for the Development of a Theme: Eliot in *Murder in the Cathedral*', *English*, Vol. XI, No. 61 (Spring, 1956), pp. 2–8.

Brooks, Cleanth, John Thibaut Purser and Robert Penn Warren, *An Approach to Literature*, Third Edition (Appleton-Century-Crofts, New York, 1952), pp. 755–7.

Brown, John Mason. 'The High Excitements of "Murder in the Cathedral"', *The New York Evening Post*, 30 March, 1936, p. 18. (Reprinted in *Two on the Aisle*, W. W. Norton and Co., New York, 1938, pp. 124–6.)

Butler, John F. 'Tragedy, Salvation, and the Ordinary Man', *The London Quarterly and Holborn Review*, CLXII (1937), pp. 489–97. (A brief but stimulating reference.)

Colum, Mary M. 'Life and Literature: Revival in the Theatre', *The Forum*, Vol. XCV, No. 6 (June, 1936), pp. 344–5, 346–7.

Dasgupta, Rabindrakumar. 'T. S. Eliot's "Murder in the Cathedral"', *The Calcutta Review*, Vol. 69, No. 3 (December, 1938), pp. 296–306.

Dean, Leonard F. (Ed.). *Nine Great Plays* from Aeschylus to Eliot. Revised edition (Harcourt, Brace and Co., New York, 1956), pp. 643–6.

Dukes, Ashley. 'A Poet Turns Dramatist', *The New York Times*, 20 February, 1938, sec. 2, pp. 1 and 3.

Eliot, T. S. *Meurtre dans la Cathédrale* traduit de l'anglais et présenté par Henri Fluchère (Les Cahiers du Rhône, Série Blanche, Éditions de la Baconnière, Neuchatel, 1944), pp. 129–33.

—— *Assassino nella cattedrale*, traduzione di C. V. Lodovici (Teatro dell' Università di Roma, Collezione di autori stranieri, I, pp. vii–xiv. (Introduction dated May, 1940.)

Eliot, T. S., and George Hoellering. *The Film of 'Murder in the Cathedral'* (Faber and Faber, 1952).

Fergusson, Francis. 'Action as Passion: Tristan and *Murder in the Cathedral*', *The Kenyon Review*, Vol. 9, No. 2 (1947), 201–21.

★—— *The Idea of a Theatre* (Princeton U.P., Princeton, New Jersey, 1949), pp. 210–22.

Bibliography

Fluchère, Henri. 'Lettres Étrangères' (Review), *La Nouvelle Revue Française*, tome XLVII (1936), pp. 556–8.

Gielgud, Val. 'Radio Play: In the Age of Television', *Theatre Arts Monthly*, XXI (February, 1937), pp. 108–12.
(Speaks briefly of its success as a radio play, p. 111.)

Gregory, Horace. 'Poets in the Theatre', *Poetry: A magazine of verse*, Vol. XLVIII, No. 4 (July, 1936), pp. 227–8.

Hoellering, George. 'Filming Murder in the Cathedral', in Braybrooke's *Symposium*, pp. 81–4.

Isaacs, Edith J. R. 'Saints and Law-makers: Broadway in Review', *Theatre Arts Monthly*, Vol. XX, No. 5 (May, 1936), pp. 341–3.

Jennings, Humphrey. 'Eliot and Auden and Shakespeare', *New Verse*, No. 18 (December, 1935), pp. 4–7.

Kenner, Hugh. 'Eliot's Moral Dialectic', *The Hudson Review*, II (Autumn, 1949), pp. 421–8.
(Pp. 429–31 and 432–3 on *Murder in the Cathedral*.)

Lannes, Roger. 'Les Spectacles de Paris', *Fontaine*, 45 (octobre, 1945), pp. 733–5.

Lemarchand, J. ' "Meurtre dans la Cathédrale" au théâtre du Vieux-Colombier,' *L'Arche*, 2ᵉ année, No. 9, Vol. 3, (septembre, 1945), pp. 121–3.

Lobb, K. Martyn. *T. S. Eliot: 'Murder in the Cathedral'* (Notes on Chosen English Texts. J. Brodie Ltd., London, 1950).

*Martz, Louis L. 'The Wheel and the Point: Aspects of Imagery and Theme in Eliot's Later Poetry', *The Sewanee Review*, LV (1947), pp. 126–47. Reprinted in Unger's *Critique*, pp. 444 ff.

Moore, Marianne. 'If I am worthy, there is no danger' (Review), *Poetry: A magazine of verse*, Vol. XLVII, No. V (February, 1936), pp. 279–81.

Mueller, W. R. ' "Murder in the Cathedral": an imitation of Christ', *Religion in Life*, XXVII (Summer, 1958), pp. 414–26.

Muir, Edwin. 'New Literature: "Murder in the Cathedral" ', *The London Mercury*, Vol. XXXII, No. 189 (July, 1935), pp. 281–3.

Nicholas, Constance. 'The Murders of Doyle and Eliot', *Modern Language Notes*, LXX (1955), pp. 269–71.

Ould, Herman. *The Art of the Play* (Pitman's Theatre and Stage Series: Pitman, London, 1938; 2nd edition, 1948), pp. 124–8, 138.

Oxenford, Mabel A. *Murder in the Cathedral*. A study (Argentine Association of English Culture. English Pamphlet Series No. 2, Buenos Aires, 1942).

Pacuvio, Giulio. ' "Assassino nella cattedrale" e ritorno al teatro di poesia', *Scenario*, Anno IX, N. 6 (giugno, 1940), pp. 297–8.

*Peter, John. 'Murder in the Cathedral', *The Sewanee Review*, LXI (1953), 362–83.

P. O. D. 'Murder in the Cathedral', *Agonia*, Año VI (primavera, 1944), pp. 72–4.
(A review of an amateur production in Buenos Aires.)

Putt, S. Gorley. 'This Modern Poetry', *Voices*, No. 85 (Spring, 1936), pp. 58–60.

Ransom, John Crowe. 'Autumn of Poetry', *The Southern Review*, Vol. I (1935–6), pp. 619–23. (Reprinted in *The World's Body*, Charles Scribner's Sons, New York, 1938, pp. 166–72.)

Rees, Richard. (Review of the book.) *The Adelphi*, Vol. XI, No. 1, N.S. (October, 1935), pp. 60–1.

Ross, Hugh. 'Mediaeval Drama Redivivus', *The American Scholar*, Vol. 5, No. 1 (Winter, 1936), pp. 49–63.
(A brief but striking reference on p. 63.)

Sayers, M. 'A Year in the Theatre', *The Criterion*, Vol. XV, No. lxi (July, 1936), pp. 653–5, 657.

Shapiro, Leo. 'The Medievalism of T. S. Eliot', *Poetry: A magazine of verse*, Vol. LVI, No. iv (July, 1940), pp. 202–13.

Smith, Grover, Jr. 'T. S. Eliot and Sherlock Holmes', *Notes and Queries*, Vol. 193, No. 20, October 2, 1948, pp. 431–2. (See also the correspondence columns of *The Times Literary Supplement* for 19 and 26 January, and 23 February, 1951.)

Smith, Stevie. 'History or Poetic Drama?' in Braybrooke's *Symposium*, pp. 170–5.

Spencer, Theodore. 'On "Murder in the Cathedral"', *Harvard Advocate*, Vol. CXXV, No. 3 (December, 1938), pp. 21–2.

Stone, Geoffrey. 'Plays by Eliot and Auden', *The American Review*, Vol. 6, No. 1 (November, 1935), pp. 121–8.

Troyat, Henri. 'T. S. Eliot: Le Meurtre dans la cathédrale', *La Nef*, 2e année, numéro 8 (juillet, 1945), pp. 157–9.

Van Doren, Mark. 'The Holy Blisful Martir', *The Nation*, CXLI (October, 1935), p. 417. (Reprinted in *The Private Reader*, Selected Articles and Reviews, Henry Holt and Co., New York, 1942, pp. 210–12.)

Watson, E. Bradlee and Benfield Pressey (eds.). *Contemporary Drama: Fifteen Plays* (Charles Scribner's Sons, New York, 1959). (Introduction and notes.)

Wilder, Amos N. *The Spiritual Aspects of the New Poetry* (Harper and Brothers, New York, 1940), pp. 211–15.

Yeats, William Butler. Introduction to *The Oxford Book of Modern Verse* (Oxford University Press, 1936), pp. xxii–xxiii. Reprinted in Unger's *Critique*, pp. 287–8.

The Family Reunion

*Barber, C. L. 'T. S. Eliot After Strange Gods', *The Southern Review*, VI (1940–1), 387–416. Reprinted in Unger's *Critique*, pp. 415–43.

Battenhouse, Roy W. 'Eliot's "The Family Reunion" as Christian Prophecy', *Christendom*, Vol. X, No. 3 (Summer, 1945), pp. 307–21.

Bodkin, Maud. 'The Eumenides and the Present-day Consciousness' (Review), *The Adelphi*, Vol. 15, No. 8 (May, 1939), pp. 411–13.

*Bodkin, Maud. *The Quest for Salvation in an Ancient and a Modern Play* (Oxford University Press, 1941).

Brooks, Cleanth. 'Sin and Expiation', *Partisan Review*, Vol. VI, No. 4 (Summer, 1939), pp. 114–16.

Brooks, Harold F. ' "The Family Reunion" and "Colombe's Birthday" ', *Times Literary Supplement*, Vol. LI, 12 December, 1952, p. 819.

Browne, E. Martin. Introduction to *Four Modern Verse Plays* (Penguin Books, Harmondsworth, Middlesex, 1957), pp. 8–10.

*Carne-Ross, Donald. 'The Position of "The Family Reunion" in the Work of T. S. Eliot', *Rivista di Letterature Moderne*, Anno I, N. 2, Nuova Serie (ottobre, 1950), 125–39.

Fergusson, Francis. 'Notes on the Theatre', *The Southern Review*, V (1939–40), 562–4.

Garrett, John. 'Drama' (review of the book), *The English-Speaking World*, Vol. XXI, No. 6 (June, 1939), pp. 278–9.

Greenwood, Ormerod. *The Playwright*. A study of form, method and tradition in the theatre (Theatre and Stage Series, Pitman, London, 1950), pp. 103–9.

Gregory, Horace. 'The Unities and Eliot', *Life and Letters Today*, 23 (October–December, 1939), pp. 53–60.

Häusermann, H. W. ' "East Coker" and "The Family Reunion" ', *Life and Letters Today*, Vol. 47 (1945), pp. 32–8.

Horton, Philip. 'Speculations on Sin', *The Kenyon Review*, Vol. I, No. 3 (Summer, 1939), pp. 330–3.

Kelly, Bernard. (Review of the book) *Blackfriars*, Vol. XX, No. 231 (June, 1939), pp. 469–71.

Knowlton, Edgar C. 'A Playwright Preoccupied with Sin', *The South Atlantic Quarterly*, Vol. XXXVIII, No. 4 (October, 1939), pp. 467–8.

L. G. D. (Review of first production) *Poetry* (London), No. 2 (April, 1939) (no pagination).

Montgomerie, William. 'Harry, Meet Mr. Prufrock (T. S. Eliot's Dilemma)', *Life and Letters Today*, Vol. 31, No. 51 (November, 1941), pp. 115–28.

Murry, J. Middleton. 'Mr. Eliot's Cocktail Party', *The Fortnightly*, No. 1008 N.S. (December, 1950), pp. 391–8.
(An essay on the relation of the later play to this one.)

*—— 'Note on the "Family Reunion"', *Essays in Criticism*, Vol. I, No. 1 (January, 1951), pp. 67–73. (Substantially reprinted in *Unprofessional Essays*, pp. 154–62.)

*Peter, John. '"The Family Reunion"', *Scrutiny*, XVI (1949), pp. 219–30.

Pottle, Frederick A. 'A Modern Verse Play', *The Yale Review*, XXVIII (June, 1939), pp. 836–9.

Ransom, John Crowe. 'T. S. Eliot as Dramatist', *Poetry: A magazine of verse*, Vol. LIV, No. v (August, 1950), pp. 264–71.

Rezzano, Maria Clotilde. *The Family Reunion*. A Study (Argentine Association of English Culture. English Pamphlet Series No. 2, Buenos Aires, 1942).

Roberts, Michael. 'Mr. Eliot's New Play', *The London Mercury*, Vol. XXXIX, No. 234 (April, 1939), pp. 641–2.

Scott, Nathan A., Jr. *Rehearsals of Discomposure:* Alienation and Reconciliation in Modern Literature (John Lehmann, London, 1952), pp. 229–37.

Spender, Stephen. 'Books and the War—VII', *Penguin New Writing*, No. 8, ed. John Lehmann (Penguin Books, 1941), pp. 125–32.

Stamm, Rudolf. 'The Orestes Theme in Three Plays by Eugene O'Neill, T. S. Eliot and Jean-Paul Sartre'. *English Studies*, XXX (1949), pp. 244–55.

Turnell, G. Martin. 'Mr. Eliot's New Play', *Scrutiny*, Vol. VIII, No. 1 (June, 1939), pp. 108–14.

*Unger, Leonard. 'T. S. Eliot's Rose Garden', *The Southern Review*, VIII (1942), pp. 667–89. Reprinted in his *Critique*, pp. 374–94, and in his *The Man in the Name* (The University of Minnesota Press, Minneapolis, 1956), pp. 168–89.

Ward, Anne. 'Speculations on Eliot's Time-World: An analysis of *The Family Reunion* in relation to Hulme and Bergson', *American Literature*, XXI (1949), pp. 18–34.

Williamson, Audrey. *Contemporary Theatre, 1953-6* (Rockliff, London, 1956), pp. 98–100.

Zabel, Morton Dauwen. 'Two Years of Poetry, 1937–39', *The Southern Review*, V (1939–40), p. 592.

The Cocktail Party

*Arrowsmith, William. 'English Verse Drama (II): "The Cocktail Party"', *Hudson Review*, III (Autumn, 1950), 411–30.

Bain, Donald. 'The Cocktail Party', *Nine*, Vol. II, No. 1 (January, 1950), pp. 16–22.

Barrett, William. 'Dry Land, Dry Martini', *The Partisan Review*, Vol. XVII, No. 4 (April, 1950), pp. 354–9.

Barry, Michael. 'Televising *The Cocktail Party*' in Braybrooke's *Symposium*, pp. 85–8.

Brown, John Mason. 'Honorable Intentions', *The Saturday Review of Literature*, XXXIII (4 February, 1950), pp. 28–32. (Reprinted in his *Still Seeing Things*, McGraw-Hill, New York, 1950, pp. 167–174.)

Dunkel, Wilbur Dwight. 'T. S. Eliot's Quest for Certitude', *Theology Today*, Vol. VII, No. 2 (July, 1950), pp. 228–36.

—— 'An exchange of Notes on T. S. Eliot: A Rejoinder', *ibid.*, Vol. VII, No. 4 (January, 1951), pp. 507–8.

(A reply to the article by Gregor Smith.)

Enright, D. J. 'On Not Teaching *The Cocktail Party*: A Professorial Dialogue', in *The Apothecary's Shop*, Essays on Literature (Secker and Warburg, London, 1957), pp. 206–11.

Hamalion, Leo. 'Mr. Eliot's Saturday Evening Service', *Accent*, Vol. X, No. 4 (Autumn, 1950), pp. 195–206.

Hamilton, Iain. 'Comments on *The Cocktail Party* (An interview and criticism)', *World Review* (November, 1949), pp. 19–22.

Hardy, John Edward. 'An Antic Disposition', *The Sewanee Review*, LXV (1957), pp. 50–60.

*Heilman, Robert B. '*Alcestis* and *The Cocktail Party*', *Comparative Literature*, V (Spring, 1955), 105–16.

Heywood, Robert. 'Everybody's Cocktail Party', *Renascence*, Vol. III, No. 1 (Autumn, 1950), pp. 28–30.

Hobson, Harold. *Verdict at Midnight* (Longmans, Green & Co., London, 1952), pp. 183–5.

Inge, W. Motter. 'The Bookshelf' (Review), *Theatre Arts*, XXXIV (May, 1950), pp. 8–9.

*Klatt, Heinz Günther. *Sanatorium einer Ehe*. Versuch einer Deutung von T. S. Eliot's "Cocktail-Party" (Lutherhaus-Verlag, Hannover, 1952).

Kramer, Hilton. 'T. S. Eliot in New York (Notes on the End of Something)', *The Western Review*, Vol. 14, No. 4 (Summer, 1950), pp. 303–5.

*Lawlor, John. 'The Formal Achievement of "The Cocktail Party"', *The Virginia Quarterly Review*, Vol. 30, No. 3 (Summer, 1954), pp. 431–51.

Lawrence, Seymour. 'Review', *Wake*, 9 (1950), pp. 120–2.

Levine, George. '*The Cocktail Party* and *Clara Hopgood*', *The Graduate Student of English*, Vol. I, No. 2 (Winter, 1958), pp. 4–11.

Bibliography

*McLaughlin, John J., S. J. 'A Daring Metaphysic: *The Cocktail Party*', *Renascence*, Vol. III, No. 1 (Autumn, 1950), pp. 15–28.

Morgan, Frederick. 'Chronicles: Notes on the Theater', *The Hudson Review*, Vol. III, No. 2 (Summer, 1950), pp. 290–93.

Munz, Peter. 'The Devil's Dialectic, or *The Cocktail Party*', *The Hibbert Journal*, XLIX (1950–1), pp. 256–63.

*Murry, J. Middleton. 'Mr. Eliot's Cocktail Party', *The Fortnightly*, No. 1008, N.S. (December, 1950), pp. 391–8.
(On the relation of the play to *The Family Reunion*. Partly reproduced in his *Unprofessional Essays*, pp. 162 ff.)

Nathan, George Jean. 'The Theatre: Clinical Notes', *The American Mercury*, Vol. LXX, No. 317 (May, 1950), pp. 557–8.

Parsons, Geoffrey. 'Solving Some of Eliot's Riddles', *New York Herald Tribune*, 12 February, 1950, sec. 5, pp. 1 and 2.
(An interview with Martin Browne.)

Peschmann, Hermann. ' "The Cocktail Party": Some Links Between the Poems and Plays of T. S. Eliot', *The Wind and the Rain*, Vol. VII, No. 1 (Autumn, 1950), pp. 53–8.

Peter, John. 'Sin and Soda', *Scrutiny*, XVII (1950–1), pp. 61–6.

Pick, John. 'A Note on "The Cocktail Party" ', *Renascence*, Vol. III, No. 1 (Autumn, 1950), pp. 30–2.

Popkin, Henry. 'Theatre Letter', *Kenyon Review*, Vol. XII, No. 2 (Spring, 1950), pp. 337–9.

Rahv, Philip. *Image and Idea*. Twenty Essays on Literary Themes (revised and enlarged. Weidenfeld and Nicolson, London, 1957), pp. 196–202.

Reed, Henry. 'Towards "The Cocktail Party" ', *The Listener*, 10 and 17 May, 1951, Vol. XLV, pp. 763–4 and 803–4.

Schwartz, Edward. 'Eliot's *Cocktail Party* and the New Humanism', *Philological Quarterly*, Vol. XXXII, No. 1 (January, 1953), pp. 58–68.

Scott, Nathan A., Jr. 'T. S. Eliot's "The Cocktail Party": Of Redemption and Vocation', *Religion in Life*, Vol. XX, No. 2 (Spring, 1951), pp. 274–85.

Sherek, Henry. 'On Giving a Cocktail Party', *Theatre Arts*, Vol. XXXIV, No. 4 (April, 1950), pp. 25–6.

Shuman, R. Baird. 'Buddhistic Overtones in *The Cocktail Party*', *Modern Language Notes*, LXXII (1957), pp. 426–7.

Smith, R. Gregor. 'An Exchange of Notes on T. S. Eliot: A Critique' *Theology Today*, Vol. VII, No. 4 (January, 1951), pp. 503–6.

Speaight, Robert. 'Sartre and Eliot', *Drama*, N.S., No. 17 (Summer, 1950), pp. 15–17.

Spender, Stephen. 'On "The Cocktail Party"', *The Year's Work in Literature 1950*, ed. John Lehmann (Published for the British Council by Longmans, Green and Co., London, 1951), pp. 17–23.

Theatre Arts, Vol. XXXIV, No. 4 (April, 1950), p. 10.
(A brief review of the New York production.)

Theatre World, Vol. XLVI, No. 305 (June, 1950), pp. 11–18.
(Photographs of the London production.)

Thurber, James. '*What* Cocktail Party?', *The New Yorker*, April 1, 1950, pp. 26–9.

Vassilieff, Elizabeth. 'Piers to Cocktails', *Meanjin: A Literary Magazine*, Vol. IX, No. 3 (Spring, 1950), pp. 193–203.

Vincent, C. J. 'A Modern Pilgrim's Progress', *Queen's Quarterly*, Vol. LVII, No. 3 (Autumn, 1950), pp. 346–52.

White, Jon Manchip. 'What a Party!', *Poetry London*, No. 19 (August, 1950), pp. 24–7.

*Wimsatt, W. K., Jr. 'Eliot's Comedy', *The Sewanee Review*, LVIII (1950), pp. 666–78.

Wool, Sandra. 'Weston Revisited', *Accent*, Vol. X, No. 4 (Autumn, 1950), pp. 207–12.

Worsley, T. C. *The Fugitive Art*. Dramatic Commentaries 1947–51 (John Lehmann, London, 1952), pp. 144–6.

Wyatt, Euphemia Van Rensselaer. 'Theater' (Review), *The Catholic World*, Vol. CLXX, No. 1,020 (March, 1950), pp. 466–7.

Yoklavich, John M. 'Eliot's *Cocktail Party* and Plato's *Symposium*', *Notes and Queries*, 8 December, 1951, pp. 541–2.

Zolotow, Maurice. 'Psychoanalyzing the Doctor', *The New York Times*, 26 February, 1950, sec. 2, p. 3.
(Interview with Alec Guinness, who played Sir Henry Harcourt-Reilly in the original production.)

The Confidential Clerk

Arrowsmith, William. 'Menander and Milk Wood', *The Hudson Review*, Vol. VII, No. 2 (Summer, 1954), pp. 291–6.

Bellow, Saul. 'Theatre Chronicle', *The Partisan Review*, Vol. 21, No. 3 (May–June, 1954), pp. 313–15.

Brooke, Nicholas. '*The Confidential Clerk*: A Theatrical Review', *The Durham University Journal*, Vol. XLVI, No. 1, December, 1953, pp. 66–70.

*Colby, Robert A. 'Orpheus in the Counting House: *The Confidential Clerk*', *Publications of the Modern Language Association*, Vol. LXXII, No. 4, Part I (September, 1957), pp. 791–802.

*Dobree, Bonamy. '"The Confidential Clerk"', *The Sewanee Review*, LXII (1954), pp. 117–31.

*Fergusson, Francis. 'Three Allegorists: Brecht, Wilder, and Eliot', *The Sewanee Review*, LXIV (1956), pp. 544–73 (pp. 562–9 and 571–2 on Eliot).

Findlater, Richard. 'The Camouflaged Drama', *The Twentieth Century*, Vol. CLIV, No. 920 (October, 1953), pp. 311–16.

*Gardner, Helen. (Review of the book) *The New Statesman and Nation*, Vol. XLVII, No. 1202 (20 March, 1954), pp. 373–4.

Hivnor, Mary. 'Theatre Letter', *Kenyon Review*, Vol. 16 (1954), pp. 463–5.

Weightman, J. G. 'Edinburgh, Elsinore and Chelsea', *The Twentieth Century*, Vol. CLIV, No. 920 (October, 1953), pp. 306–8.

Wilkinson, Burke. 'A Most Serious Comedy by Eliot', *The New York Times*, 7 February, 1954, Section 2, p. 1, col. 5.
(An interview with E. Martin Browne.)

Williamson, Audrey. *Contemporary Theatre, 1953–6* (Rockliff, London, 1956), pp. 22–6.

The Elder Statesman

Note: Since the bibliography for this play is as yet very slight, I have included more items from weekly and daily publications.

Brien, Alan. 'The Invisible Dramatist', *The Spectator*, 5 September, 1958, pp. 305–6.

*Dobree, Bonamy. 'The London Stage', *The Sewanee Review*, Vol. LXVII, No. 1 (Winter, 1959), pp. 109–15.

*Paul, Leslie. *See* Salmon.

Salmon, Christopher and Leslie Paul. 'Two Views of Mr. Eliot's New Play', *The Listener*, 4 September, 1958, pp. 340–1.

Saturday Review of Literature, The. 13 September, 1958, pp. 30–2. 'T. S. Eliot at Seventy' (includes an interview with Eliot by Henry Hewes).

Stanford, Derek. 'Mr. Eliot's New Play', *The Contemporary Review*, No. 1114 (October, 1958), pp. 199–201.

—— 'T. S. Eliot's New Play', *Queen's Quarterly*, Vol. LXV, No. 4 (Winter, 1959), pp. 682–9.

The Times. 26 August, 1958, p. 11, 'Mr. Eliot's Most Human Play'.

Weightman, J. G. 'After Edinburgh', *The Twentieth Century*, Vol. 164, No. 980 (October, 1958), pp. 342–4.

*Worsley, T. C. 'Mr. Eliot at Colonus', *New Statesman and Nation*, Vol. LVI, No. 1433, Saturday, 30 August, 1958, pp. 245–6.

Index